The Economics of Sex Differentials

The Economics of Sex Differentials

Cynthia B. Lloyd
and
Beth T. Niemi

1979
Columbia University Press
New York

Library of Congress Cataloging in Publication Data

Lloyd, Cynthia B   1943–
    The economics of sex differentials.

    Bibliography: p.
    Includes index.
    1. Women—Employment—United States.   2. Sex
discrimination in employment—United States.   3. Sex
discrimination against women—United States.   I. Niemi,
Beth T., 1942–   joint author.   II. Title.
HD6095.L558   331.4'0973   79-9569
ISBN 0-231-04038-5

Columbia University Press
New York   Guildford, Surrey

To Our Mothers
Mary Thacher Brown and
Margaret Morris Tilghman

Contents

Figures

Tables

Preface

The seed from which this book eventually grew was planted five years ago, at Barnard's first annual Scholar and Feminist Conference in May 1974. There the authors were assigned the task of leading a discussion with a group of scholars, largely from other disciplines, on the economics of sex differentials. The enthusiastic response to the substance of the discussion, as well as the general thirst for knowledge about economics displayed by those interested in women's issues, ultimately persuaded us to pursue the project further and develop it into a book. As we initially approached this task, we felt in full command of the material, but this feeling rapidly dissipated as questions led to more questions rather than to easy answers. As the project grew in scale and lengthened in time, our initial thesis was strengthened by the actual changes in sex differentials which were simultaneously unfolding, as well as by the burgeoning empirical and theoretical literature on various aspects of men's and women's labor market roles.

The working relationship we have developed in the writing of this book is a very special one and has itself become one of the creative outcomes of the project. It is often assumed that a coauthored book requires only half the effort from each coauthor, and consequently each receives only half the credit or the blame, as the case may be. It is not unusual for the separate contributions of each author to be listed by chapter in the preface. Ideally, on the other hand, the coauthored book can be seen as an opportunity to create a product which is at least twice as good as what could be written by one scholar alone. In this book, each page has been written by both of us, until our separate contributions are no longer distinguishable, even to ourselves. This is in the true spirit of feminist scholarship and we believe that, in this case, the product is far superior to the sum of two independent inputs because of the interaction from which we have both benefited greatly. Thus each of us accepts full responsibility for the entire book.

As must be the case with any project of this size, we have quite a number of people to thank for help and support. First there are those who have generously given their time to comment on earlier drafts. In this connection, we particularly acknowledge Mark Killingsworth's painstakingly thorough comments at every point in the book's evolution. In addition, detailed comments from Charles Brown, Myra Strober, Estelle James, Duncan Foley, Aline Quester and Judith Layzer were extremely helpful.

We were fortunate to have extremely competent research assistance at every stage of the book's development. Our thanks go to Andrea Shepard, Angela Dambrie, and Bonnie Caroit, and most especially to Mary O'Neill Berry, who carried through not only all the final data analysis, reference checking, and proofing, but has shown her heretofore latent artistic flair in the preparation of all the book's figures. We also acknowledge the typing assistance of Liz Gewirtzman, and of Ruth Saccomanno, who typed and retyped the entire final draft.

Funding for this project has come from several different sources. Both the Rutgers Research Council and Barnard College have provided us each with support in the form of research grants and paid leaves of absence at different crucial points in the project's development, which we gratefully acknowledge. Cynthia received a special junior faculty leave from Barnard College in the fall of 1975, when the project was just getting under way. Beth received a summer fellowship in 1976 and a year's leave from Rutgers under their faculty academic study plan in 1978. Finally, the Ford Foundation provided essential support for the completion of the book through its grant covering the initial three years of the Program in Sex Roles and Social Change of the Center for the Social Sciences at Columbia University. We are grateful for the extensive financial, intellectual and moral support provided by the program and the center during this crucial final stage.

The Economics of Sex Differentials

Chapter 1

Women's Secondary Economic Status

Women's secondary status is at least as striking in the labor market as it is everywhere else. Every standard labor market statistic shows marked differentials on the average between men and women, in both the level of economic participation and the distribution of economic rewards. Although the existence of these differentials between the sexes is widely known, their causes and exact nature are not well understood. Rapid increases in women's labor force participation rates have been accompanied by a widening of the wage and unemployment gaps between men and women and continued sharp contrasts in the occupational distribution. Thus, although it has been widely recognized that the focus of women's economic activity has been shifting from the home to the market, as yet there has been no fundamental change in the division of labor in the home, or the division of rewards in the market place, between the sexes.

How is it possible for traditional sex stereotypes to continue to prevail in the face of rapid increases in women's role in the labor market? This paradox must be directly confronted. Attitudes change much more slowly than economic conditions, and, even as individual behavior changes in response to economic signals, attitudes lag behind. The accumulation of knowledge itself may be slowed because statistical definitions and theoretical assumptions are rooted in past experience.

The purpose of this book is to describe and explain the relative economic status of women and men and how this has changed over time. One necessary input must be a critical analysis and review of the economic literature on sex differentials as it relates to the realities of the past thirty years. The major sex differentials to be analyzed are those in labor force participation rates, hours and weeks of work, levels and

1

types of education, job experience and on-the-job training, occupational distribution, earnings, and unemployment rates. Each of these differentials is a key indicator of either relative participation or relative rewards in the market economy. Taken together, they give a multidimensional picture of male and female economic status.

There has been a tremendous increase in recent years in the literature on women's place in the economy. But the analysis of women's behavior and women's position is too often segregated for special treatment, because women are seen to be fundamentally different from men. This has reinforced the notion that their patterns of behavior are, in fact, different. By analyzing men's and women's decisions symmetrically, we recognize that men and women are basically people with the same innate abilities and patterns of response to incentives, whose different opportunities have led to different labor market outcomes.

Economic Perspectives

The discipline of economics brings a particular point of view to the analysis of individual decisions and consequent market outcomes. Its emphasis is on choice. Whether individuals, firms, or governmental units are making the choices, the assumption is that choices are available and that the direction ultimately chosen is the one that provides the maximum output (measured either in terms of profit or utility), given the resources and opportunities available. Each individual choice that is confronted involves the weighing of alternative opportunities. For example, the decision to go to college involves weighing the net gains, in terms of increased future income (total gains minus direct schooling costs) and increased knowledge, against the value of alternatives forgone (opportunity costs), such as working full time or raising a family. Thus the concept of opportunity cost is synonymous with the availability of choice.

However, within the context of this general framework, economists disagree in their assessment of the importance of freedom of choice, relative to institutional constraints, in the determination of market outcomes. The dominant orthodox approach to labor market analysis assumes that roughly the same wide array of choices lies before each individual. The observed dispersion in both the quantity and quality of labor supplied must thus be essentially voluntary, resulting from differences in preferences and/or nonmarket opportunity costs. The recently developed labor market segmentation approach, on the other hand, places primary emphasis on the various ways in which free individual choice is constrained. Each individual is seen to have only a small number of options, and this feasible opportunity set is quite dissimilar for different individuals and/or groups. Although each individual engages in maximizing behavior, two people with identical preferences and nonmarket opportunities may well end up making completely different decisions in the labor market, because they are choosing from different sets of available alternatives.

Men's and women's choices about labor force participation, hours of work, education, experience and training acquired, and occupational selection can all be examined within the framework of opportunity costs. This simple analytic framework will be used throughout the book in discussing the supply side of the labor market. The relative weights attached to various goals by men and women may differ because of differences in preferences stemming from the socialization process but, even with no differences in preferences, we would expect that men and women would make dissimilar choices because of substantial objective differences in the range and types of opportunity available. Men and women do face different opportunities in both the market and nonmarket sectors. Women's fecundity adds both an additional option and an additional constraint to the choice equation. Child rearing has traditionally devolved upon women, and thus the desire for children within families constrains women's choices in other areas, because of the time-consuming nature of child rearing.

The labor supply decisions of individual women and men, however, are only part of the picture. Closely related to the differing emphasis on freedom versus constraint in the context of individual choice is the question of whose choices are most important in determining labor market outcomes—those of individual workers on the supply side, of firms as employers on the demand side, or of governmental units, whose policies influence behavior on both sides of the market? Under orthodox assumptions, the demand for labor plays an essentially passive role in the determination of sex differentials. Although both labor and product markets are usually assumed to be competitive, the supply side of the labor market remains the source of earnings and unemployment differentials, even when this assumption is dropped. A firm with monopoly power will restrict output and employment, but this does not entail the power to differentiate workers by sex and pay them unequal wages. Even a firm with monopsony power, that has control over wages by virtue of its large size relative to the labor market in which it operates, can reward male and female workers differently only if their labor supply behavior differs.

If labor markets are segmented, so that men and women are channeled into largely noncompeting groups, or if firms maximize not money profits, but rather a more complex utility function that has other dimensions as well, then the demand for labor may be differentiated by sex. Thus women and men with the same characteristics will be faced with different opportunities in the labor market. Firms do make significant choices about the allocation of resources, including the selection of applicants for available jobs, and their preferences and resources also determine the final outcome. To the extent that women and men on the average differ, or are believed to differ, in types and levels of characteristics which are valued by employers as indices of potential productivity, they will be hired for different jobs and paid different wages. If employers themselves also have preferences as to the sex composition of their work forces, this will affect male/female hiring and promotion patterns. When discrimination takes this form, it reflects a preference on the part of the employer but, for those discriminated against, it becomes an additional constraint on their free choice.

Government policymakers also make choices based on scarce resources and competing goals. Governments have traditionally viewed women not only as a labor resource but, often more importantly, as a source of population growth and youth education. When population growth is seen as a stimulant to economic growth rates rather than a deterrent, women's role as reproducers may be viewed as relatively more important than their role as producers in the market. Policies to encourage their family role (e.g., welfare, joint income taxation, etc.) will create constraints on women's pursuit of their role in the labor market. Again, implicit choices are being made that have opportunity costs attached. Resulting policies will affect men and women's labor market choices by differentially changing the relative rewards of market versus nonmarket work.

From our point of view, the most enlightened (and enlightening) approach to an understanding of existing sex differentials involves a synthesis of a variety of useful theoretical tools, and gives roughly equal emphasis to supply, demand and policy decisions. The concepts of segmented labor markets and discrimination are used to broaden, rather than to replace, the orthodox theory. The same modes of analysis are applicable to each of the relevant actors on the economic stage—the individual, the firm and the government. Opportunity costs in each case are the key to choices, with the degree of available choice being determined by the level and distribution of resources. This is the theoretical framework within which sex differentials will be viewed. In analyzing each sex differential within this context, it will become clear that resource constraints and preferences are not always independent of each other, as is usually assumed in the theory. Systematic differences between men and women in certain resources will, through time, be translated into different preferences. While resources will always reflect current reality, preferences may be partially determined by past realities such as, in this case, traditional sex roles.

Myth and Reality

The usefulness of this mode of analysis will be tested against actual trends and patterns in sex differentials. However, these trends and patterns themselves cannot always be readily observed from average statistics, not only because of the way these are defined, but, most importantly, because they may disguise the amount of variation in the underlying distributions. In fact, certain myths about men and women have been allowed to persist despite changing patterns in sex differentials, and can only be dispelled with a detailed exploration of facts and figures. For example, differences in average labor force participation rates between men and women give a picture of a "typical" man, who works at least 90 percent of the time, and a "typical" woman, who works only half the time. Whether or not such patterns are really typical depends on the dispersion of labor force participation rates within each sex. If the dispersion is large, which it is in this case, then average labor force participation rates can create a mythology about sex differentials which does not correspond to the facts.

One myth that has been most successfully reinforced by statistical averages is the myth that the typical woman is a secondary worker and a secondary earner and the typical man is a primary worker and a primary earner. As secondary workers, women are typically assumed to work for pay during only 50 percent of their active lives and to time their participation to conform with family demands. Within the family, the work decision is assumed to be sequential rather than simultaneous, with the husband committing himself to full-time work and choosing an occupation and geographic location which maximizes his career options. Then the wife is viewed as accommodating herself and her work life to that decision and, therefore, adjusting of necessity to a second-best solution. If it is assumed that men work almost all of their active adult lives and that family decisions are made sequentially, it logically follows that women will be secondary workers, whose pattern of labor force participation is intermittent and discontinuous, and whose contribution to family income is small and undependable.

This myth of the typical woman and man is perpetuated by a superficial view of certain labor market indicators. For example: (1) The much-quoted aggregate female labor force participation rate had just reached the 50 percent level in mid-1978 (50.0 percent in May and 50.1 percent in June), even though it increased tremendously during the postwar period. (2) Women in the child-bearing ages (25–44) have labor force participation rates which, even in 1978, fell at least 8 percentage points below those of women aged 20–24 (U.S. Department of Labor, Bureau of Labor Statistics, Report 544, p. 2), and this is often interpreted as documentation of the "drop-out" phenomenon of women who interrupt their careers to have children. (3) Aggregate job turnover rates, which measure the percentage of the labor force that moves between jobs or in and out of the labor force during a given time interval, are higher for women than for men. (4) Employed women contribute on the average only about a quarter of total family income.

Such statistics are powerful and persuasive. They serve to reinforce the myth described above. They give support to the traditional assumptions made by economists in their empirical research, and they have even determined in important ways the systems of classification under which the Census Bureau collects and codes labor force data. In fact, this traditional view of the division of labor between the sexes prevents a truly symmetrical analysis of male and female labor force characteristics. For instance, the definition of head of household as described in the 1970 Census is as follows:

One person in each household is designated as the "head"—the person who is regarded as the head by the members of the household. However, if a married woman living with her husband was reported as the head, her husband was considered head for the purpose of simplifying the tabulation. (U.S. Bureau of the Census, *1970 Census*, p. 8)

The Census provides labor force participation rates for women according to their husbands' income and the presence and ages of children, but comparable statistics are not available for men. This has helped to justify economists' assumptions that such variables are important in women's labor force decisions but not in men's, and has severely limited the possibility of doing comparable research on the determinants of male and female labor supply until quite recently, when comparable panel data on men and women has become available.

If we look beneath summary statistics, we encounter a more complex reality. Any statistical average tends to divert attention from the underlying distribution or, in this case, the extent to which both men and women differ one from another. Although it is true that every group of men has a higher labor force participation rate than the corresponding group of women, the differences across groups of men and groups of women, subdivided by such characteristics as age, race or marital status, are sometimes almost as great as the differences between the sexes.

It cannot be emphasized too strongly that the total labor force participation rate for all women aged 16 and over, even though it has been over 50 percent since May 1978, is still deceptively low, because of the relatively large proportion of the female population which is over the typical retirement age, as a result of low mortality rates. Among women of working age, those in the labor force have been in the majority for some time, and the labor force participation of those aged 20–24 is rapidly approaching 70 percent. In addition, a recent study using longitudinal data indicates that women fall roughly into one of three groups: one-third work continuously, one-third work intermittently, and one-third never work (Heckman and Willis 1977). Therefore, a labor force participation rate of 50 percent for all women does not tell us much about the typical woman. There actually appear to be relatively few women whose lifetime participation in the labor force is accurately reflected in the aggregate statistics.

The dramatic increases in labor force participation rates among women of all ages, but particularly among younger women, in the last ten years have meant that for the young cohorts of women (that is, women born in the same year), labor force participation rates appear to be rising almost continuously over the life cycle. This presents a sharp contrast to the cross-sectional picture, which implies that women are dropping out in their child-bearing years. The deception arises because the labor force behavior of different women of varying ages is being used to simulate the life cycle of a hypothetical woman. However, because of dramatic changes in behavior among younger women, it is not accurate to look at older women today and assume that that is where younger women will be a certain number of years down the road. Thus, the fact that the labor force participation rate of mothers of preschool children has grown 111 percent since 1960 is not an indication of the increasingly marginal nature of women's work, but rather of their increasing career attachment.

In fact, serious questions can be raised concerning the notion that a woman is more likely to leave a particular job than a similarly placed man. Women's participation appears to be becoming more continuous throughout the year, and their movement in and out of the labor force is decreasing. Women's records of attendance and labor force turnover are similar to men's when they are compared on the basis of similar job levels and under similar circumstances (U.S. Dept. of Labor, 1969). Therefore, their higher average rates of turnover relative to men must be explained by the types of jobs they do—jobs which offer less reward in terms of career development and wage growth and which, therefore, provide less incentive to stay for all employees, whether they be men or women.

The importance of women's contribution to family income is also greatly understated by the average figures quoted above. Recent research provides strong evidence that working wives' earnings tend, on the average, to raise their family income up to the level of non-working wives' family income in the same reference group (defined on the basis of age, educational level and geographic region). (Strober 1977:417). This attests to the crucial importance of wives' earnings in maintaining a desirable standard of living for the family. And, when comparing all families, it is also true that families where the wife has a full-time job enjoy a median income more than 40 percent higher than those where the wife is not in the labor force. When all working women are included, even those working part-time, median family income is 20 percent higher than in families with nonworking wives (Hayghe 1976:17–18). In many cases, that contribution, however measured, is necessary to pull a family above the poverty line or establish it firmly in the ranks of the middle class.

Although the myth of the secondary worker continues to have some reality for certain women, the gap between myth and reality is growing as the labor force participation rates of young women undergo dramatic change. This gap creates increasing problems in the interpretation of contemporary phenomena. Widening wage and unemployment gaps between men and women and a relatively un-changing occupational distribution are explained in terms of the myth of women as secondary workers. If one assumes that women have high turnover rates and a marginal attachment to the labor force, then it would be expected that a rapid increase in their labor force entry would reduce their relative wages and increase their unemployment rates. It would also be expected that they would choose traditionally "féminine" occupations, and therefore their entry would not dra-matically affect the distribution of men and women across occupa-tions. However, a closer examination of economic reality, which we will undertake in the course of this book, suggests that labor force participation rates are rising, not because of the increased entry of marginal workers, but largely because of reduced exit rates on the part of young women, who are embarking on careers and, therefore, maintaining a much more continuous attachment to the labor force.

Myth or conventional wisdom not only disguises and understates the radical changes that have taken place in sex differentials in labor supply, but also disguises the notable lack of change in other areas. Thus the growing inconsistencies in patterns of sex differentials are blurred rather than brought into sharp focus. For example, the media would have us believe that occupational barriers have fallen and that women have successfully entered traditionally masculine fields. Here again, however, reality is more complex and differs in many essential ways from stereotypical beliefs, but in this case the misconception is the result of reliance on anecdotal evidence as opposed to aggregate data on the overall situation, rather than the misuse or misinterpretation of such data.

Although the distribution of both women and men across occupations has changed significantly over time, these changes have not been such as to place women and men in the same occupations. Despite examples such as rising female enrollments in professional schools and the well-publicized male telephone operators and female linepersons, overall the labor market remains sharply sex-segregated. There are still "masculine" and "feminine" occupations, and the degree of overlap remains minimal.

When we examine recent trends in earnings and unemployment rates, we encounter two opposing mythologies, with an elusive reality lying somewhere in between. With respect to labor force participation, exclusive attention to the average female participation rates creates a myth which overshadows the reality of substantial heterogeneity and dispersion around the mean. With respect to actual returns (wages and employment stability), however, the crucial problems of interpretation involve the distinction, not between the mean and the entire distribution, but rather between unadjusted and adjusted mean values. Women still earn only 60 percent of what men earn on average, and have unemployment rates that are 30 to 40 percent higher than men's, and these unadjusted differentials have, in fact, widened somewhat in the past twenty years. On the one hand, women's advocacy groups point to the deterioration of average wage and unemployment differentials as proof that discrimination is getting worse. On the other hand, many orthodox economists and government policymakers point to the fact that these gaps are unadjusted for either changes in the composition of the labor force or for changes within groups in average earnings-related characteristics—adjustments which, if combined, would not only narrow the gap but might even reverse the trends in these differentials. It is a mistake to go to extremes, either immediately taking the widening of the unadjusted gaps in earnings and unemployment rates at face value, or bending backwards to explain away the observed trends by adjusting for any and all factors that appear to reduce the differential. This is because many of the factors which are statistically correlated with earnings are themselves determined by a market process which provides different (but nonetheless overlapping) sets of opportunities to men and women.

An understanding of current economic phenomena and predictions about the future requires that myths be dispelled and the complexity of current reality explored in depth. This is particularly crucial for two related reasons: (1) employers often justify discriminatory behavior in hiring and promotion on the basis of women's higher average turnover rates and, therefore, secondary status—claims which are documented not just by women's lower labor force participation rates but by their lower wages and higher unemployment rates as well: (2) the design of government policy makes implicit assumptions about the role of wives in the economics of the family and the proper occupational division of labor between the sexes. The first phenomenon is what economists call "statistical discrimination" and results from the tendency on the part of employers who lack full information to assign characteristics to an individual which are average characteristics of his or her sex, without taking account of individual differences. The second phenomenon sets up incentives in such a way as to slow the inevitable process of change by rewarding those men and women who conform to traditional stereotypes. For example, progressive income taxes tax wives' earnings at the higher marginal rates determined by their husbands' income bracket, rather than as individuals in their own right, thus penalizing the contribution of secondary earnings. In addition, social security, by providing for the nonworking wives of working men without additional contributions, penalizes the working wife who makes contributions to the system which yield little if any incremental gain to her old-age income. Employment and training programs also reward men and women who choose traditional jobs but discourage women's participation in nontraditional areas, not only because of unfounded assumptions about sex differences in job preferences, but also because of realistic awareness of actual discriminatory barriers.

Although behavior conforming to the myths we have been discussing can still be found, it should be clear that this is only one aspect of a wider and more complex reality. The failure to recognize these facts appears to be a classic example of the intervention of belief in the development of conventional wisdom. In some cases, generalizations become widely accepted only shortly before changing circumstances make them no longer accurate. In other cases, however, hasty generalizations based on nonrepresentative examples may develop and be accepted before the underlying realities have changed significantly.

The Vicious Circle

Neither supply factors, such as a relative lack of experience and training, nor demand factors, such as the segmentation of labor markets and direct discrimination against women, can tell the whole story of the strong persistence over time of women's secondary economic status, even in the face of the dramatic and continuing increase in their labor market activity. Productivity-enhancing job experience and differential access to such experience are the keys to the vicious circle of constrained opportunities in which the woman worker is still trapped. It is through the dynamic interaction of supply and demand in the labor market that patterns based on past discrimination, behavior, and experiences are perpetuated. In fact, the question of whether individual choice on the supply side or employer discrimination on the demand side came first in a particular case is actually almost irrelevant, because the circular process, once set in motion, affects individual, employer, and even government behavior, and its self-perpetuating character is extremely difficult to short-circuit at any point.

Do the lower earnings, higher unemployment, and occupational segregation of women result from their higher turnover and lack of continuous job experience? Or are discontinuous work histories and high turnover the inevitable result of being restricted to secondary occupations, characterized by low earnings, unstable employment and little or no opportunity for advancement? The answer to both questions is yes. The same observed variables, such as occupation and work experience, simultaneously represent both different opportunities *and* different qualifications. Different opportunities arise in part because of employers' perceptions of the different qualifications of women and men, and different qualifications, in turn, are the result of different opportunities for skill acquisition.

Until this vicious circle breaks down, not only will women experience a disadvantage, on the average, relative to men, in earnings, unemployment, and occupation, but any individual woman, judged and stereotyped on the basis of perceived group behavior, will continue to find substantial barriers, however great her ability and commitment, to acquiring the quality of job experience necessary to realize her potential. We all know that young people first entering the labor market "can't get jobs because they have no experience, and can't get the experience because they can't get jobs." This stalemate evaporates fairly rapidly for most young white men once they land their first jobs and begin to acquire relevant experience, but it tends to haunt women (and minority) workers indefinitely, as jobs with the essential component of training simply do not open up to them. This is the essence of the vicious circle of women's economic status which we will develop in our sequential analysis of the various sex differentials and their interrelationships.

That analysis of the dimensions and sources of sex differentials will begin with a thorough discussion of sex differentials in individual choices. Then, by examining employer behavior and government policy, we will show the extent to which men's and women's choices are differentially constrained. It will become clear that all parts of the economic system are interdependent. For example, men's and women's labor supply is dependent on the market wage but the market wage offered is affected by past labor force experience (i.e., labor supply). Therefore, the extent to which sex differentials are a function of different choices under similar circumstances and the extent to which they are affected by different opportunities is not always clear.

Chapter 2 analyzes the labor force participation choices of both men and women within a family context. Wage differentials between the sexes are taken as given here. The major differences between men and women in labor force participation rates, average hours and weeks worked, and total years spent in the labor force are carefully detailed and explained in terms of individual responses to wage rates and income levels.

Chapter 3 uses the theory of investment in human capital to highlight the major determinants of men's and women's choices of education, occupation and skill level. Human capital theory is seen as a key link between labor supply decisions and occupational choices because of close connections between the accumulation of work experience and the acquisition of training (both in school and on the job). Systematic differences between men and women in access to specific occupations or types of training are not specifically dealt with here, but are introduced in the following chapters.

In chapter 4, the predictions implied by the various sex differentials in labor supply discussed in chapters 2 and 3 are analyzed within a market context. We begin by assuming no differences by sex in market opportunities and use the pure human capital model, which can be labeled the orthodox approach, to predict wage and unemployment differentials as a function of differential supply alone. Actual wage and unemployment differentials are compared with those predicted by the theory, and inconsistencies are pointed out. The lack of correspondence between theory and reality in this case leads us to search for alternative or additional explanations of market differentials, and to consider specifically the importance of differences in the demand for male and female workers, over and above any differences already discussed in their labor supply behavior. The first step in this direction is to drop the assumption of free and perfect mobility, and to introduce the idea of labor market segmentation, which may channel women and men into different, noncompeting areas.

Chapter 5 extends this crucial concept of demand-based sex differentials by developing and exploring the theory of discrimination and its implication for sex differentials in wages and unemployment. Because no theory of discrimination predicts a persistence of discrimination over time, we develop a dynamic explanation for the widening of the wage and unemployment gaps through the interaction of discrimination and differential supply behavior over time. A review of the empirical literature shows that the attempt to measure the relative importance of discrimination has been largely unsuccessful. This is partly due to the methodology, which assumes that objective and discriminatory factors are mutually exclusive, and thus ignores the importance of feedback effects. It is these very feedback effects—these dynamic, mutually determining supply and demand interactions—of course, that are the essence of the self-perpetuating process that we call the "vicious circle."

Chapter 6 provides a comprehensive review of government programs and policies which impinge on sex differentials, either intentionally or unintentionally. It becomes clear that government policy reflects past social and economic realities, but is decidedly slow to respond to dramatic changes in the economic role of women. In this light, the enactment of recent antidiscrimination legislation is a hopeful sign, but one which has unfortunately been largely ineffectual in combatting pervasive labor market practices.

All in all, these chapters build on one another in telling a compelling story of women's continuing secondary economic status, despite rapid change in some areas. This is ironic, given the high visibility of the movement for women's liberation in recent years. Obviously, liberation "is easier said than done" in a society in which every major institution, through custom or law, inhibits the process of inevitable change through anachronistic assumptions about sex roles. The critical question that remains is how and when the vicious circle which has perpetuated itself for so long will break down. Chapter 7 takes a look at likely trends in labor supply, occupational distribution, and wages, with an eye to pinpointing the key areas where stress will come and where real change is most likely.

Chapter 2

The Economics of Labor Supply: Work in the Market versus Work in the Home

The quantitative dimensions of an individual's supply of labor to the market are summarized in the concepts of labor force participation and hours of work. The major differences observed between the sexes in all dimensions of labor supply have been seen to reflect a traditional division of labor between man the provider and woman the homemaker. However, long-term declines in the labor force participation rates of younger and older men and rapid increases in these rates for women suggest the possibility that the traditional division of labor may be changing, at least during some phases of the life cycle. This chapter will analyze these choices for both men and women within a family decision-making context, in order to explain differences.

As is generally known and as will be seen in detail shortly, women supply less labor to the *market* sector than men do. This is not, of course, the same thing as saying that women do *less work* than men. Much productive work takes place in the home sector, and to categorize all nonmarket time under the rubric of leisure distorts reality and leads to paradoxical interpretations of labor supply behavior. This is particularly so in the case of women, who still perform the vast bulk of nonmarket or household work in our economy.

The other side of the question of why men do so much more market work than women is the complementary question of why women do so much more nonmarket work than men. How is the division of labor between the sexes determined, and how does it change over time in response to changing economic conditions? How does this division of labor in turn influence the substantial differentials by sex in education, training, mobility, earnings, and unemployment rates? Not only are their different rates of labor force participation a crucial component of the unequal economic status of men and women, but labor supply is closely linked to all other components of economic status. Thus it is essential to consider the levels and determinants of labor supply in considerable detail.

Much has been written about postwar trends in women's labor force participation rates, and only the most important points need to be repeated here. Labor force participation rates for the female population over 16 have climbed steadily from 31.8 percent in 1947 to 50.1 percent in 1978 (see table 2.1 and figure 2.1). During the 1950s, the most rapid increases in participation were among women aged 45–64, whereas since 1963 the most dramatic growth has been among the 20- to 34-year-olds, with particularly strong increases since 1971. The teenage group has also experienced rapid increases recently.

Table 2.1 and figures 2.1 and 2.2 give us at least the outline of a very interesting story. The past thirty years have clearly been characterized by dynamic changes in labor force participation and a dramatic narrowing of the sex differential. The male labor force participation rate is now less than 1.6 times as great as the female rate, as compared to a ratio of 2.7 in 1947. About two-thirds of the observed narrowing of the participation gap has been the result of rising female labor force participation while the steady, but less dramatic, decline in the participation rate of men accounts for the remaining third.

However, pronounced as this change has been, we are still far from a convergence. The trends for men and women in figure 2.1 are not yet close to intersecting, and the age-participation profiles in figure 2.2 highlight the continuing sharp contrast between the lifetime participation patterns of women and men. Figures 2.1 and 2.2, taken together, amply demonstrate the coexistence of both substantial change in the direction of greater similarity, and continued significant dissimilarity, between the sexes in labor supply behavior.

This brief look at current patterns and recent trends in labor force participation may well raise more questions than it answers, but at least the importance of these questions is indisputable. While more detailed data on labor supply behavior than we have so far examined

Table 2.1

Labor Force Participation Rates by Sex, 1947–1978

Year	Male	Female	Differential (M-F)	Ratio (M/F)
1947	86.8	31.8	55.0	2.73
1948	87.0	32.7	54.3	2.66
1949	86.9	33.2	53.7	2.62
1950	86.8	33.9	52.9	2.56
1951	87.3	34.7	52.6	2.52
1952	87.2	34.8	52.4	2.51
1953	86.9	34.5	52.4	2.52
1954	86.4	34.6	51.8	2.50
1955	86.2	35.7	50.5	2.41
1956	86.3	36.9	49.4	2.34
1957	85.5	36.9	48.6	2.32
1958	85.0	37.1	47.9	2.29
1959	84.5	37.2	47.3	2.27
1960	84.0	37.8	46.2	2.22
1961	83.6	38.1	45.5	2.19
1962	82.8	38.0	44.8	2.18
1963	82.2	38.3	43.9	2.15
1964	81.9	38.7	43.2	2.12
1965	81.5	39.3	42.2	2.07
1966	81.4	40.3	41.1	2.02
1967	81.5	41.2	40.3	1.98
1968	81.2	41.6	39.6	1.95
1969	80.9	42.7	38.2	1.89
1970	80.6	43.4	37.2	1.86
1971	80.0	43.4	36.6	1.84
1972	79.7	43.9	35.8	1.82
1973	79.5	44.7	34.8	1.78
1974	79.4	45.7	33.7	1.74
1975	78.5	46.4	32.1	1.69
1976	78.1	47.4	30.7	1.65
1977	78.3	48.5	29.8	1.61
1978	78.4	50.1	28.3	1.56

SOURCES: 1947–1977: U.S. Dept. of Labor, *Employment and Training Report of the President* (1978), p. 182, table A-2.
1978: *Employment and Earnings*, January 1979, p. 22, table A-2.

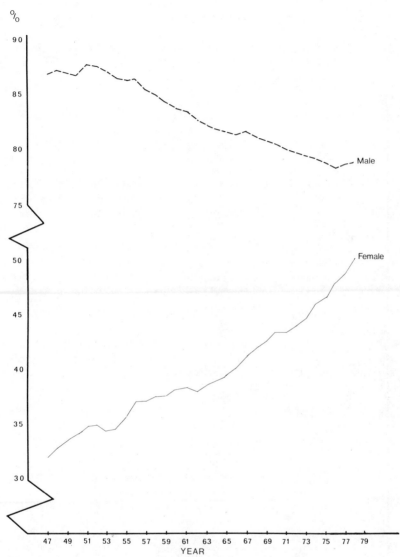

Figure 2.1.   Labor Force Participation Rates by Sex, 1947–78

SOURCE: 1947–1977: U.S. Dept. of Labor, *Employment and Training Report of the President* (1978), p. 182, table A-2.

1978: *Employment and Earnings*, January 1979, p. 22, table A-2.

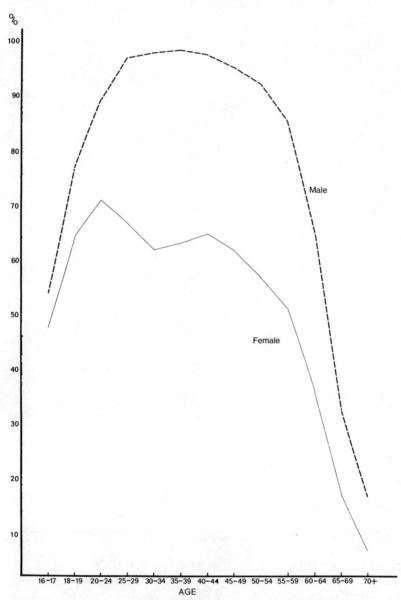

%

100

90

80

Male

70

60

Female

50

40

30

20

10

16–17 18–19 20–24 25–29 30–34 35–39 40–44 45–49 50–54 55–59 60–64 65–69 70+
AGE

Figure 2.2.   Age-Participation Profiles of Men and Women, 1978

SOURCE: *Employment and Earnings*, January 1979, pp. 156–57, table 3.

are clearly called for, the marginal returns from looking at yet another table or figure of labor force participation rates, in the absence of a theoretical framework to facilitate arranging the information available and making predictions, diminish very rapidly. The purpose of this chapter is to develop and apply that necessary theoretical underpinning.

First, existing theories of labor supply and time allocation will be used to provide a consistent and symmetrical framework for interpreting and predicting labor force participation decisions of both men and women. We assume that all individuals work, and therefore, a move into or out of the labor force is seen as an "interindustry" job change. The major differences between men and women in labor force participation rates, average hours and weeks worked, and total years spent in the labor force, will be shown to relate to their common concern for efficient time allocation.

These theoretical tools will be used in a critical examination of detailed labor market statistics and important empirical research on labor supply. No one statistical measure can adequately capture all the dimensions of labor supply, which include not only the identification of the relative number of labor force members at a point in time, but also the extent and continuity of labor force attachment over the year, over the business cycle and over the life cycle. Therefore, in addition to labor force participation rates, measures of hours and weeks worked and labor market experience will be used both in cross section and over time. Thus the consistency of theoretical predictions and previous research can be checked against the observed facts.

We will also find that, although the economic literature abounds with various empirical tests of labor supply theory, the many available studies differ from each other in terms of both the types and sources of data used and the methodology, with some looking exclusively at either males and/or females, while others use sex as an important differentiating factor. The types of questions economists have asked and the assumptions they have made must be carefully defined and critically evaluated. The many questions that remain unanswered can be identified only after the most significant findings to date have been summarized.

Labor Supply Theory

The original neoclassical theory of labor supply (e.g. Robbins 1930; Marshall 1938: 528–29; Lewis 1956) was designed to explain and predict the participation and hours decisions of men. Because men represented the dominant group in the labor force at that time, an explanation of their behavior was sufficient to analyze changes and predict trends. Men have traditionally spent the bulk of their productive years in continuous full-time labor market activity and, although everyone engages in some productive work outside the market sector, it did not originally seem a severe distortion of reality to assume that such nonmarket work represented a negligible portion of men's time. Leisure and income are the two sources of utility which an individual seeks to maximize, subject to the constraints of his earning capacity and his total available time. The usual substitution and income effects of consumer demand theory are easily derived.

An increase in an individual's wage rate leads to two opposing effects on labor supply. Because of an increase in the opportunity cost of time, the demand for leisure will fall and hours of work will increase. On the other hand, income will increase for a given number of hours worked, which will lead to a decline in the supply of hours if leisure is a normal good. This leads to the prediction that for individuals with lower levels of participation, the substitution effect is more likely to outweigh the income effect because the size of the increase in income is dependent on hours worked. The opposite would be true of individuals with high levels of participation.[1] However, the net impact of the income and substitution effects on labor supply is an empirical question, and the effect of the upward trend in real wages cannot be predicted from the theory alone.

Figure 2.3 (pages 24–25) illustrates the derivation of the income and substitution effects of a change in the wage rate, on the assumption that market work and leisure are the only two possible uses of time. Leisure is assumed to be a normal good, and thus the positive income effect and the negative substitution effect on leisure, when the wage rate rises, are in opposite directions.

For individual A, who works relatively few hours (TL_1) and has a relatively large amount of leisure (OL_1) at the original wage rate, the substitution effect outweighs the income effect. Thus hours of work increase (to TL_3) and hours of leisure decrease (to OL_3) when the wage rate increases, and the individual A's labor supply curve slopes upwards. Individual B, on the other hand, has relatively little leisure (OJ_1 hours) and works relatively long hours (TJ_1) at the original wage rate. In this case, the income effect outweighs the substitution effect, and the increase in the wage rate causes a decline in hours of work and an increase in leisure hours. The labor supply curve of individual B is backward bending.

Mincer (1962a) expanded the simple model described above to include productive uses of time outside the market sector. His extended theoretical framework was designed to explain the participation decisions of married women, whose pattern of increased participation rates differed sharply from the downward trend in labor force participation for men. Despite the relatively small number of women in the labor force, their rates of increase began to dominate total labor force trends in the mid-sixties and, therefore, an explanation of the behavior of married women became an increasingly important element in understanding and predicting labor force trends.

In Mincer's model, all women work. The total number of hours of work is determined by family income, but the distribution of those hours between the home and market sectors is determined by a woman's productivity in the market (that is, her earning capacity) relative to her productivity in the home. An optimal allocation of time requires that the marginal hour yield the same productivity in each use. If an hour of time worked in the market yields a wage which exceeds the value a woman implicitly places on her time at home, she will supply labor to the market sector. She will continue to do so until the incremental wage earned equals the marginal value of her time at home. The law of diminishing returns predicts that marginal productivity in the home will rise as the time allocated to work in the home declines. If time in the home is more productive than time in the market, a woman will withdraw hours from the market until marginal productivities are equalized or until all hours are withdrawn from the market sector. In the latter case, the value of her marginal productivity at home exceeds her wage in the market.

This three-way model of choice leads to an additional substitution possibility as wage rates change. An increase in the wage rate not only implies an increase in the price of leisure and an increase in income for those who work, but also an increase in the productivity of time in the market relative to time at home. For working women, a rise in the opportunity cost of leisure will lead to increased work, and an increase in the relative productivity of market work will lead to an increase in the proportion of total work done in the market sector. However, for many women who do not engage in market activities, a rise in their potential wage rate will lead to no change in behavior if the value of their home productivity remains higher than the increased wage. Although this theory was designed to explain the labor force behavior of married women within a family context, the same substitution possibilities are equally relevant for men, particularly at the younger and older ages, where acceptable alternatives to labor market activity exist in the form of schooling and retirement.

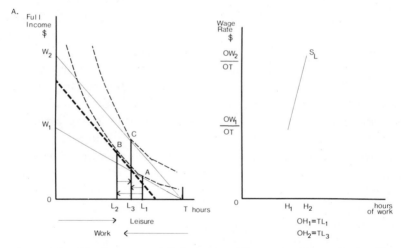

Figure 2.3. The Income and Substitution Effects of a Change in the Wage Rate

A.   The Substitution Effect Outweighs the Income Effect, and the Supply Curve of Labor Slopes Upward

NOTE: OW_1/OT = original wage rate.
OW_2/OT = higher wage rate.
L_1L_2 = substitution effect.
L_2L_3 = income effect.
L_1L_3 = net wage effect.

Becker (1965) expanded and generalized the theory of time allocation, which applies to any individual and includes a wide range of
productive nonmarket activities. An individual's utility is assumed to
derive from certain basic commodities (i.e., a dinner, a trip) which are
produced by combining goods and services bought in the market with
his or her own time. An individual's own time outside the market sector is an essential ingredient, both because market goods and services
in many cases must be further processed to yield desirable commodities, and because time is needed to consume and enjoy the
household commodities produced. Although work time yields the
income necessary to purchase the desired market goods and services, it
competes with time needed to produce and consume commodities at
home.

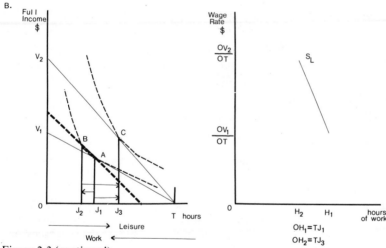

Figure 2.3 (continued)

B. The Income Effect Outweighs the Substitution Effect, and the Supply
    Curve of Labor Bends Backward

NOTE: OV_1/OT = original wage rate.
$\quad\quad OV_2/OT$ = higher wage rate.
$\quad\quad J_1J_2$ = substitution effect.
$\quad\quad J_2J_3$ = income effect.
$\quad\quad J_1J_3$ = net wage effect.

In this model, which is perfectly general in its applicability to either sex, a rise in the market wage will have the usual income and substitution effects. However, they are derived differently. A rise in income leads to an increased demand for household commodities. In order to produce these additional commodities, an individual must withdraw some time from the market. An increase in the opportunity cost of time leads to an increase in the relative price of time-intensive commodities and a shift in demand toward relatively less time-intensive commodities. In addition, the production of all commodities will become less time-intensive as the relative price of the time input increases. As in Mincer's theory, a change in the wage will lead to a reallocation of work time until the marginal hour yields the same productivity in each use. Although it may be easier, for example, to substitute market goods and services for time in the production of a meal than in the care of a child, the net substitution effect of a rise in the opportunity cost of time will be a reduction in the total nonmarket time used to produce any given set of household commodities. Substitution is possible in both production and consumption, but the net effect of a rise in wages on labor supply cannot be predicted a priori and remains an empirical question, because of the countervailing income effect on hours of work.

The general theory of time allocation can easily be extended from the individual to the multiperson household:

Instead of simply allocating time efficiently among commodities, multiperson households also allocate the time of different members. Members who are relatively more efficient at market activities would use less of their time at consumption activities [i.e., work in the home] than would other members. Moreover, an increase in the relative market efficiency of any member would effect a reallocaton of the time of all other members towards consumption activities in order to permit the former to spend more time at market activities. In short, the allocation of time of any member is greatly influenced by the opportunities open to other members. (Becker 1965: 512)

Within the household, the time of all members is pooled and considered a joint resource available for the production of income and household commodities. In the husband-wife family, each household commodity now has three potential types of input: market goods and services, husband's time, and wife's time. The time of children or other adults is also available in larger households. Considerations of efficiency will determine each family member's allocation of time. The broad division of labor between market work and home production will be determined by the productivity of time in the market relative to time in the home for each member. This model does not necessarily predict the specialization of men in market work and women in home work, although this has been the typical pattern. A family with several earners is perfectly consistent with the model, and would imply that the wage rate available to each partner exceeded each earner's valuation of his or her marginal home productivity at zero hours of market work. The division of labor within the household sector will also depend on relative productivities. The members spending relatively more time in the market will spend relatively less time at home but, within that home time, each member will allocate time to those tasks at which he or she is most productive. Men and women may be potential, although not necessarily perfect, substitutes in some household activities, such as cooking, cleaning, and laundry, whereas they may tend to engage in others, such as child rearing and leisure activities, together, and thus be complements.

Although the continuum of uses of time implied by time allocation theory appears to be a step forward to a higher level of generality, in practice it has tended to result in the blurring of the important distinction between leisure and nonmarket work emphasized by Mincer. Very recently, as detailed time budget evidence has made it possible to analyze the components as well as the total amount of nonmarket time, the distinction between consumption and work time in the nonmarket sector has again been drawn (e.g., Gronau 1977).

Consumption time is a direct source of utility, while work at home is an input in the production of goods and services produced at home. It is possible to hire others to do one's nonmarket work, but leisure time cannot be transferred from one individual to another. Obviously, the work-leisure distinction *within* the nonmarket sector remains especially crucial in the case of women's time allocation.

Until recently, all labor supply theory, including the theory of the allocation of time, was set in a one-period framework in which average lifetime levels of labor force participation were based on certain average or "permanent" levels of income and wages. This theory was mainly used empirically to explain differences among individuals in their levels of participation at a point in time. However, over the working life of an individual, the wage rate usually rises rapidly at first, then the rate of growth decreases until the peak is reached, and eventually the wage levels off or even declines. The life cycle approach to time allocation, as developed by Ghez and Becker (1975), considers the determination of the general level of labor force participation as well as the timing of participation over the life cycle in response to seasonal, cyclical and life cycle changes in wage rates. Lifetime levels of labor supply and household consumption and production are determined by permanent income, but the timing of a given lifetime level of labor force participation is determined by the current wage rate. When the wage rate is rising, goods will be substituted for time in current household production, and present consumption will be substituted for future consumption because consumption in the present is relatively cheaper than consumption in the future. Both substitution effects will lead to an increase in hours of work as the wage rate rises. In the theory's simplest form, there would be no income effect to counteract these substitution effects, because permanent income is assumed to be perfectly foreseen at the beginning of the life cycle and therefore does not change. Thus, wages would be positively correlated with labor supply over an individual's life cycle, on the assumption that capital markets are perfect and therefore positive or negative transitory income will have no effect on either consumption in general or the consumption of leisure in particular. Since actual capital markets are far from perfect, the desired smoothing of income and consumption may not be attainable through judicious borrowing and saving alone. Thus, even in a world of perfect foresight, there will be a positive (transitory) income effect on leisure, which will work in the direction of increasing hours of work when the wage rate is relatively low.

J. P. Smith (1977) applies this life cycle model of time allocation in the family context. Over the life cycle of the family, the possibility of intertemporal substitutions in production and consumption complicates the effects of a general rise in wage levels on the division of labor within the household. The labor supply of each family member will be determined by both his or her own wage and the wages of other family members. For the reasons previously discussed, the labor supply of the husband or wife is generally expected to vary positively with wage rate changes over the life cycle. However, again in this more complex model, there are opposing forces at work and the net effect of a rise in the husband's wage on the wife's labor supply cannot be predicted *a priori*. The rise in the cost of future commodities will cause a decrease in the quantity demanded, and thus also a decrease in the derived demand for other inputs, including the wife's time. This would leave more of the wife's future time available for market work. However, the strength of this effect will depend on the share of husband's time in total production costs. In the typical household, this is likely to be relatively small. On the other hand, an increase in the husband's wage will lead to a cross-substitution effect in production toward wife's time, leading to a decline in her labor supply. The same analysis can be applied perfectly symmetrically to the effect on the husband's labor supply of a rise in the wife's wage over the life cycle.

The assumption that lifetime wage rates and income are known with perfect foresight is obviously unrealistic, although it is not surprising that it is made, given the complexity of the theory. In reality, uncertainty exists because of dispersion in possible future wage rates as well as in the incidence and duration of possible unemployment. As Block and Heineke (1973) show, a high degree of uncertainty about wage rates could lead to a reduction of market labor supply and the substitution of hours toward home production, where the value of output is more predictable, but increased uncertainty with regard to nonwage income will definitely lead to increased labor supply. In a family context, each individual responds to the earnings of other family members as nonwage income. Thus an increase in the uncertainty of one member's wage will cause others to increase their labor supply in order to compensate for this uncertainty.

The general theory of time allocation which is now evolving into the more complex areas of the life cycle, uncertainty, and finer distinctions within the nonmarket component of time, can be used as a starting point to analyze and explain the typical differences between male and female labor force participation and hours of work, as well as deviations around the average and changes that have taken place over time.

Empirical Evidence on Labor Supply

All empirical studies of labor supply estimate the direction and degree of change in labor force participation and/or hours of work induced by changes in individual and family characteristics and market conditions. Both because the very levels of participation characteristic of different groups may affect the degree of flexibility in response to changing circumstances, and because these levels are of great interest in their own right, differentials between men and women in labor force participation and hours of work must be carefully examined. This examination of recent differentials and trends in labor supply for men and women provides the background against which an understanding of the determinants of these trends can be developed through a review of the empirical research on labor supply responsiveness. Thus we can not only comprehend how labor supply behavior has varied in the past, but also attempt to project future patterns in the face of continuing economic, social and demographic change.

Separating the labor force participation and hours of work decisions is somewhat misleading, as the individual should ideally be viewed as making these decisions simultaneously, or as making one rather complex labor supply decision involving several dimensions. The decision as to how many hours of work to supply to the market, which is represented in figure 2.3, necessarily incorporates the labor force participation decision, for it is always possible to choose the "corner solution" of supplying zero hours (i.e., not participating in the labor force). However, here as elsewhere, it will be necessary to sacrifice some analytic precision in the interest of ease of presentation. Since the vast bulk of both available data and empirical studies deals with labor force participation and hours of work separately, we will also deal first with the levels and determinants of labor force participation and afterward with hours and weeks of work. The reader should keep in mind, however, that this separation is an artificial one for the sake of convenience, and that the two decisions are actually simultaneous rather than sequential. A third important dimension of labor supply, the continuity of labor force attachment, is also analyzed separately. Although the available information here is scanty at best, this is a key variable in determining sex differentials, and is the subject of both speculation and heated debate.

LABOR FORCE PARTICIPATION

All published data on labor force participation, which are cross-tabulated according to various personal and family characteristics, come from the Census Bureau. Monthly and annual data come from the Current Population Survey (CPS), which is based on interviews of a stratified sample of 47,000 households. Once a year, in March, inter-viewees are asked a detailed set of questions relating to marital and family characteristics, work experience and educational attainment. Once every ten years the Census provides similar information on labor force participation based on a sample of the total population enumerated.[2] In addition, the Census data provides information on hours worked in the sample week, and weeks worked in the previous year, for different labor force groups. Each of these samples is used to estimate the size of the labor force and its components for the country as a whole, with sex, race and geographic weights based on current census information.

Standard definitions of labor force status are used in each of these samples, and only those of working age—16 and older—are included. The employed are those working for pay or profit at least one hour a week, or working at least fifteen hours a week on the farm or in a family business, as well as those "with a job but not at work" for some temporary reason. The unemployed are those who are without a job but currently looking for work and available for work, plus all those on temporary layoff from a job. Members of the noninstitu-tional population not categorized in either of these two groups are defined as "out of the labor force," and thus the total labor force is defined as the sum of the employed and the unemployed. The labor force participation rate is simply the ratio of the labor force to the total noninstitutional population.

In many cases, the ways individuals are categorized and the types of cross-classification that are available reflect a very traditional view of the division of labor between the sexes, and prevent a truly symmetrical analysis of male and female labor force characteristics. For example, labor force participation rates are available for women according to their husbands' income and the presence and ages of children, but comparable statistics are not available for men. Current interest in women's issues has expanded the special cross-classifications available for women without in any way changing the traditional concept of men's unwavering attachment to the labor force. The arbitrary designation of the husband as the head of the household, as discussed in chapter 1, is another good example of the fact that the data collection process itself is not value-neutral.

In the last few years, there has been a renewed interest in an empirical study of the economic determinants of labor supply because of many policy makers' concern for the possible work disincentive effects of income maintenance programs. Although work incentive and disincentive effects have always been implicit in government tax and welfare policies, the debate in the 1960s concerning the optimal design of income maintenance programs to alleviate poverty inspired many economists to attempt new and more sophisticated estimating procedures to isolate the income and substitution effects of economic theory on the labor supply of low-income individuals. A wealth of new data sources, including the 1967 Survey of Economic Opportunity (SEO), the 1970 Census, experimental data and several longitudinal samples, such as the National Longitudinal Survey (NLS) and the University of Michigan Panel Study of Income Dynamics (MID), have reinforced interest in labor supply research, as it has recently become possible to test responses over portions of the life cycle and to reestimate previously estimated relationships with less restrictive assumptions.

The majority of published studies of labor force participation have used cross-sectional data to estimate, across individuals or geographic regions, the responses to changes in wages and income and to many other personal and family characteristics, for either a moment in time or over the life cycle. The application of such results to the explanation of trends in participation requires the fairly strong assumption that differences in labor force participation between individuals in differing economic circumstances at a point in time correspond to the changes any one individual would make in labor force participation if his or her circumstances should change. Although cyclical and time series data would be preferable to answer some of these questions, such data have not been collected with sufficient detail to test fully the questions raised by the economists' theory of optimal household decision-making. However, these data can be used to explore the responsiveness of the labor force to certain changes in labor market conditions. The recent availability of longitudinal data sets provides, for the first time, both the individual detail characteristic of cross sections and the ability to follow changes over time in the behavior of the same individuals or groups characteristic of time series data.

Because the available data lend themselves to different kinds of questions, the evidence on labor force participation will be reviewed in three basic parts. The first part will describe recent trends and patterns in labor force participation; the second part will deal with the explanations of these patterns and trends that have been formulated and tested using cross-sectional data; finally, analysis of time-series data will be examined and utilized to provide some of the necessary links between observed cross-sectional patterns and trends over time. These comparisons will enable us to distinguish differential responses to temporary and more permanent changes in economic conditions, and to synthesize various pieces of information concerning labor force participation into a cohesive overview.

Trends and Patterns in Labor Force Participation

Table 2.1 and figure 2.1 displayed the trends in the aggregate labor force participation rates of men and women. We will now examine the components and determinants of the dramatic upward trend in female labor force participation and the decline in male labor force participation. Figures 2.4 and 2.5 provide a breakdown of the trends in labor force participation by age and race.

Although sex differentials in labor force participation rates have been narrowing within all groups, the reasons often differ. For men and women under 55, the primary cause has been the rise in women's labor force participation, whereas declining male labor force participation has been largely responsible for the narrowing differential among those aged 55 and over. Among white workers, the major

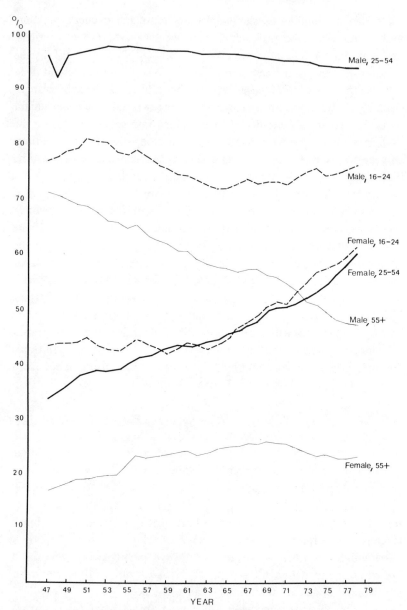

Figure 2.4.   Trends in Labor Force Participation by Age and Sex

SOURCE: 1947–77: U.S. Dept. of Labor, *Employment and Training Report of the President* (1978), pp. 181–182, table A-2.

1978: *Employment and Earnings*, January 1979, pp. 156–57, table 3.

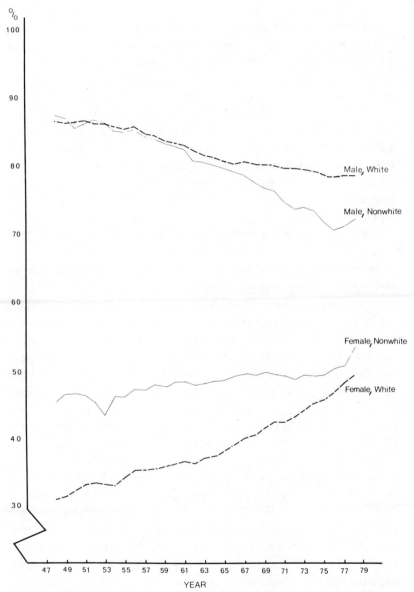

Figure 2.5.   Trends in Civilian Labor Force Participation by Race and Sex

Source: 1948–1953: U.S. Dept. of Labor, *Employment and Training Report of the President* (1977), pp. 142–144, table A-4.
1954–1977: U.S. Dept. of Labor, *Employment and Training Report of the President* (1978), pp. 186–188. table A-4.
1978: *Employment and Earnings*, January 1979, pp. 156–57, table 3.

35

reason for the narrowing of the gap has been the rise in female labor force participation, but the decline in male participation has dominated the narrowing differential among nonwhites. As can be seen in figure 2.5, the labor force participation rate of nonwhite women has shown little upward trend.

When men and women are classified according to marital status, the only group that shows a consistent decline in differentials for every age is the married group. Among single men and women, the differentials are never large and in several years, particularly among the 20- to 24-year-olds, women's labor force participation rates exceed men's. Among those widowed, divorced and separated, sex differentials are not as large as those in the married group and the only group among whom differentials have narrowed is the 45- to 64-year-olds.[3]

The decline in fertility since 1957 and the rise in average educational attainment among women throughout the period (see chapter 3) have been significantly related to the dramatic postwar rise observed in the labor force participation rates of married women. The assumption is traditionally made, as in Becker (1973), that the presence of children is the primary determinant of the division of labor between the sexes and, therefore, the changing role of women can be explained by the changing importance of children in the family. However, even among women with children at home there has been a dramatic increase in labor force participation. The labor force participation rate of married women with children under 6 was 39.3 percent in 1977, as compared to 18.6 percent in 1960, an increase of 111 percent. The labor force participation rate of married women with children from 6 to 17 increased 43 percent and that of those with no children under 18 increased only 23 percent over the same period.[4] It is clear that the "rules of the game" are changing and that children are no longer the deterrent they were traditionally assumed to be. For more and more women the pull of market opportunities is stronger than the demands of young children in the home.

Labor force participation rates vary much more by education among women than among men. For example, among those 25 to 34, 36.7 percent of women with an eighth-grade education were in the labor force in March 1977, as opposed to 72.4 percent of women with a college education. Among men in the same age group, the participation rate of college-educated men was only 8.7 percentage points higher than the rate of grade-school graduates.[5] Therefore, we would expect that rising educational attainment for both men and women would lead to a narrowing of the differential between their labor force participation rates.

May 1978 was a significant month in that the total female labor force participation rate passed the halfway mark for the first time; 50.1 percent of all women aged 16 and over were in the labor force. However, as we saw in chapter 1, this rate is actually deceptively low. For women aged 20–64, those in the labor force are more strongly in the majority; 58.5 percent of women in these prime ages were in the labor force in 1978.

A comparison of age-participation profiles, such as those presented in figure 2.2 for men and women in 1978, is a useful way of visualizing differences in labor force participation between the sexes. However, these must be interpreted with extreme caution, particularly for women, because dramatically changing trends make it unrealistic to assume that a young woman who is 20 in 1978 will follow the pattern of participation over her life cycle which is characteristic of women of older ages in 1978. Therefore, the smaller differences between men and women in the younger age groups observed in figure 2.2 must be interpreted partly as a life-cycle phenomenon, but partly as a result of the long-run trend in the direction of greater labor force participation by women. We shall return to the question of life-cycle participation and the continuity of labor force attachment shortly.

Additional detail on cross-sectional patterns of labor force participation is presented in figures 2.6 and 2.7, which deal with differences by race and sex in age-participation profiles, and shifts in the female age-participation profiles over the past 28 years, respectively. Significant differences emerge when racial comparisons are made. The differential between black men and women is narrower at every age and, although it widens in the middle years, the change is small compared to the change among whites. In fact, only white women show a drop in participation rates during the childbearing years. Although lower throughout, the participation rates of black women follow a pattern similar to that of men, rising to a peak between the ages of 35 and 44,

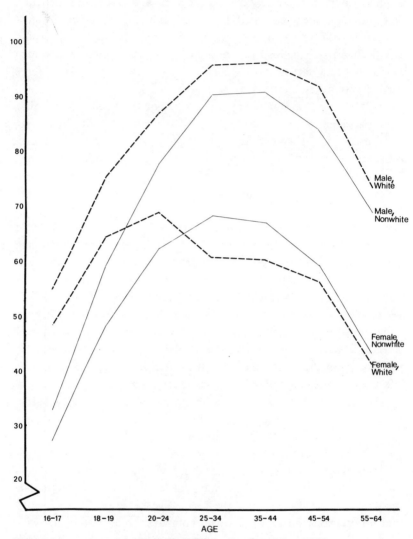

Figure 2.6.　Age-Participation Profiles by Race and Sex, 1978

SOURCE: *Employment and Earnings*, January 1979, pp. 156–57, table 3.

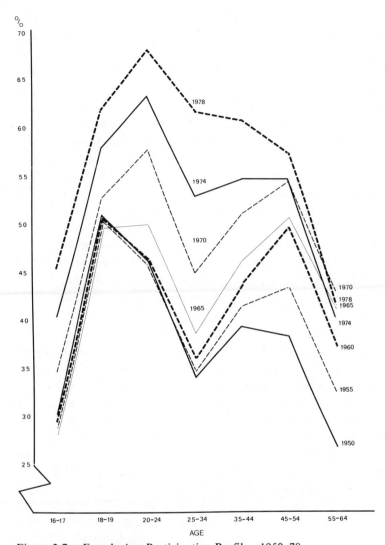

Figure 2.7.   Female Age-Participation Profiles, 1950–78

Source: 1950–74: U.S. Dept. of Labor, *Employment and Training Report of the President* (1978), pp. 181–82, table A-2.
1978: *Employment and Earnings*, January 1979, p. 159, table 4.

and falling off thereafter. Sharp contrasts also appear in the comparison of current age-participation patterns of men and women by marital status. Not surprisingly, the most pronounced sex differentials in both the levels of participation and the shapes of the profiles occur in the married group.

The pattern of shifts in female age-participation profiles over time, as shown in figure 2.7, provides some of the links between cross-sectional patterns and long-run trends, and tells a fascinating story. The steady upward movement of the entire profile from 1950 to 1978 is of course consistent with the observed upward trend in female labor force participation, and confirms the fact that, although the relative contribution of different age groups to the growth in participation has varied considerably over time, every age group from 16 to 64 has exhibited a substantial increase over the past quarter-century. By 1950, the "two-peaked" pattern of female labor force participation was already established, although the second peak, after age 35, was not very pronounced and much lower than the first peak at age 18–19. For the next fifteen years, when the growth in female labor force participation was concentrated in the age groups 35 to 64, this second peak grew rapidly, and was only marginally lower than the first peak by 1965.

In the past thirteen years, although strong growth in female labor force participation has been continuous, the pattern of that growth has undergone major changes. Between 1965 and 1970, pronounced growth in the participation of women under 35 appeared for the first time, while that for older women continued, with the result that the entire profile shifted upwards in roughly parallel fashion; the 1965 and 1970 profiles are quite similar to each other in exhibiting a pronounced "two-peaked" or M-shaped pattern. By 1970, however, the exceptionally strong growth in the participation rate of women aged 20–24 resulted in two changes that foreshadowed developments to come in the 1970s: the first peak was once again substantially above the second, and the peak participation age had moved up from 18–19 to 20–24.

By 1978, we find that the familiar double peak in female labor force participation has disappeared. It was already much less pronounced by 1974, due to a rapid upward shift in the "trough" at ages 25–34 and much slower growth among women aged 35 and over. If we project the patterns of change of the 1970s into the future (admittedly a questionable procedure at best), continued rapid increases among those aged 25–44 might well transform the shape of the female age-participation profile into the familiar inverted U exhibited by male profiles.

Clearly there have been rapid and continuous changes in both the level and pattern of female labor force participation. While the dramatic nature of these changes guarantees that even a straightforward description will be of interest, it is even more desirable to be able to explain as well as describe what has been happening, and thus to be able to predict future behavior as well. We turn now to the wealth of empirical work on the economics of labor force participation, in search of such consistent explanations and predictions.

The first apparent anomaly we encounter is that, while the most fascinating aspect of the labor force participation decision is the phenomenon of pronounced secular change, the vast majority of detailed studies make use of cross-sectional samples for a particular year. Furthermore, among those studies that do analyze time-series data directly, the tendency is to focus the main attention on short-run fluctuations rather than on long-run trends, with the necessity of examining the underlying causes of the latter eliminated by the use of some form of trend variable. Thus our examination of the determinants of levels of and changes in labor force participation will be subdivided along lines dictated by the nature of the data used in the various studies: we will look first at studies using aggregate cross-sectional data, then at those using individual cross-sectional data, and finally at studies involving the direct analysis of time-series data.

Aggregate Data

Much of the earlier research of labor supply for both men and women relied heavily on aggregate data for Standard Metropolitan Statistical Areas (SMSAs), industries or occupations to test the effect of various market conditions and average group characteristics on labor supply. Although none of these studies provide a truly symmetrical and comparative analysis of men and women, the broad outlines of our present knowledge of sex differences evolved from this research, as did the major questions and concerns of most contemporary research.

Although the secular decline, at least through 1955, in hours worked per week in industry is clearly consistent with the existence of a backward-bending supply curve of labor, where the income effect of a rise in wages dominates the substitution effect, as in figure 2.3B (see Lewis 1956), the rapid rise in the labor force participation rate of married women in the postwar period raised questions about the universal applicability of this concept. Mincer's (1962a) pioneering article on the labor force participation of married women called attention to the family context in which labor market decisions are made, and provided empirical results which confirmed the general applicability of labor supply theory. In order to use differences in labor force participation rates across SMSAs as a proxy for individual differences in labor supply, Mincer assumed that the labor force participation rate for a region could be considered an approximation of the fraction of working life that women in that region spend, on the average, in the labor force. Then differences between regions in labor force participation rates can be interpreted as differences in average labor supply over the life cycle. Using data from 1950, he found that a rise in the median income of women working full time (a proxy for their wage rate) had a positive effect on labor force participation which significantly outweighed the negative effect of husbands' income. These results were then interpreted as life cycle responses to long-run or "permanent" changes in relevant variables, given that the age and family-type mix in different regions is similar at a given time. Cain's (1966) results from the 1940, 1950, and 1960 Censuses basically confirmed Mincer's results, although the effect of wage changes on labor supply was not always as large. In addition, Cain analyzed the higher rates of participation for black women and suggested several explanations, including (1) less job discrimination against black women than black men; (2) housing patterns which facilitate child care; (3) marital instability; and (4) more part-time jobs for black women.

Bowen and Finegan (1969), using data from the 1960 Census, produced the first major attempt to analyze the labor supply behavior of both men and women, using similar techniques of analysis. The effects of individual characteristics and market conditions on labor force participation were explored for each age and sex group. However, because the traditional division of labor between the sexes was assumed, women's "individual" characteristics included her husband's income and occupation and the presence of children, whereas the man's individual characteristics included only his own personal attributes. His family circumstances, including the income of his wife, were assumed to play a negligible role in his labor supply decision. Although differences between the sexes in the factors included as determinants of market behavior make consistent comparisons impossible, Bowen and Finegan's results imply that women and other secondary groups (such as younger and older men) are more responsive to wage rate changes than are prime-age males. It is interesting, if not surprising, to note that a positive relationship between labor force participation rates and wages was found for every age-sex group. Black prime-age males and young people were also found to have a slightly lower participation rate than similar whites, even when various explanatory variables had been controlled for. The opposite was true for black and white married women.

More recent results reported by Bell (1974), using the 1967 SEO, raise new questions concerning racial differences in participation rates, with the finding that if black women had had the characteristics of white women, they would have participated even more than they actually did. The important role of long-term family income prospects is a possible explanation of these differentials. The degree of discrimination faced by black men in the labor force reduces their income prospects, and thus induces greater participation among black women, even during childbearing years.

When Heckman and Ashenfelter (1974) retested Bowen and Finegan's aggregate analysis of the 1960 Census data, they used a family labor supply model in which the wage of each spouse and total family nonwage income are assumed to be the three primary determinants of the labor supply of married men and women aged 25–54. That is, the labor supply of each member of the family is now seen as subject to an income effect and *two* substitution effects: the pure substitution effect of a change in one's *own* wage rate, which has a positive effect on labor supply, and the cross-substitution effect of a change in one's *spouse's* wage rate, which is positive or negative depending on whether spouses' nonmarket hours are, on balance, complements or substitutes. It is, of course, possible, and in fact intuitively plausible, that these nonmarket hours could be complementary in some activities (leisure, which is not transferable between individuals), and substitutable in others (nonmarket work).

Although they continue to assume that the presence of children is a determinant of female labor supply but not of male labor supply, their results provide the only reasonably comparable estimates, based on aggregate data, of the responsiveness of male and female labor force participation rates. The results show that an increase in a husband's wage has no net effect on the husband's labor supply and a significant negative effect on the wife's labor supply. An increase in the wife's wage, on the other hand, has a negligible net impact on the husband's labor supply and a significant positive effect on the wife's labor supply. These results lead to the conclusion that, in the prime-age groups, men's labor supply is unaffected by differences in family wages and income, whereas women's labor supply could not be predicted without knowledge of these average wage and income differences between regions.[6]

The application of the coefficients derived from these aggregate cross-sectional studies to an explanation of the ongoing secular increase in female labor force participation involves examining the relative sizes of the elasticities with respect to income levels and wage rates. The observed growth is interpreted as resulting from the fact that the positive wage effect on labor force participation exceeds the negative income effect in absolute value, since the wages of married men and women have grown at roughly the same rate. (See chapter 4 for information concerning trends in the earnings of men and women.)[7]

In fact, it is actually impossible to imagine how an increase in wages could have anything but a positive effect on labor force participation rates, because those women who are out of the labor force entirely receive no income gains as wages rise. The size of the positive relationship between labor force participation rates and wages would depend on the distribution of the groups according to tastes and/or reservation wages. If a normal distribution of reservation wages is assumed for a group, then, as the wage rises, the absolute response of that group's labor force participation rate should increase up to the point where the market wage is equal to the mean of the group's reservation wage, at which point half the group should be in the labor force. After that point, as wages continue to rise, the responsiveness of the labor force participation rate should decrease. The implication is that groups with very low or very high labor force participation will exhibit a lower wage elasticity than groups such as women with labor force participation rates closer to 50 percent (Ben-Porath 1973:703).

The interpretation of all these results, which consistently find that the net elasticity of female labor force participation with respect to the wage rate is significantly positive, raises important and complex questions regarding the continuity of labor force attachment and the amount of turnover. The simple framework of individual labor supply theory, as described earlier, "must be supplemented by further assumption specifying how one moves from the individual to the population if the theory is to be used with data describing many individuals and the estimates are to be applied to market phenomena" (Ben-Porath 1973:698). The assumption originally made by Mincer (1962a) is that, within race, sex, and other groups, people have equal tastes for market work, and thus wish to offer the same amount of labor under the same set of market circumstances. This implies that the labor force participation rate for a particular group is a reasonable estimate of the proportion of time that each member of that group will spend in the labor force, and that individual differences at any point in time are thus the result of variations in timing. This assumption of roughly homogeneous groups means that a considerable degree of turnover will be characteristic of those groups with relatively low rates of labor force participation.

However, other plausible hypotheses concerning the individual behavior patterns underlying the observed group averages are certainly possible. Ben-Porath suggests two versions of such an alternative hypothesis concerning the sources of individual differences: (1) differences in tastes and/or nonmarket productivity, both of which result in differences in the reservation wage or shadow price of time, and (2) differences in the wage rates that apparently similar individuals could actually get, because of unmeasured differences in personal characteristics. Either of these would imply relatively low turnover and a positive correlation between an individual's labor force participation across different periods. Data from the 1960 Census (Ben-Porath 1973:701) as well as some panel data (Heckman and Willis 1977) indicate a high correlation between an individual's labor force status across successive years.[8] This evidence raises serious questions about the proper interpretation of the empirical results based on aggregate data discussed above, because a labor force participation rate can no longer be considered an estimate of the average percentage of the life cycle spent in the labor force by a member of the group in question. Microdata sets, which provide information on the characteristics of specific individuals, form a basis for the testing of alternative hypotheses.

Individual Data

Census and other sample data on individuals and family units provide a wealth of information on personal, family and economic characteristics which are not similarly available on an aggregate level. Because labor supply theory is built up from an analysis of the individual decisionmaker or the utility-maximizing household, this microdata provides an important basis for the testing of labor supply responsiveness. It is also important because it provides the opportunity to test the economic determinants of the division of labor between the sexes. However, large variations in tastes among individuals make it impossible for the economist to account for the major portion of the total variation in labor supply within these samples. In aggregate data, on the other hand, variations in tastes are largely washed out in the averaging process.

On the individual level, labor force participation becomes a dichotomous variable with each individual categorized as either in or out of the labor force. When using regression analysis to explain labor force status, the effect of each variable is measured in terms of a change in the probability of an individual's participation. Because of the statistical difficulties inherent in examining the determinants of labor force status on an individual basis, where the independent variable is not continuous,[9] most studies using microdata have focused on continuously variable "time" dimensions of labor supply, such as hours worked per week or per year. However, a minority of these studies do attempt to predict the probability of participation, in addition to or instead of hours of work, for individuals.[10]

We find that essentially three basic forms of a labor supply equation have been estimated: the labor force participation equation, with a dichotomous dependent variable, as discussed above; the hours worked equation, estimated by using only those who actually worked in the market; and the total labor supply equation, which predicts expected hours worked by all persons, included those currently outside the labor force. Each of these approaches is characterized by specific problems related to such factors as missing variables, selectivity bias, and difficulties in estimation. At this point, we will discuss only the determinants of the labor force participation decision, leaving the latter two forms of the labor supply equation to be considered in the subsequent discussion of hours and weeks of work. As it turns out, the vast majority of studies which have used microdata to explore the labor force participation decision have focused only on women,[11] and particularly on those family characteristics which are predicted to affect their work decision, such as husband's income and education, and the presence of children. Gramm (1973) expanded the dichotomous analysis of the labor force participation decision to include three alternatives—no work, part-time work and full-time work—instead of the usual two.[12] She argues that if the wage for part-time work differs from the wage for full-time work, the labor supply decision becomes a discrete choice in which the utility of alternative combinations of hours of work and earnings must be compared. Unfortunately, the fact that the wage rate is itself a (positive) function of current hours of work must often be ignored, given data limitations and the need for simplifying assumptions.

The lack of wage observations for nonworking women makes it impossible to derive a labor force participation equation by using actual wage rates as one of the determinants of labor force participation; somehow a predicted or potential wage rate must be estimated for all women. This missing variable problem can be evaded (although, as we shall see, at the cost of creating additional serious biases) in the context of predicting hours of work by simply restricting the sample to labor force participants only and using the actual wage rate. However, no such escape route, however imperfect, exists if one wishes to predict probabilities of participation; nonworking women must be included in the sample. The usual procedure (e.g., Cain 1966) has been to assign to nonworking women a "potential" wage which is equal to the average market wage earned by working women with the same individual and family characteristics. Alternatively, women's wage is not included as a predictor of labor force status, and education is considered a proxy for wage (e.g., Bowen and Finegan 1969). Although the results tend to confirm findings from aggregate data on income and substitution effects, there are major problems in the interpretation of these results, and neither of these solutions can really be considered satisfactory.

An individual's decision about whether to go out to work is assumed to depend on a comparison between the wage available to that particular individual in the market and the productivity of that same individual's time at home. For a given home productivity, an increase in the market wage should increase the probability that an individual will participate in the market sector. The presence of children, particularly of preschool age, is assumed to provide a proxy for home productivity because of the increased demands on the mother's time. Without exception, every study of female labor force participation has controlled for the presence of children and has found that children are a deterrent to women's labor force participation, although this effect is less important for black women. However, even when children are included as a proxy for women's nonmarket productivity, education is not an adequate proxy for the market wage, because education also enhances productivity in other nonmarket activities.[13]

The imputation of wages for nonworking women has seemed a more promising approach. However, the fact that a woman is not in the labor force implies that the market wage available is not sufficiently attractive. This could be because the market wage available to her is lower than that offered to other women with similar characteristics and/or because, although the wage available is the same, the value she places on her time at home is higher relative to other women in her group. If the second hypothesis were correct and home productivity were properly controlled for by including variables such as children, education and family income, then an estimated wage could provide an acceptable approximation. However, it is also likely that the first hypothesis is correct and that wages are incorrectly estimated (see Gronau 1973). Because labor force status in one period is highly correlated with labor force status in preceding and subsequent periods, the market wages potentially available to women currently out of the labor force may well be low relative to the wages of working women because of a lack of market experience. In fact, wages are not a truly independent determinant of labor supply because past participation decisions will have implications for present wages.[14] Recent studies have included some measure of market experience in their estimate of market wages, as the first stage in a two-stage estimation procedure of labor force status, under more dynamic assumptions.

Before we return, in the context of the determination of hours of work, to many of the questions concerning measurement and interpretation raised above, we must complete our survey of empirical studies of labor force participation by examining the actual use of time series data. As we noted above, although it appears safe to say that the most interesting aspect of labor force participation is the long-run increase in the labor force participation rate of married women, the lack of detailed data such as is available in cross-sections, combined with the identification problem of distinguishing between supply and demand factors, has led to the paradoxical result that time-series analysis has tended to concentrate on short-run fluctuations, rather than long-run trends, in labor force participation rates.

Short-Run Versus Long-Run Responses

Life cycle theory predicts that individuals and family units plan their total lifetime commitment to the labor force on the basis of expectations of "permanent" income, but time their participation to take advantage of short-run fluctuations in economic conditions. In the long run, individual preferences for leisure versus income will determine how labor force participation will respond to increasing productivity in both the market and the nonmarket sectors, which causes real income and wages to grow. In the short run, the substitutability between husbands and wives in both home work and market work will determine the responsiveness of labor supply to changes in general economic conditions, as well as to changing circumstances within the family. The phrase "discouraged worker effect" is used to identify the reaction of the individual to temporary changes in labor market conditions specifically affecting his or her employability. The assumption is that reduced demand for labor and increased unemployment will temporarily "discourage" workers from entering the labor force and will accelerate their withdrawal. On the other hand, the phrase "additional worker effect" is used to identify the reaction of the individual to temporary changes in the economic circumstances of his or her family. The assumption is that the unemployment of a family member or a temporary decline in his or her income will induce labor force participation of other family members.

Because of the national preoccupation with levels of unemployment and their proper measurement, the cyclical aspect of labor force participation has received primary focus in the literature. Both cross-section and time-series data have been used to explore differences in response patterns to short-run versus long-run change, and to calculate the net effect of "discouraged" and "additional" workers on patterns of labor force participation over the cycle.

Both aggregate and individual data on a cross-sectional basis have been used to test the effect of temporary changes on labor force participation. In aggregate data, the unemployment rate is used as a proxy for labor market conditions in a region, and the measured relationship between unemployment and labor force participation rates across regions is interpreted as a measure of the responsiveness of labor force participation rates to the cycle, as in Bowen and Finegan (1969), Cain (1966), and Mincer (1962a). In every study, for both men and women in all age groups, a significant negative relationship has been found between unemployment and labor force participation rates. This has been interpreted as evidence that the discouraged worker effect is greater than the additional worker effect. In addition, women were found to be more responsive to labor market conditions than men. However, Mincer (1966) suggested that cross-section data lead to an overestimate of short-term labor supply elasticities because of the persistent structural differences between area labor markets. In other words, migration to favorable labor markets and permanent withdrawal from depressed labor markets creates a strong negative correlation, which reflects permanent as well as short-run responses, between unemployment and labor supply across regions.

The discouraged worker effect should primarily affect labor force participation rates, whereas the additional worker effect may affect hours and weeks of work as well. Individual cross-section data provide information on family income and earnings which permit an analysis of the relationship between husband's income and wife's market work. Although temporary changes in the wife's employment status or income should also affect the husband's propensity to work, no empirical studies have yet investigated this question, probably because "additional" workers are assumed to be secondary workers who are associated with a primary male earner.

Mincer (1962a) did look at the differential response of women to temporary and permanent changes in the husband's earnings. For a given number of weeks worked, an increase in earnings was interpreted as an increase in permanent income generated through additional hours of work. He found wives much more responsive to temporary than to permanent changes in income. Given imperfect capital markets, the wife's labor force participation may serve as a buffer to help maintain a consistent pattern of family consumption in the face of a change in the income of the husband. "Mincer's results are significant, not only in emphasizing the dependence of wives' activities on their husbands' economic status, but more importantly, in highlighting the flexibility of the division of labor between the sexes under changing economic circumstances" (Lloyd 1975:10). Bowen and Finegan also found that, other things being equal, wives were more likely to work if their husbands were unemployed than employed.

The net effect of additional and discouraged workers on aggregate labor supply can most easily be tested using time-series data. Since the late 1950s, numerous studies[15] have estimated the relationship between labor force participation rates and various measures of labor market demand, of which the aggregate unemployment rate has been the most frequently used, for different age and sex groups, using annual, quarterly, and monthly data, and some of these earlier studies, covering the postwar cycles through the early 1960s, were reviewed by Mincer (1966). They generally confirmed the procyclical behavior of the labor force. In addition, regression results broken down by age and sex indicated that all women, and men under 25 and over 55, exhibit substantial positive sensitivity to the business cycle, whereas prime-age males show little response. However, as Mincer argued, because labor force participation rates for a particular age-sex group are related to unemployment rates for that same group, the responsiveness of labor supply to the business cycle was seriously overestimated.[16]

More recent studies have extended the data through the early 1970s.[17] These results are in some ways inconsistent and puzzling but, in general, they confirm Mincer's suspicion that short-run supply elasticities were overestimated. However, it is to be expected that labor force behavior will differ substantially between a period of many short cycles (1950s) and a period of unbroken prosperity (1960s).

We have compared labor force responsiveness in the last decade (1966-76), which includes two cycles, to the previous decade (1956-65) (Lloyd and Niemi 1978). We found a statistically significant increase in the sensitivity of the total labor force to cyclical fluctuations in the employment rate between the two periods, which was the result of increased procyclical responsiveness on the part of the male labor force. Because of sex differences in occupational and industrial distributions, secular and cyclical changes in the composition of demand impact differently on men and women (R. E. Smith 1977). Evidence in our results suggests that recessions in the 1970s had a greater negative impact on employment in male-dominated sectors than was the case earlier.

These results confirm that the simple employment rate elasticities, which are usually interpreted as supply responses to short-run changes in employment conditions, are in fact a joint measure of supply responses to fluctuations in both employment rates and sectoral shifts in demand, so that what first appeared to be a statistically significant shift in supply elasticities was in fact the result of a sectoral shift in demand over the business cycle, unfavorable to men and favorable to women. In addition, however, there remain shifts in labor supply behavior in response to the expected wage which probably represent long-run changes, in the direction of men's labor supply behavior becoming more procyclical (or less countercyclical) and women's becoming less procyclical. However, these results are still preliminary, and further investigation is under way. This analysis suggests that discouragement is not solely a function of employment rates, but rather of all the demand factors which affect employment conditions over the business cycle.[18]

On the individual level, short-run fluctuations in market and non-market opportunities and demands will determine the timing of periods of market and nonmarket work. For those who choose to spend virtually all of their lifetime in market work, these questions of timing are not relevant. However, for most women, and for increasing numbers of men who are postponing labor market entry or anticipating early withdrawal, questions of timing are crucial. The smaller the percentage of time individuals plan to spend in the market, the greater their flexibility and their willingness to respond at any point in time to fluctuations in business conditions and family circumstances.

The results of the New Jersey Graduated Work Incentive Experiment (1968–72), as described in Pechman and Timpane (1975), are a clear indication of these individual differences. Families were provided with cash payments ranging from 50 to 125 percent of poverty-line income, with penalty rates which implicitly taxed family earnings at a rate of 30 to 70 percent, on a temporary experimental basis. There was only a small reduction of hours of work among male family heads. Among white and Spanish-speaking working wives, who had low participation rates to begin with, work effort was reduced significantly, by about one-third to one-half. It is clear that it was not worthwhile for the men with high expectations for lifetime participation to adjust to this temporary change in economic circumstances, whereas many women found it an appropriate occasion for temporarily reducing participation rates. A permanent income maintenance program would be more likely to affect males, by changing their expectations of *lifetime* income possibilities.

There is some evidence that individual responsiveness to the business cycle varies by race and previous labor market experience among women. Blau (1978), using NLS data on women aged 30–44, found significant discouraged worker effects for whites and significant additional worker effects among blacks. This may well be due to differences in the incidence of unemployment among white and black husbands. Previous labor market experience was found both to reduce the likelihood of leaving the labor force when unemployment is high and to increase the probability of entering during prosperity, suggesting systematic differences among women in labor market attachment.

However, there is some evidence indicating that "discouragement" which results from cyclical downturns can have long-term repercussions for labor supply, and should not be considered merely a matter of optimal timing. Schweitzer and Smith (1974), using longitudinal data on young men, found that the experience of unemployment and unsuccessful job search increases the probability of withdrawal in the current period, and in subsequent periods as well. In fact, one's expectation of the future is colored by current opportunities and the ultimate level of lifetime participation is very much affected by labor force experience. If this is true, then it is likely that those groups facing higher rates of unemployment and job discrimination may experience long-term discouragement, and permanently lower participation.

We have seen a dramatic narrowing of sex differentials in labor force participation over time. Furthermore, the most dramatic change has been concentrated among the very group of women—those of childbearing age—whose past patterns of discontinuous participation have been the primary source of stereotyped images of the "typical" division of labor between the sexes. These trends have not yet been fully explained by the abundant empirical literature on the determinants of labor force participation. Although the observed positive net wage effect for women, both cross-sectionally and over the business cycle, is consistent with the actual trends, there are problems of measurement and interpretation which cloud our understanding of even the static relationship between labor force participation and wages. A complete explanation of the nature of the secular trends in labor force participation requires a fuller analysis of the other dimensions of labor supply, as well as the dynamic implications of increasing labor force participation.

HOURS AND WEEKS OF WORK

The accurate measurement of differences between groups requires information on various dimensions of labor supply. As we have seen, the labor force participation rate measures the percentage of a group who, during a survey week, was working or was willing to work. Clearly it is possible for two groups with similar labor force participation rates to experience different degrees of participation because of differing hours of work per week, weeks per year, years over the life cycle, or rates of unemployment. Therefore, within the working population, it is interesting to observe differences between groups in weekly hours and annual weeks worked. Empirical studies using cross-section data have usually focused on either labor force participation rates or hours of work, although more recently some studies have included both dimensions of labor supply in a model of sequential, or ideally simultaneous, decision-making.

Trends and Patterns in Hours and Weeks of Work

After the ongoing growth in female labor force participation, the most interesting and dramatic change in labor supply has been the secular decline in the full-time work week. The form this decrease has taken deserves further comment: in contrast to the 35 percent decline from 1900 to 1940, the full-time work week was not found to have changed significantly since 1940 (Kniesner 1976:7). The data on average weekly hours of work in selected years that appear in table 2.2 illustrate this trend. Table 2.3 presents average weekly hours by sex for the most recent ten years, and also the percentage of the civilian labor force working part-time. It is certainly not startling to observe that the average work week of women is consistently about 18 percent shorter than the male work week, and that part of this difference stems from the fact that the fraction of the female labor force in part-time employment is roughly three times as great as the corresponding fraction of the male labor force. It is also the case, however, that even among those who work a full-time week of over thirty-five hours, men still average more hours per week than women.

Thus there are clearly major differences between the sexes, not only in participation rates, but in average hours of work among labor force participants. Because most prime-age men are in the labor force, the main source of variation in their labor supply has been hours of work. For this reason, the bulk of research on men has focused on hours of work per week or per year. On the other hand, much research on

Table 2.2

Average Weekly Hours of Work,[a] 1900–1977.

Year	Nonagricultural Payrolls[b]	Manufacturing
1900	58.5	55.0
1905	57.2	54.5
1910	55.6	52.2
1915	53.4	50.4
1920	50.6	48.1
1925	49.0	47.9
1930	47.1	43.6
1935	41.7	36.4
1940	42.7	37.6
1947	40.3	40.4
1950	39.8	40.5
1955	39.6	40.7
1960	38.6	40.1
1965	38.8	41.2
1970	37.1	39.8
1975	36.1	39.4
1976	36.2	40.0
1977	36.1	40.3

Sources: 1900–1940: Kniesner (1976), p. 4, table 1.
1947–1977: U.S. Dept. of Labor, *Employment and Training Report of the President* (1977), p. 221, table C-3; and *Employment and Earnings*, March 1978, p. 93, table C-1.

[a] These figures are based on establishment data and reflect hours paid for by firms, rather than hours actually worked. The pre-1940 series is probably a more accurate representation of hours actually worked than is the post-1940 series. The latter series tends to overstate actual hours worked because of the growth of paid leisure in the form of holidays and vacations.
[b] For 1900–1940, this includes all nonagricultural wage and salary workers, while for 1947–1977, it includes "production or nonsupervisory workers on private payrolls."

women has focused on the labor force participation decision, and only recently have some studies incorporated both decisions in a comparative analysis of male and female responses.

As has been pointed out, the juxtaposition of radical change in the level of female labor force participation with virtually no (or very little) change in the earnings, unemployment rates, and occupational distribution of women relative to men is paradoxical. A possible explanation is that the dramatic participation changes we have observed significantly overstate growth in the average market labor supply of women because either (1) the percentage of women working part-time has increased and average hours of work per woman have decreased, and/or (2) inter-labor force turnover has increased, so that more women are working fewer weeks and/or shorter and less continuous periods. In the extreme, either of these hypotheses could imply that a group's labor supply remained unchanged despite an increase in their labor force participation rate, because of a reduction in average hours per week or per year. Under less extreme assumptions, the effect of increased labor force participation on total labor supply would be weakened by these other changes, but not completely eliminated. Thus average weekly hours and the continuity of labor force attachment of women must be analysed before we can speak with complete confidence about trends in female labor supply.

Part-time work is becoming more prevalent among both men and

Table 2.3

Part-Time Status of the Civilian Labor Force and Average Hours of Work for Those at Work, by Sex, 1968–1978

	Men, 16+		Women, 16+	
	% of LF part-time	Av. Hrs./Wk.	% of LF part-time	Av.Hrs./Wk.
1968	7.3	43.0	23.2	34.9
1969	7.7	42.9	23.5	34.9
1970	8.0	42.0	24.1	34.2
1971	8.1	42.2	24.4	34.3
1972	8.2	42.3	24.5	34.5
1973	8.0	42.4	24.6	34.4
1974	8.1	42.0	24.4	34.3
1975	8.2	41.6	24.2	34.1
1976	8.2	41.7	24.2	34.1
1977	8.4	41.9	24.2	34.2
1978	8.3	42.1	24.0	34.5

SOURCE: Unpublished BLS data.

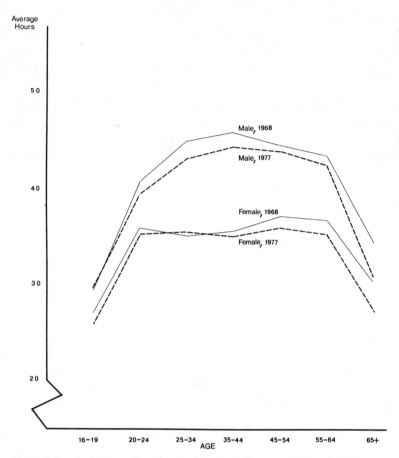

Figure 2.8.   Age-Hours Profiles for Men and Women, 1968 and 1977
SOURCE: Computed from unpublished BLS data.

women, but the rate of increase in recent years does not appear to
have been more rapid for women than for men.[19] It is significant to
note that women aged 25–34 show no decline in average hours over
that same period. The percentage working part-time in this group has
actually fallen during the 1970s and this is the only age-sex group for
which this is true. This finding is of particular interest because this
group has been at the low point on the traditional two-peaked age-participation profile. There is no evidence whatever that the vanishing dip

in participation rates at age 25–34 is being replaced by a dip in hours of work. As shown in figure 2.8, age-hours profiles for men and women do not present nearly as sharp a contrast as the age-participation profiles. The female profile is consistently lower, and flatter across the prime working ages, than the male profile, and both profiles have shifted downward slightly in the past ten years.

Data from the 1970 Census on the distribution of hours worked provide additional details on this dimension of labor supply by sex and other characteristics, and the distribution of hours shows some significant differences. Whereas 11.6 percent of women and 36 percent of men work more than forty hours, 29.8 percent of women and 14.1 percent of men work less than thirty-four hours. Interestingly enough, a greater proportion of women (54.4 percent) than men (47 percent) work thirty-five to forty hours (see table 2.4).

Differences in timing, for individuals who spend less than 100 percent of their available time in the labor force, can take place not only in hours worked per week but also in weeks worked per year.

Table 2.4

Percentage Distributions of Weekly
Hours of Work by Sex, 1970

	Male	Female
Total	100%	100%
Part-time	14.1%	29.8%
1–14 hrs.	3.8	8.5
15–29 hrs.	5.4	12.9
30–34 hrs.	4.8	8.3
Full-Time	83.9%	66.2%
35–39 hrs.	4.8	11.2
40 hrs.	42.7	43.2
41–48 hrs.	17.1	7.4
49–59 hrs.	9.8	2.2
60+ hrs.	9.1	2.0
With a job but not at work	2.6	3.9

SOURCE: U.S. Dept. of Commerce, *1970 Census*, table 17.

Work in Market vs. Work in Home

Table 2.5

Weeks Worked Per Year by Sex, 1959–1977

	Men		Women	
	full-time	part-time	full-time	part-time
1959	45.87	31.70	39.03	29.65
1960	45.87	30.19	39.33	28.99
1961	45.44	30.40	39.23	28.80
1962	45.57	29.45	39.50	28.74
1963	45.98	28.79	39.40	28.63
1964	45.97	29.20	39.66	28.31
1965	46.26	29.43	39.87	28.16
1966	46.47	27.65	39.94	29.92
1967	46.38	31.73	40.37	30.48
1968	46.23	31.83	40.38	30.38
1969	46.23	31.55	40.46	30.90
1970	45.73	31.48	40.72	30.26
1971	45.64	31.74	40.92	31.37
1972	45.86	31.17	40.99	31.10
1973	46.17	31.32	41.04	31.47
1974	45.84	32.69	41.66	32.25
1975	44.83	32.19	41.22	32.62
1976	44.99	31.48	41.42	31.89
1977	43.43	31.51	41.82	32.01

SOURCE: Mean figures computed from frequency distributions found in: 1959–1976: Special Labor Force Report nos. 11, 19, 25, 38, 48, 62, 91, 107, 115, 127, 141, 162, 171, 181, 192 and 201 (Washington, D.C., various years). 1977: Unpublished BLS data. Figures for 1959–1965 are for men and women aged fourteen and over, while the figures for 1966–1977 are for men and women aged sixteen and over.

Variations in these two dimensions of labor supply are not perfect substitutes for one another. Part-year work allows nonmarket time to be concentrated during certain portions of the year, whereas year-round part-time work allows nonmarket time to be spread evenly throughout the year. Because of child rearing responsibilities and school vacation schedules, women may be more likely to use weeks as a variable in their labor supply decision than men. Although it is the case that on the average, women work four or five fewer weeks per year than men, there is no sign that women's increased labor force participation has been accompanied by a reduction in their average weeks per year. On the contrary, table 2.5 suggests that, if anything, these have increased. Given the evidence concerning trends in hours per week and weeks per year among women workers, we conclude that the dramatic increases in female labor force participation have not been offset by declines in these other dimensions of labor supply.

Labor Supply Curve Estimation

Early studies of the relationship between hours of work and wages for men, such as Douglas (1934) and Schoenberg and Douglas (1937) hinted at the possibility of a backward-bending supply curve of labor. Certainly, the aforementioned secular decline in hours per week worked in industry suggested this relationship. Finegan's study (1962) of variations in hours of work across industries and occupations, based on 1940 and 1950 data, represented the first comprehensive test of the backward-bending supply curve using multiple regression analysis. This confirmed the negative relationship between hours and wages, but also found other determinants of differences in hours, including the proportion of females and the proportion of married men in different industries and occupations, to be important. Since Finegan's study, questions have been raised about the proper interpretation of the negative relationship between hours and wages. When comparing means in different labor markets, it may be incorrect to assume that these observations represent points on a supply curve. Both demand and supply may shift, and wages may be just as much a consequence of hours as a determinant. Figure 2.9 illustrates the nature of this "identification problem," which is not adequately dealt with in studies such as Finegan's. Although Finegan does control for many factors affecting supply, the interpretation of his results is dependent on the assumption that "in the majority of occupations and industries the length of the normal work week is determined primarily by the preferences of the workers therein" (p. 454).

However, as we can see, an observed negative relationship between wage rates and hours of work could be tracing out a backward-bending supply curve (such as $a''b''c'$ on S'_1), a downward-sloping demand curve (such as abc or $a'b'c'$ on D_1), or simply the locus of points of

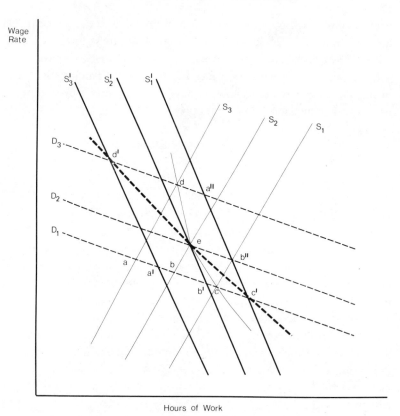

Figure 2.9.   The Identification Problem

intersection of the different demand and supply curves in different labor markets (such as d'ec' or dec), and therefore does not necessarily have any direct implications regarding the shape of the supply curve (see Feldstein 1968). Rosen (1969) confronts the identification problem explicitly, and uses 1960 industry data to test the simultaneous determination of hours worked by men by both supply and demand. Although the supply relationship between hours and wages is negative, the elasticities are small, and demand for hours of work is shown to be more elastic than the supply.

Even when demand can be properly controlled for, the estimation of labor supply functions is plagued by significant measurement error in both wages and labor supply, and also by selectivity bias. Observed wage rates are rarely measured directly, but are derived in most cases by dividing earnings by hours of work, so that any errors in reporting hours worked are transmitted inversely to the measured market wage rate. Wage rates may also be subject to substantial measurement error even when reported directly, and permanent and transitory components of the observed wage are frequently not distinguished. Measurement problems also arise with respect to the dependent labor supply variable, which can take a variety of forms, such as weeks worked last year, hours worked last week, hours worked last year, weeks worked last year times hours worked last week, or weeks worked plus weeks unemployed last year (see Cain and Watts 1973: 350–51). As Kalachek, Mellow and Raines (1978) emphasize, measures like weeks worked or hours worked last week are arbitrarily selected aspects of labor supply. Since, like the number employed, these measures are determined by demand as well as supply, labor supply will be underestimated to the extent that workers experience unemployment and/or underemployment, and thus work fewer hours than they would prefer. They argue that these misspecifications have been responsible for the substantial differences among various estimates of the elasticity of hours of work with respect to the wage rate.[20] In addition to their finding of apparently different labor supply responses among mature men to the permanent and transitory components of wages, they also reach the interesting conclusion that wages have only a modest influence on labor supply for this group, whose behavior appears to be dominated by attitudes, health, and demographic variables.

Most studies of the determinants of hours of work, at least until very recently, have included only the currently employed in the group used to estimate the labor supply function. The obvious advantage of this pragmatic approach is that wage information, albeit subject to considerable measurement error, is available for all individuals in the sample. However, there are several disadvantages which tend to result in biased and inconsistent estimates. When the labor force participation rate of a group is well below 100 percent, truncation of the sample to exclude nonworkers introduces selectivity bias due to this sample censorship. In addition, there is a related problem of simultaneous equations bias, also of particular relevance for those groups with lower rates of participation. Past decisions regarding participation and training, which are jointly and simultaneously determined with current labor supply, will be reflected in current wage offers. Thus these two variables are jointly and simultaneously determined; in other words, the wage rate itself, like labor supply, is endogenous. We will return shortly to the simultaneity problem of the effect of labor supply on the wage rate in our discussion of continuity of labor force attachment. For the moment, however, we will focus on the static single-equation specification, and on the inherent problems that exist even in the absence of simultaneous equations bias, namely sample censorship and the measurement errors described above.

The question of what is the best solution to the problem of sample censorship is closely related to the issue of whether the estimation of a labor supply function should be treated as a two-stage decision—participation and then hours worked, conditional on participation—or whether these decisions are appropriately viewed as generated by the same function, truncated at zero hours supplied for nonparticipants. While the latter approach certainly does have wide appeal and support (e.g., Killingsworth 1979a; Heckman 1974), the question as to whether the joint decisions of participating in the labor force, and of working a certain number of hours once there, are in fact determined by the identical combination of factors has not been conclusively answered (T. P. Schultz 1975:73).[21] Given the fact that over 95 percent of prime-age men are in the labor force, the problem of censorship bias, and any difference between the labor supply function estimated for a sample including only labor force participants and that estimated for the entire population group, will tend to be insignificant. Thus it has been almost exclusively within the context of studies of female labor supply that these issues have been raised, debated, and dealt with in various ways.

Given the sex differential in participation levels, it is not surprising to find that most studies have focused exclusively on either men or women, and therefore only the crudest kind of comparison between the sexes is possible. Although there has been a wide range of estimates of income and wage elasticities for men and women, it can be broadly concluded that the total effect of a wage change on male labor supply is small and negative, whereas its effect on female supply is positive. (See, for example, Kosters 1969; Cain and Watts 1973; and Lewis 1975.) Certain family characteristics, such as the presence of children of different ages and husband's income, are shown to have an important effect on the wife's labor supply (Leibowitz 1972; Zellner 1974), whereas comparable variables are not usually included when analyzing male labor supply. A study of male labor supply that did include the number of dependents found this variable to have a significant (positive) effect (Hill 1973).

Studies of both men and women that do use the same independent variables to explain the labor supply decision obtain results similar to those described above. Hall (1973) found that wives and older men are very sensitive to wage and income changes, whereas husbands of both races and single men and women are unresponsive to wage changes. It appears that marriage is a primary correlate of sex differences in labor supply, with the presence of school-age children positively correlated with male hours of work, and the presence of preschool children negatively correlated with female hours. Boskin (1973) basically confirms these results and finds additionally that the income effect works primarily to decrease hours of work for both husbands and wives, but has little effect on labor force participation. In addition, the presence of children has opposite effects on male and female labor force participation, but in every case the number of dependents has a positive effect on hours of work for members of the labor force.

To return to the rather complex methodological issues that have arisen with respect to estimation of hours of work functions for women, a significant proportion of whom supply zero hours to the market sector, there are three basic approaches.[22]

1. The least satisfactory approach involves estimating a simple hours of work function by using a sample composed solely of working women, with the observed market wage as an independent variable. This implicitly assumes that women with the same observable nonmarket characteristics (age, education, number of children) have identical tastes and nonmarket productivities, and thus the same reservation wage.

2. The "imputed wage" approach, which has been used in a number of studies,[23] includes all women, whether or not they are

employed, in the sample on which the labor supply function is estimated. A wage equation is estimated across the subsample of the employed, and then used to generate a predicted wage for each woman in the total sample. This predicted wage replaces the observed market wage as the independent wage variable, and nonparticipants are included as supplying zero hours. This approach implicitly assumes that all women with given labor market attributes (the independent variables in the wage equation) face identical wage offers. In particular, unbiased results will be obtained only if there are no unobserved differences between participants and nonparticipants which are systematically related to wage rates. Since this is not in fact the case, bias due to sample censorship results here as well. Both this approach and the following one incorporate labor force participation into the overall labor supply decision.

3.   The most original and satisfactory approach is the maximum likelihood procedure developed by Heckman (1974), which estimates the wage and labor supply functions simultaneously. Although econometrically very sophisticated, it is based on the simple relationship between wages offered in the market (demand) and the value of time ("shadow price") in the home (supply), and the simultaneous estimation of these two functions.

Since the problem of how to deal with those whose hours of work in the market are equal to zero is most important in the case of married women, Heckman concentrates on this group. However, the methodology is a general one, and would be applicable to any group containing some nonparticipants. Labor force participants adjust their hours of work so that the shadow price of time equals the hourly wage rate. For nonparticipants, on the other hand, this shadow price, when hours of market work equal zero and all available time is used in the home sector, is *at least* as great as the market wage rate. Labor supply can be seen as a function of both demand and supply factors, including education and experience, which affect productivity in the market, and education, children, family assets, and the wage rate of the husband, which affect the demand for home time and the value placed on it. Heckman's results show that education increases market productivity more than home productivity and thus is an inducement to labor participation.

The Uses of Nonmarket Time

Although not everyone works in the paid labor force in a given week, everyone spends time in the nonmarket sector to varying degrees.[24] Home time can be seen as a complement to market time and, therefore, incorporates within it the mirror image of labor supply (labor force participation, and hours and weeks of work). Differences between individuals in home time can be estimated as a residual assuming some fixed amount of total time, as in J. P. Smith (1977), or can be derived from time budget studies.[25] The latter approach also makes it possible to distinguish among the various components of nonmarket time. In particular, the important distinction between leisure and nonmarket work may be made. Most studies in this area have focused on women and show the importance of education and the number and age of children in the time worked at home. More educated women put in less time on all home activities, except children (Leibowitz 1975; Hill and Stafford 1974). Although they have fewer children, they spend more time per child. The more educated the woman, the more difficult it apparently is for her to buy adequate substitutes for her time in child care.[26]

All time budget studies show that married men devote only a small amount of time to nonmarket work, both in absolute terms and relative to married women (Vanek, 1974; Leibowitz, 1975). A study of time budgets in forty-four metropolitan areas in the United States in 1965–1966 (Hedges and Barnett 1972) found that working wives work longer hours in total than working husbands, with married women spending an average of 71.4 hours per week on paid work, commuting, housework and family tasks, compared to 66.5 hours for married men. Married men work more hours in the market and married women work more hours at home, but this translates into relatively longer working hours for wives because of the relatively small amount of housework done by men.[27] Evidence from Israeli data (Gronau 1976) indicates that married people of both sexes have less leisure than single people, and this effect of marriage is stronger for men than for women. For men, the effect of marriage is to strongly increase market work and to slightly increase work at home. For women, on the other hand, the fall in leisure with marriage is the net result of a great increase in nonmarket work swamping a decrease in market work. Although these results are disturbing, more information is needed to analyze the interrelated responses of husbands and wives to changes in economic variables.

Both J. P. Smith (1977), using home time estimated as a residual, and Bloch (1975), using housework time estimates from a time budget study, tested the effect of husband's and wife's wage on male and female home time and, as expected, found both negatively related to own wage and positively related to spouse's wage. Because J. P. Smith's data include leisure and nonmarket work in one category, Bloch's results are easier to interpret. He found that the time spent by wives doing housework is strongly affected by their own wage but totally unaffected by their husband's wage, whereas the husband's contribution to housework is more strongly affected by the wife's wage than by his own. This is corroborated by Gronau, who found that the husband's allocation of time is more affected by the wife's education than his own. However, Bloch finds that an increase in the wife's wage leads to a net reduction in housework, because the reduction in the wife's time devoted to housework is not fully compensated for by the husband's increase, with the likely result that market goods and services are used as substitutes for the wife's time in the home.

Results reported by Leibowitz (1974a) highlight the nature of substitutability and complementarity in various household tasks. Mothers and fathers appear to be true complements in both the physical and other (i.e., social and educational) care of children, which means that increased inputs of the father's time to these functions actually raise the marginal product of the mother's time in these same functions, and thus result, on the average, in her increasing the time she spends in physical and other child care by four and three minutes, respectively, for each ten minutes the father supplies to these tasks. On the other hand, men and women appear to be imperfect substitutes in the task of meal preparation. For each twenty minutes devoted to meal preparation by the husband, the wife reduces her time input by an average of ten minutes. It would appear that male time substitutes for female time in a ratio of two to one in this activity, or that it takes a man twice as long as a woman to produce a (supposedly edible, although quality is not explicitly discussed) meal!

Observed trends in hours and weeks confirm that increases in labor force participation rates among women do not just reflect a change in the composition of labor supply toward more women working for shorter periods but, in fact, suggest positive growth in their labor supply. Rising real income appears to be the primary cause of the long-term decline in average hours for both men and women. However, on balance, the observed positive response of women's working hours to rising wages appears consistent with their relatively steady pattern, over time, of hours per year (hours per week times weeks per year), given the countervailing influence of the income level. On the other hand, the small negative response of men's labor supply to rising wages found in the literature appears consistent with their steady decline, over time, in hours per year. There is little evidence to suggest, however, that these long-term changes have significantly affected the division of labor in the home. Husbands appear to be imperfect substitutes for their wives in the home, leading to a net reduction in home work as women's labor force participation increases. To some extent this may be due to smaller family size, but is likely to reflect as well the substitution of market goods and services for women's time in the home.

CONTINUITY OF LABOR FORCE ATTACHMENT

Although we have seen that average weekly hours of work among women have not declined sufficiently to eliminate the effect of increasing female labor force participation on their total labor supply, the question of the relationship between levels of participation and continuity of attachment among women remains to be answered. Differences between groups in average weeks per year cannot be interpreted as a complete measure of differences in continuity, although they may well be part of the story. Some jobs, such as teaching, are part-year by their very nature; even if, for example, all teachers worked without interruption from year to year, they would be counted correctly as working less than the maximum number of weeks per year.

The relationship between labor force participation and inter-labor force turnover is not a simple one, and could conceivably take a variety of forms. Although inter-labor force turnover is necessarily low among groups with very high participation rates (i.e., if 90 or 95 percent of a group is always in the labor force, there is simply very little leeway for movement in and out), such turnover may be either high or low among groups (such as women) with participation rates significantly below 100 percent. A group with a labor force participation rate of 50 percent, for example, would be characterized by no inter-labor force turnover and continuous labor force attachment on the part of participants in the case of complete heterogeneity and specialization, where the same 50 percent of the group is always in the labor force and the other half of the group never enters the labor force. On the other hand, there would be considerable turnover and discontinuity if such a group were completely homogeneous, so that each member's behavior conformed to the average of spending exactly half of his or her working life in the labor force.

Within the intermediate range (approximately 30 to 50 percent) over which female labor force participation rates have been rising during the past thirty years, one can easily visualize higher levels of participation being linked to either increasing or decreasing labor force turnover. The question of whether today we have more women working, but for shorter and less continuous periods, or more women entering the labor force and then remaining there longer, is crucial, and must be answered if we are to understand dynamic changes in female labor supply.

Evidence concerning actual labor force turnover on an annual basis, as presented in table 2.6, shows no indication that female labor force turnover has been rising. Inter-labor force turnover among women, as measured by the ratio of the labor force experience rate (the percentage of total women working sometime during the year) to the annual average labor force participation rate, has decreased as labor force participation has risen over the past twenty years, both in the aggregate and within each age group, and particularly in the prime ages 35–64 (Niemi 1977:26). This implies that not only are more women in the labor force but the average woman worker is more permanently attached. This is also confirmed by Census data on the distribution of weeks worked, which shows a rise in the proportion of married women working fifty to fifty-two weeks a year, from 39.8 percent in 1959 to 44.1 percent in 1969.[28]

Table 2.6

Civilian Labor Force Participation Rates, Labor Force Experience Rates, and Indices of Labor Force Turnover for Men and Women, 1957–1977

YEAR	Total			Men			Women		
	LFP	LFE	LFE/LFP	LFP	LFE	LFE/LFP	LFP	LFE	LFE/LFP
1957	57.8	66.8	115.7	81.9	88.2	107.8	35.8	47.3	132.1
1958	57.5	66.0	114.8	81.2	86.4	106.4	36.0	47.4	132.0
1959	57.4	65.8	114.6	80.9	86.0	106.4	36.1	47.4	131.3
1960	57.5	66.9	116.4	80.4	86.6	107.8	36.7	49.0	133.6
1961	57.2	65.4	114.5	79.5	84.9	106.8	36.9	47.7	129.4
1962	56.5	66.0	116.8	78.4	85.1	108.5	36.6	48.7	132.9
1963	56.4	65.7	116.5	77.9	84.3	108.3	37.0	48.9	132.3
1964	58.7	68.0	115.8	81.0	87.2	107.7	38.7	50.7	130.9
1965	58.9	67.4	114.5	80.7	86.2	106.8	39.3	50.5	128.6
1966	59.2	68.4	115.5	80.4	86.5	107.5	40.3	52.3	129.8
1967	59.6	68.9	115.6	80.4	86.7	107.8	41.1	53.1	129.2
1968	59.6	69.3	116.2	80.1	86.8	108.4	41.6	53.9	129.4
1969	60.1	69.7	116.0	79.8	87.1	109.0	42.7	54.4	127.4
1970	60.4	69.6	115.3	79.7	86.5	108.6	43.3	54.7	126.1
1971	60.2	69.5	115.5	79.1	86.5	109.3	43.3	54.5	125.7
1972	60.4	69.1	114.4	79.0	86.7	108.5	43.9	54.3	123.9
1973	60.8	69.8	114.8	78.8	85.6	108.6	44.7	55.7	124.5
1974	61.2	69.9	114.1	78.7	85.0	108.0	45.6	56.4	123.5
1975	61.2	69.0	112.8	77.9	83.6	107.0	46.3	56.1	121.0
1976	62.3	68.5	110.0	77.7	82.0	105.6	47.3	57.2	121.0
1977	62.3	70.1	112.6	77.7	83.4	107.4	48.4	58.2	120.1

SOURCE: Labor force experience figures are taken from Bureau of Labor Statistics Special Labor Force Reports nos. 11, 19, 25, 38, 48, 62, 91, 107, 115, 127, 141, 162, 171, 181, 192 and 201 (Washington, D.C., various years). Civilian labor force and civilian noninstitutional population data for 1957–1963 are from U.S. Depat. of Labor, *Manpower Report of the President* (1966), p. 153, table A-1, and those for 1964–1977 are from U.S. Dept. of Labor, *Employment and Training Report of the President* (1978), pp. 179–80, table A-1.

NOTE: Figures for 1957–1963 are for men and women aged fourteen and over, while the figures for 1964–1977 are for men and women aged sixteen and over. The three variables that appear in this table are defined as follows: (1) LFP = the average civilian labor force participation rate for the group in question for the year; (2) LFE = the proportion of the civilian noninstitutional population in question that was in the civilian labor force at some time during the year (the civilian labor force *experience* rate); (3) LFE/LFP = the index of labor force turnover, which is the ratio of the civilian labor force experience rate to the average civilian labor force participation rate for the year. The larger the value of this index, the greater was the amount of inter-labor force turnover during the year.

Additional evidence that the trend has been for women to remain in the labor force longer and more continuously than was the case in the past can be seen in table 2.7. Neither the exit rate nor the proportion of new entrants in the labor force has changed much for men, although there have been changes within age groups, with prime age and older men showing some increase, and young men a strong decrease, in the amount of movement in and out. On the other hand, despite an increase in the absolute number of female entrants, especially in the prime age group, these entrants represent a decreasing proportion of the female labor force. This is the case because, as can be seen from the strong decline in exit rates, more and more women are remaining in the labor force, and thus experienced workers make up a larger proportion of the female labor force.

The crucial area of labor supply behavior over the life cycle requires further investigation. This is a new area in labor supply literature, as the theory of life cycle phenomena and the data to test it have been developed only recently. To test life cycle phenomena, it is ideal to have sample data on individuals over a period of time. This can be retrospective data that relies on a person's memory, longitudinal data from interviews with the same individual in successive years, or some combination of the two. An alternative approach is to use cross-sectional Census data to simulate life cycle data by stratifying the sample by age. "Each observation represents a separate cohort at one point in its life cycle path. The entire profile captures both movements along life cycle paths and across profiles of different cohorts" (J. P. Smith 1977). This procedure, however, involves the implicit (and rather strong) assumption that the life cycle pattern does not differ between cohorts. If this is not the case, then the simulated life cycle pattern is simply a series of observations, each one lying on the profile of a different cohort, which does not accurately describe the behavior of any one cohort or individual.

An obvious simple example of this type of analysis would be the age-participation profiles for men and women found in figure 2.2. As was noted above, these should not be casually interpreted as descriptive of life cycle participation patterns. Because of the dynamic changes that have been taking place, estimation of life cycle patterns of participation with cross-section data can be seriously biased for women, and, to get a truer picture of their experience through time, it is necessary to follow the labor force participation rates of individual birth cohorts of women, as is done in figure 2.10. In general, we find that successively younger cohorts have higher rates of participation at each age in the life cycle, so that the cohort profiles have been shifting upwards. In addition, the dip in participation at age 25–29, indicative of discontinuous participation (dropping out during the childbearing years and reentering afterwards), has become successively less pronounced, and appears to have disappeared completely among the cohort that reached this age in the mid-1970s. This is an additional indication that labor force continuity, as well as participation, is increasing among women. (It should be noted that the simulation of male life cycle labor supply behavior from cross-sectional data is not subject to *caveats* described above, as the age-participation profile for men does not appear to have shifted over time. The profiles are virtually identical for successive cohorts, and closely approximate the cross-sectional male age-participation profile at a moment of time.)

Two studies that attempt to test the life cycle theory of labor supply using cross-sectional data are Ghez and Becker (1975), which uses data on men from the 1960 Census, and J. P. Smith (1977), which uses essentially the same statistical technique, on data from the 1967 Survey of Economic Opportunity and the 1960 and 1970 Censuses, in a symmetrical analysis of life cycle labor supply for men and women. The empirical results of both these studies conform generally to the predictions of life cycle labor supply theory, but many serious questions concerning measurement and interpretation make it impossible to accept these results as a conclusive test of the theory.

Recently there has been an increasing availability of longitudinal data, which is most appropriate for analysis relating to continuity and patterns of life cycle behavior, and this information is being utilized in ways that creatively address these questions. Three major longitudinal data sets that have been used to study continuity of labor force attachment and labor supply behavior over the life cycle are: (1) the Continuous Work-History Sample (CWHS) maintained by the Social Security Administration (Mallan 1974); (2) National Longitudinal Surveys (NLS), designed by the Ohio State University Center for Human Resource Research under a contract with the Manpower

Table 2.7

Proportion of Labor Force Made Up of New Entrants and Probability of Labor Force Exit, by Sex and Age, 1967–1978

	Male				Female			
Year	Entrants[a] No. (1000's)	As % of LF	Exits[b] No. (1000's)	As % of LF	Entrants No. (1000's)	As % of LF	Exits No. (1000's)	As % of LF
				Total, 16+				
1967–68	3970	8.06	3424	6.95	7173	24.9	6329	22.0
1968–69	4357	8.73	3669	7.36	7815	26.2	6507	21.8
1969–70	4634	9.14	3660	7.22	7478	24.1	6470	20.9
1970–71	4533	8.78	3707	7.18	6963	21.9	6392	20.1
1971–72	4806	9.13	3562	6.77	7248	22.2	6062	18.5
1972–73	4652	8.66	3714	6.91	7562	22.3	6329	18.7
1973–74	4759	8.70	3776	6.90	7810	22.2	6495	18.5
1974–75	4323	7.80	3894	7.03	7392	20.3	6218	17.1
1975–76	4467	7.98	3723	6.65	7377	19.6	5961	15.8
1976–77	4873	8.56	3783	6.65	7677	19.6	6139	15.7
1977–78	4796	8.27	3703	6.39	8169	20.0	6243	15.3
				Age 16–24				
1968–69	2771	30.9	2370	26.5	3322	44.7	2799	37.6
1969–70	2867	30.4	2304	24.4	3135	39.7	2716	34.3
1970–71	2920	29.1	2280	22.7	3000	36.4	2752	34.4
1971–72	2938	27.3	2141	19.9	3106	36.0	2587	30.0
1972–73	2797	24.4	2205	19.3	3215	35.2	2708	29.6
1973–74	2564	21.5	2233	18.7	3211	33.4	2779	28.9
1974–75	2410	19.9	2327	19.2	2968	29.8	2682	26.9
1975–76	2501	20.3	2161	17.5	2917	28.4	2606	25.4
1976–77	2586	20.4	2222	17.5	3029	28.5	2624	24.7
1977–78	2458	18.9	2179	16.8	3152	28.5	2653	23.9

Age 25–59

Year								
1968–69	839	2.3	549	1.5	3850	19.4	3121	15.7
1969–70	986	2.7	583	1.6	3657	17.9	3155	15.3
1970–71	855	2.3	607	1.7	3320	15.9	3047	14.6
1971–72	1087	2.9	623	1.7	3462	16.2	2844	13.3
1972–73	1225	3.3	661	1.8	3779	17.1	2994	13.6
1973–74	1316	3.5	689	1.8	4053	17.7	3087	13.5
1974–75	1178	3.1	739	1.9	3778	15.9	2931	12.3
1975–76	1266	3.2	709	1.8	3870	15.6	2789	11.3
1976–77	1463	3.7	749	1.9	4026	15.5	2902	11.2
1977–78	1475	3.7	718	1.8	4330	16.0	2974	11.0

Age 60+

Year								
1968–69	766	15.1	762	15.1	642	25.0	587	22.9
1969–70	763	15.1	773	15.3	687	26.1	619	23.5
1970–71	757	15.0	819	16.3	649	24.1	599	22.3
1971–72	780	15.6	797	15.9	681	24.9	632	23.1
1972–73	630	12.9	849	17.4	568	20.8	627	22.9
1973–74	880	18.4	855	17.9	546	20.5	629	23.6
1974–75	734	15.5	828	17.4	646	24.5	606	23.0
1975–76	702	15.2	853	18.4	588	22.0	565	21.1
1976–77	821	18.0	811	17.8	618	23.0	613	22.8
1977–78	866	18.9	807	17.6	693	25.4	617	22.6

SOURCE: *Employment and Earnings*, various dates.

[a] The number of entrants is calculated as the sum of the number who left and the net change in the civilian labor force.

[b] Estimated from persons out of the labor force who left a job within the previous 12 months. For example, to estimate the number who left between mid-1968 and mid-1969, an average was taken of the four quarterly figures for 1969. Because these four quarterly figures include persons who left jobs from the beginning of 1968 to the end of 1969, an average gives a more accurate estimate of the flow between two mid-years.

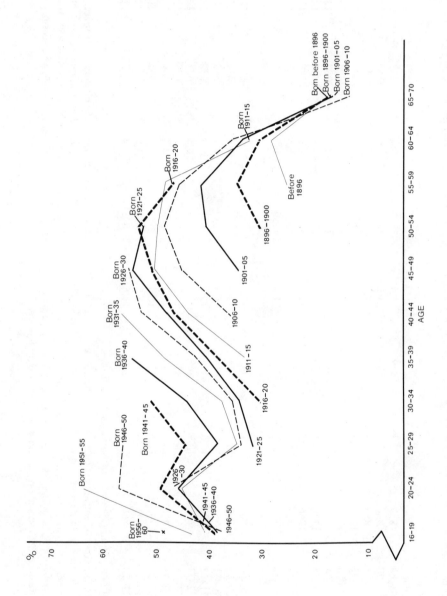

Administration (Blau 1976; Maret-Havens 1977; Sandell 1977; Mincer and Ofek 1979); and (3) the University of Michigan Panel Study of Income Dynamics (MID) (Heckman and Willis 1977; Heckman 1979). The CWHS has the advantage of providing truly longitudinal earnings and employment information, without resorting to the use of error-prone retrospectively reported data, in annual detail from 1951 and in cumulated form since 1937. However, this is outweighed by the disadvantage of providing almost no additional information concerning either basic demographic characteristics, such as marital status and educational attainment, or workers' activities other than covered employment. (The alternative statuses of being unemployed, being out of the labor force, and working in noncovered employment cannot be distinguished from one another.)

Both the NLS and the MID provide longitudinal information covering periods spanning the late 1960s and early 1970s, a wealth of detailed personal data on the sample members, and retrospective work histories. The NLS and the MID clearly confirm that past experience is in fact strongly related to current labor force status for women (Blau 1976: 53; Heckman 1979), which appears inconsistent with the hypothesis of a homogeneous female population characterized by high rates of movement into and out of the labor force. Heckman (1979) provides the most complete delineation of the reasons for and implications of this phenomenon.

The two major explanations for the relationship between previous and current work status are heterogeneity and the investment effect of previous work experience. These are not by any means mutually exclusive, and in fact Heckman finds considerable evidence that both effects exist. The assumption of heterogeneity means that unobserved differences among women in tastes and productivities result in different propensities to participate in the labor force. Past experience and present status will be positively correlated, and thus a woman's work history will be helpful in predicting the probability that she will be in

Figure 2.10.   Cohort Labor Force Participation of Women

SOURCE: 1950: U.S. Census Special Report PE No. 1-A: "Employment and Personal Characteristics," pp. 1A–16, table C.
1955–75: *U.S. Working Women: A Databook*. (Washington, D.C.: U.S. Dept. of Labor, BLS 1977), p. 6, table 4.

the labor force. Because of heterogeneity, the labor force participation rate cannot be used as an unbiased estimate of the fraction of her life an individual women will spend in the labor force. Heckman and Willis (1977) tested this model and found ". . . evidence of considerable heterogeneity. According to parameter estimates, the distribution of participation probabilities is U shaped. Thus, loosely speaking, there tend to be two groups of women in the sample: workers, whose participation probabilities are near unity, and nonworkers, whose participation are near zero. Relatively few women in the sample have probabilities near the mean participation rate of 40 percent" (p. 53). However, this rather extreme statement of their conclusion can be and has been criticized (Mincer and Ofek 1979) for not referring specifically to the length of the period covered, and thus implying that the degree of heterogeneity observed over a period of approximately five years would still hold over much longer periods. The absence of homogeneity does not necessarily imply the existence of a near-dichotomy of "workers" and "nonworkers."

In addition to this innate heterogeneity, additional heterogeneity is created by differing labor market experience; such a relationship is referred to as "state dependence." Heckman's (1979) model is a truly dynamic one, and is consistent with human capital theory. Since that theory of the acquisition of skills via investment in training is the subject of the following chapter, we will not describe it in detail here. Very simply, the process that occurs is that work experience provides women with training that raises their wage rates and thus makes future participation more likely. The continuity or discontinuity of labor force attachment is thus the key connecting link between current labor supply and the acquisition of human capital, which has extensive implications with respect to occupation, earnings and unemployment.

The mere existence of a positive relationship between past and present labor force participation is not sufficient to establish causation in the form of state dependence. It could, as we have seen, simply be the result of initial heterogeneity. More sophisticated techniques are needed to discriminate between these two phenomena, and these are developed and applied by Heckman (1979). The evidence thus obtained ". . . lends considerable support to the notion that there is genuine state dependence in individual probabilities. The data also display considerable evidence of heterogeneity in the population. This evidence is consistent with human capital theory and a model with fixed costs of labor force entry" (p. 11).

Although longitudinal samples such as the NLS and MID are now available to provide information on the continuity of individual workers' attachment to the labor force in recent years, evidence sufficient to discern changes over time in patterns of continuity is more difficult to come by. However, the available information from the NLS (Blau 1977) and CWHS (Mallan 1974) does not show any evidence of increasing turnover and decreasing amounts of experience among women workers accompanying rising female labor force participation. The average age of members of the labor force has been falling since the late 1950s, with the steady growth in the size of young cohorts of workers entering the labor force. This necessarily implies fewer average years of work experience, because younger workers have had less time to accumulate such experience. However, since average age fell by about three years for both women and men between 1957 and 1977,[29] this effect would be expected to apply equally to both sexes and does not imply a decrease in experience or continuity for women relative to men.

Certainly the dynamic model developed by Heckman implies that increased labor force participation will eventually (although perhaps with a time lag) result in an increase in accumulated labor market experience. Thus the current all-time high in the participation rate of 20- to 24-year-old women has long-run implications for higher and more continuous future female labor force participation. All the available evidence appears to imply that recent increases in female labor force participation, particularly among women with young children, are the result of a trend toward long-term career commitment rather than an increase in marginal workers with high turnover rates as has sometimes been suggested. (Cf., for example, the *1973 Economic Report of the President*, ch.4, p. 100.)

Conclusion

Certain themes emerge from a review of the labor supply literature. No matter how participation is measured, every study brings out strong differences between men and women in labor market behavior.

Women's market labor supply is both lower than men's and more responsive to labor market conditions, such as wages and employment levels. Within the family context, the traditional division of labor still appears to predominate, with marriage and children being deterrents to women's participation at certain stages of the life cycle, and incentives for men to participate more. However, the direction of causation here is by no means clear. Women's willingness to participate more in the nonmarket sector may be in part the result of their perception of limited opportunities open to them in the market sector, as a result of discrimination. It is also true that sex differences in response patterns differ according to race and marital status. Differences between single men and women and black men and women are much less sharply drawn. Clearly, the white middle-class concept of the traditional division of labor between the sexes is not applicable to all groups. Those groups with higher levels of participation, whether they be male or female, show less flexibility in response to market conditions and home time demands.

It is still true, as economists have traditionally assumed, that women *on average* participate in the labor force less frequently, less continuously and for shorter hours and fewer weeks than men. It is also true that women *on average* do significantly more nonmarket work than men. However, the sharp narrowing of the differential between men and women in labor force participation rates has corresponded to a narrowing of the overall differences between men and women in labor supply, in terms of both hours per year and continuity of work over the life cycle. Strong trends in the direction of greater career attachment for women are indicated by such evidence as the rapid increase in the labor force participation rates of young mothers. New evidence from longitudinal data that past work experience increases the probability of future labor force participation reinforces this interpretation of recent trends.

Although men do not appear to be perfect substitutes for their wives in the nonmarket sector, men do nonmarket work, and empirical findings suggest that their time allocation is significantly affected by the economic position of their wives. As the traditional division of labor between the sexes continues to break down in response to economic and social changes, we would expect the analysis of men's labor force participation decisions to become increasingly complex. Not only will proper analysis require such extensive data on male family characteristics as are now abundantly available for women, but it will involve grappling with all the methodological problems that exist in the analysis of female labor supply.

We now move from the quantitative dimension of labor supply to the qualitative dimension, with emphasis on occupational choice and skill acquisition. Here, wages are no longer seen to be an independent determinant of labor supply, but are themselves partly determined by past participation decisions. Systematic differences between the sexes in the quantity of human capital investment and its rate of return, which are closely related to the crucial question of labor force continuity, will affect unemployment and wage differentials and subsequent differences in labor supply. We shall see that narrowing sex differentials in labor supply have not led to an immediate decrease in these other differentials, largely because barriers to skill acquisition and occupational mobility remain, even in the face of increasing labor force attachment among women. In fact, these barriers may well be factors inhibiting an even more rapid increase in continuous female labor force participation.

NOTES

1.   See, for example, Barzel and McDonald (1973), p. 622.

2.   In 1970, it was 5 percent.

3.   In the interest of avoiding an infinite series of tables and charts of labor force participation rates, complete documentation has been presented only for the most important breakdowns by age and race. The reader who wishes to examine the details of the trends in labor force participation by marital status and age briefly described in this paragraph is referred to tables B-1 and B-2 of the most recent *Employment and Training Report of the President*.

4.   See *Employment and Training Report of the President* (1978), p. 238, table B-4.

5.   Michelott (1977), p. 56, table 3.

6.   The pure substitution effect of an own wage rate change was positive for both men and women, but significantly larger for women. The cross-substitution effects of wage on husband's labor supply and vice versa are small, positive (indicating that

spouses' nonmarket hours tend to be complementary), and not significantly different from one another. An increase in family income, assuming no change in wages, has a negative effect in both cases, but is only significant in the case of the wife. The total effect of a change in wages on labor supply obviously includes the effect of the increased income earned at the original labor supply. Because of the significantly lower labor force participation rates of married women, the income effect of a change in their wage will be smaller than the income effect of a change in the wage of married men. These results were not significantly affected when account was taken of possible shifts in demand and wage rates were calculated as endogenous to the model rather than being taken exogenously.

7. Although the "true" market wage rate has unmeasured dimensions, such as fringe benefits and desirable working conditions, these may be at least partially captured by a measure of educational attainment. If so, as Cain (1966, p. 118) points out, the rising level of educational attainment and its positive relationship to labor force participation, especially for women, is consistent with the above interpretation.

8. The available evidence on continuity of labor force attachment versus inter-labor force turnover will be discussed in detail in a later section. Our concern at this point is with the implications concerning the interpretation of the income and wage coefficients in a standard labor supply function, with the labor force participation rate as the dependent variable.

9. Not only is wage estimation for nonworkers a problem, but the statistical techniques necessary for consistent estimation are more complex than standard multiple regression.

10. For example, see Bowen and Finegan (1969), especially chs. 3, 5, 8, 9 and 12; Boskin (1973); Cohen, Rea, and Lerman (1970); Gramm (1973); Kalachek and Raines (1970); and T. P. Schultz (1975).

11. Bowen and Finegan (1969) is one exception to this statement, although they did not use exactly the same variables in the equations for men and women, and thus their analyses of male and female decisions are not directly comparable. Another study that examines the participation decision for men is Cohen, Rea, and Lerman (1970).

12. Cain also differentiated part-time from full-time work by assigning part-time workers the value ½ and full-time workers the value 1. Adding these up for a group of women would give an estimate of the number of full-time equivalent workers, on the assumption that two part-time workers equal one full-time one.

13. Various studies have looked at the relationship between the wife's education and various dimensions of home production and consumption. For example, Michael (1973) examines the efficiency effect on consumption, Leibowitz (1974b) looks at effects on the quality of children, and Benham (1974, 1975) examines the effect on the husband's income.

14. A full discussion of these relationships can be found in chapter 3.

15. For example, Long (1958), Tella (1964, 1965), Strand and Dernberg (1964), and Dernberg and Strand (1966).

16. First, since employment is a large fraction of labor force, any sampling errors in one will be duplicated on the other, biasing the regression coefficients toward unity. Second, specific labor force groups may experience demand or supply fluctuations

which are independent of the overall state of the market. This will create an upward bias in estimates of the effect of the cycle on labor force participation.

17. For example, Barth (1968); Bowen and Finegan (1969), chapter 16; Butler and Demopoulos (1971); Bonin and Davis (1971); Fair (1971); and Wachter (1972, 1977).

18. The discussion above is based on Lloyd and Niemi (1978). Another interesting time-series analysis of labor force participation patterns can be found in Wachter (1977). He concentrated on the largely neglected question of intermediate swings (as opposed to either short-run fluctuations or long-run trends) in labor force participation rates, which he argues arise from such interrelated demographic factors as the large cohort of young workers, the drop in their income, and the decline in fertility rates. He has the following to say with regard to the changing cyclical responsiveness of male and female labor force participation:

"[T]he tendency of the discouraged-worker variable to be more significant in the equations for prime-age men than in those for secondary workers sharply reverses the results of previous discouraged-worker models. As noted earlier in connection with the poor predictions of these equations for recent years, one may conjecture that changing government regulations have reduced the cyclical sensitivity of secondary workers and that these recent years dominate the regression estimates. For prime-age males the presence of a significant discouraged-worker effect may reflect an asymmetric cyclical response for this group. For males 25 and over, participation rates have declined secularly, with the largest declines heavily concentrated in the older groups. The data suggest that periods of high unemployment speed the secular decline, but that participation rates for these groups do not recover as the labor market improves" (p. 569).

19. To measure correctly the supply of part-time labor, the part-time labor force must be defined to include only those on *voluntary* part time, which includes those unemployed who are seeking only part-time work. The other category of part-time workers, those employed part time for economic reasons, is essentially an indicator of deficient aggregate demand and underemployment. Those in this category should be included among the full-time labor force because they want to work full-time but were only able to obtain part-time work. Since this category exhibits substantial cyclical fluctuation (analogous to the fluctuation in the unemployment rate), adding these workers to the voluntary part-time workers can easily result in mistaking these cyclical variations for a trend in the importance of part-time work. Although Morgenstern and Hamovitch (1976) clearly distinguish the two categories of part-time employment, their description of dramatic recent growth in the importance of part-time work among women relative to men appears too strong to be supported by the evidence. Deutermann and Brown (1978) describe these recent trends more accurately, but point out that although part-time employment has grown substantially since the early 1950s, this growth has slackened a bit in recent years. "The employment of married women continues to rise, *but this group has shown little or no tendency to increase its propensity to seek part-time work*" (pp. 8–9, italics ours).

20. "Although investigators have used similar time periods, data bases and theoretical models, parameter estimates have varied disturbingly. For prime-age males, quite competent efforts have provided a full range of substitution elasticities: high, low, zero and negative" (p. 356).

21. A related question has to do with the relationship between the hours per week and the weeks per year decision. Hanoch (1976) has recently expanded labor supply theory by viewing utility as being derived from two different types of leisure, one enjoyed during working days and weeks and the other during nonworking days and weeks. These two types of leisure are not perfect substitutes and, therefore, individuals must make distinguishable choices with respect to hours and weeks of work.

22. The following discussion draws heavily on Cogan (1975) and Killingsworth (1979a), to which the reader is referred for more detail concerning these issues.

23. For example, Boskin (1973); Hall (1973); Leibowitz (1972); and Kalachek and Raines (1970), to name only a few.

24. This assumes that no amount of market work actually exhausts the total amount of time available.

25. See, for example, Leibowitz (1975); Hill and Stafford (1974); Bloch (1975); and Gronau (1977).

26. The sharp drop in labor force participation, between the ages of 20 to 24 and 25 to 34, for women with four years of college, is particularly striking to observe. Although more educated women have higher labor force participation rates at all ages, it appears the trade-off between productivity in the home and the market shows up very clearly for college-educated women. However, those with one to three, or five or more years of college display only a slight drop in participation rates at this stage of the life cycle.

27. This is corroborated in several other studies. See Bloch (1975) and Gronau (1976). The survey used in the latter study was conducted by the Institute of Social Research of Jerusalem in May-June 1970.

28. U.S. Bureau of Census (1973), table 21.

29. The average age of the female civilian labor force, computed from unpublished BLS data, was approximately 39.5 in 1957 and 36.4 in 1977. The corresponding figures for men were 40.7 and 37.7.

Chapter 3

Education, Training, and Occupational Selection

Differences between the occupational distributions of men and women present an even more striking picture of sex differentials than the differing rates of labor force participation and labor supply elasticities discussed in the previous chapter, and this situation has remained remarkably stable over time. In 1960, nearly half (47 percent) of employed women were in "feminine" occupations, where women represented at least 80 percent of total employment, while only 2 percent of employed women were in occupations where they represented less than one-third of total employment (the fraction they represented of the aggregate labor force), but almost 90 percent of all employed men were in these "masculine" occupations (Zellner 1975). These differences would be even more striking if housework had been included as an additional occupational category. Even in the period between 1960 and 1970, the Council of Economic Advisors, using an index of occupational dissimilarity, found only a very small change in the direction of greater occupational similarity.[1] Since 1970, no further gains have been observed in the direction of greater occupational similarity between the sexes. Table 3.1 shows several alternative estimates of the index of dissimilarity for different years, all of which show the same basic trends. Because the changes to date have been so insignificant, the overall distribution of men and women between occupations remains sharply dissimilar.

Both the actual occupational distribution at any point in time and its change over time result from the interaction of supply and demand in many different markets and a complete explanation requires a dynamic analysis of various simultaneous adjustments. The strong and persistent differences in occupational distribution between men and women reflect systematic differences between the sexes in

Table 3.1

Alternative Measures of the Index of Occupational Segregation

	1950	1960	1970	1977
197 occupations[a]		.629	.598	
183 occupations[b]	.727	.738	.707	
236 occupations[c]			.645	.643

SOURCES: [a] U.S. President, *Economic Report of the President* (1973), p. 155.
[b] Computations were based on a sample of 183 detailed census categories on which comparable data were available for all three years. Because not all detailed occupations were included and all residual categories were excluded, the estimated index is larger in size than other indexes. This is because residuals would be expected to mask some existing dissimilarity and they were not included here (Blau and Hendricks 1979).
[c] These two indexes were computed by the authors. The 1970 data were taken directly from the 1970 Census (table 38 of the Subject Report-Occupational Characteristics, PC (2)-7A). The 1977 data were taken from *Employment and Earnings* (January 1978). Because the 1977 data were slightly less detailed than the 1970 data, certain assumptions had to be made in constructing comparable categories. In any case where information was provided in one year but not the other for a particular occupation, residual categories were created. The alternative would have been to omit those categories for which figures were not provided in both years. It was deemed preferable to retain as many categories as possible, even if this meant collapsing several categories into a lesser number of residuals, rather than lose the information contained therein by elimination. For example: the category "Engineers" had five subcategories in 1977, but eleven in 1970. The five which matched in both years were entered separately for 1970 and for 1977. The remaining six in 1970 were combined to form a residual (engineers, n.e.c.) and corresponded to the residual figure in 1977 which emerged when the combined five were subtracted from the overall total of engineers.

preferences, economic circumstances and economic opportunities. Radical changes in women's labor force participation and career attachment juxtaposed against only gradual changes in the occupational distribution could reflect long lags in the response of sex-specific preferences to economic change and/or lags in the equalization of access to jobs for men and women across occupations.

This chapter will focus on the determinants of the individual's choice of occupation and level of skill. At this point, we do not attempt to explain the forces shaping differential job opportunities for men and women, but assume that such differences exist. Chapter 4 will examine the market consequences of these individual decisions under the assumption of equal opportunity in the market place. This provides an opportunity to evaluate the relative strength of differences in individual choice as an explanation of differences between the sexes in market outcomes. Chapter 5 explores discrimination explicitly as the major factor affecting differential access to jobs, and analyzes the dynamic interaction over time of differences in choice on the one side, and differences in opportunity on the other, in determining unemployment and wage differentials.

Over the life cycle, individuals maximize utility subject to resource constraints. This maximization process produces optimal decisions about labor supply, occupational choice and the amounts of education and training sought. Although all these dimensions of choice are jointly determined, for ease of exposition we choose to deal with the determinants of each choice separately. In this chapter, we use the theory of investment in human capital as the key connecting link between labor supply and occupation. Labor supply decisions have certain obvious implications for human capital investment, because time in the market necessarily involves the accumulation of experience which will enhance productivity relatively more in some occupations than others. Human capital theory is commonly used to explain the major differences between men and women in types and amounts of education and training that they seek, and consequently the types of jobs that they choose to enter and the types of careers they pursue. Therefore, a review of human capital theory as it applies to these decisions is the obvious point of departure for any discussion of occupational choice. After reviewing the theory, we will take a critical look at the empirical work on education and training, in terms of the types of questions economists have typically asked, the assumptions they have made, and the empirical results as they relate to sex differentials. This chapter will conclude with a critical reappraisal of the theory of occupational choice as it relates to the actual distribution of men and women across occupations and their job mobility.

Human Capital Theory

Human capital is a relatively new research area in economics, having developed almost entirely within the past fifteen to twenty years,[2] largely in response to the unexplained rise in the economic value of labor. Various studies in the 1960s indicated clearly that a mere head or hours count inevitably underestimates increases in the effective labor force (e.g., Denison 1962; Jorgenson and Griliches 1967). Thus the concept of human capital was introduced into economic analysis to provide a measure and an explanation of human productive capacity. Its appeal to scholars was immediate, and the analysis of investment in human capital rapidly burgeoned into a major field of study in economics.

As Becker (1964) so clearly states in his seminal work, *Human Capital*, any activity that raises future productivity as a result of current direct and/or opportunity costs incurred can be usefully analyzed within the framework of investment theory. Increased future productivity refers to higher real wages in the market[3] (which would possibly include a reduction in wage loss due to unemployment), or a higher standard of living due to nonmarket productivity, or both. These productivity-enhancing investments can take many forms, including schooling, on-the-job training and experience, medical care, migration, and the search for price and wage information. The most obvious and readily observable example of investment in human capital is education, and much of the early empirical work done by economists in the human capital area concentrated on the estimation of monetary rates of return to various levels of education. Although there are many forms of human capital in addition to education, and although investment in human capital also yields substantial nonmarket and psychic returns, economists have paid the most attention to monetary returns to schooling because these are relatively easy to measure. More recently, as we shall see, economists have shifted their attention from schooling to training, which is a more comprehensive concept, including schooling as a general type of training, as well as specific on-the-job training and job experience. This shift in emphasis has given the human capital approach more generality but has been accompanied by new and more difficult measurement problems.

THE CAPITALIZATION FORMULA

A person's human capital is simply productive capacity—the ability to produce goods and services in the market or outside. Human capital not only enhances an individual's earning power in the market, but may provide access to jobs with more prestige and better surroundings as well as enhancing the satisfaction derived from nonmarket work and leisure activities. Human capital is by definition embodied in human beings, who cannot be bought and sold within our modern legal framework. Therefore, human capital does not have a value established in the market and its value has to be estimated indirectly through the capitalization formula, which expresses in mathematical terms an individual's expectation of the value of a stream of future production. The present value of a stream of future production is calculated by discounting the expected value of future gains in earnings and nonpecuniary benefits by the interest rate: the further in the future a particular return lies, the more heavily it is discounted and the lower its expected present value will be. The capital value of income stream H is equal to $CV(H)$.

$$CV(H) = \frac{H_0}{(1 + i)^0} + \frac{H_1}{(1 + i)^1} + \frac{H_2}{(1 + i)^2} + \frac{H_3}{(1 + i)^3}$$

$$+ \cdots + \frac{H_n}{(1 + i)^n} = \sum_{t=0}^{n} \frac{H_t}{(1 + i)^t}$$

Where i = the interest rate

       n = the time period over which the income stream is calculated (0, 1, . . . , n)

       H_t = expected benefits (earnings and nonpecuniary benefits) in year t.

Before making any particular investment in human capital, an individual evaluates all the alternatives available. For purposes of illustration, we simplify the choice to two alternatives in our examples. The choice of a particular career path H can be viewed as the outcome of a process which involves comparing the expected present values of benefits deriving from two alternative careers, where H = total expected stream of benefits if career H is chosen, and L = expected stream of benefits otherwise. The present value of the expected gain (G)—or loss, if G is negative—from choosing H is $G = CV(H)$ $-CV(L) = \sum_{t=0}^{n} \dfrac{H_t - L_t}{(1 + i)^t}$

If there are no direct costs involved, the investment in career H will be made if the expected G is positive, but will not be made if G is zero or negative. This would be the situation if H and L were two alternative careers with different expected earnings streams, either of which the individual is qualified to enter. It should be emphasized at this point that to say there are no *direct* costs involved is not to say that making the investment in H is completely costless—far from it. Choosing career H involves substantial *opportunity* costs—namely *earnings foregone* by not choosing L. However, these opportunity costs are already included in the calculation of net gain.

Some investments in human capital involve direct costs as well as opportunity costs. Obvious examples of such direct costs are payments for tuition and books in the case of college education, travel expenses in the case of geographic mobility, or doctor's fees in the case of investment in health. Psychic or nonmonetary costs, such as the unhappiness and loneliness experienced in moving from a familiar area to a new location for school or a job would also be included here.[4] Although in practice it is difficult or impossible to measure this component of costs quantitatively, it clearly exists and is not infrequently large enough to outweight apparently substantial monetary returns. Direct costs as well as earnings can be distributed over time. In this case, expected costs as well as expected benefits must be discounted. The general formula for the net gain (net of both direct and opportunity costs) now becomes

$$G = \sum_{t=0}^{n} \frac{H_t - L_t - C_t}{(1 + i)^t}.$$

Uncertainty and imperfect knowledge further complicate the calculation of capital values. Investment in human capital is a gamble, and the future gains and costs from any investment cannot be predicted with certainty. Imperfect knowledge of the future is built into the capitalization formula in two ways. First, the streams of earnings and costs in the numerator are not *actual* values for the particular individual, but *expected* values. Second, an uncertainty premium is added to the interest rate in the denominator used to discount future earnings and costs.

Within the context of the basic discount formula, an alternative to the net gain approach just discussed can be used to examine profitability. This approach involves the *internal rate of return* on the investment. The internal rate of return (r) is simply the percentage rate of profit on the particular investment or, in this case, the rate which equates the present values of the two income streams. Once computed, r can be compared to the interest rate in order to determine profitability. Using this approach, an investment is profitable if $r > i$ and unprofitable if $r < i$. The procedure is to set the net gain, G equal to zero, substitute r for i in the formula, and then solve for r.[5]

INDIVIDUAL DEMAND AND SUPPLY

The model of career choice described above refers to the choice of various hypothetical options for a *given* individual. This process is unfortunately not observable and, instead, available data provide us only with information about differences *between* individuals in actual earnings, as well as years of schooling and job experience. In order to analyze systematic differences between men and women in levels of investment in training and rates of return, we must examine the sources of individual differences in the supply of and demand for human capital. Here, we are no longer directly comparing alternative career paths for a given individual, but are instead comparing the life cycle implications of alternative *levels* of investment in schooling and other types of training for the earnings profile, assuming that each level of investment is associated with an expected career path. An individual demand curve for human capital shows the marginal rate of return (r) for each incremental dollar of investment, while the supply curve shows the rate of interest (i) or the marginal cost of financing, for each dollar invested.

The demand curve for human capital is assumed to slope downwards. That is, marginal net benefits decrease as additional capital is accumulated, largely because additional accumulation entails rising opportunity costs as well as a shortening and postponement of the payoff period.[6] If markets were perfect, the supply curve of human capital would be horizontal for all at the competitively determined interest rate for human capital investment funds. In reality, this market is highly segmented, so the supply curve for the financing of investment in human capital slopes upward, in a discontinuous fashion. Some sources of funds, such as free public education or gifts from parents, are considerably cheaper than others, such as commercial bank loans, but are available to each individual only in limited amounts. As the less expensive sources of funds are exhausted, the individual who is in the process of accumulating human capital must utilize successively more costly methods of financing. For many people, however, a point may come when no funds are available at any price. This happens when individuals are directly barred from obtaining training because of discriminatory admissions policies in higher education or discriminatory hiring practices by employers providing training necessary for upward career mobility. In this case, the supply curve will become vertical, and no further investment in human capital can take place. The value of total benefits is measured by the area under the demand curve, the amount of financing costs by the area under the supply curve, and the maximum difference of benefits over costs is obtained by investing up to their point of intersection (Becker 1967: 11). See figure 3.1.

Differences in either demand or supply conditions among individuals will cause the amounts invested in human capital to vary, with those with lower supply curves and/or higher demand curves investing more than others. The implication of the observed differences between men and women in investments such as education and training is that supply or demand conditions, or possibly both, are characterized by substantial variation. It is worthwhile to examine the meaning of variations in supply and demand separately, and then to combine both types of variation into a general framework.

Differences in supply curves represent differences in opportunity due to differences in wealth and the availability of funds. Differences in demand curves represent differences in innate capabilities or the ability to benefit from investment in human capital. These differences in demand may also be affected by discrimination in the labor market.

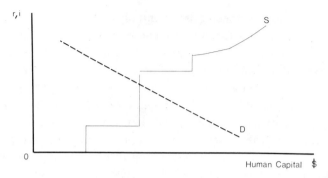

Figure 3.1.   The Supply of and Demand for Human Capital

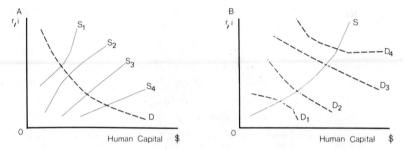

Figure 3.2.   A. Equal Ability and Different Opportunities: One Demand Curve, Many Supply Curves B. Equal Opportunity and Different Abilities: One Supply Curve, Many Demand Curves

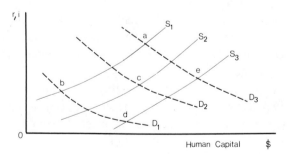

Figure 3.3.   Differences in Both Abilities and Opportunities: Many Demand and Supply Curves

The assumption that people are essentially equal in "ability,"[7] but that the opportunities for funding vary considerably, implies that everyone has the same demand curve for human capital, but that people face different supply curves. On the other hand, the assumption that everyone has essentially the same opportunities for funding, but that people vary widely in "ability," implies that everyone faces the same supply curve of human capital, but that demand curves differ among individuals. As can be seen from the points of intersection in the two diagrams in figure 3.2, the assumption of equal ability and different opportunities implies that those who invest more receive a lower rate of return on their investment, while assuming equal opportunity and different abilities leads to the opposite implication, that those who invest the most also receive the highest rate of return.

In his original presentation of this framework, Becker (1964) implicitly assumed that differences between individuals in the demand for human capital were entirely due to differences in IQ or innate ability and were not related to differences in work life expectancies or opportunity costs. Although this formulation may relate well to an understanding of differences among men in amounts of human capital investment, it clearly breaks down when attempting to explain investment differences among women or between men and women, because the great variation that exists in both the extent and continuity of labor force participation will affect the rate of return to any level of investment, by affecting the amount and distribution of returns and opportunity costs. In addition, because the demand for human capital is derived from the demand for labor services, rates of return may differ if men and women systematically enter occupations which differ in terms of opportunities for employment and advancement. If there is discrimination against women, the variation in demand curves between men and women will also be due to differences in labor market opportunities.

In the real world, we would reasonably expect both supply and demand curves to vary considerably. As can be seen in figure 3.3, if both supply and demand curves vary, then the possibilities for combinations of amounts invested and rates of returns are myriad, and the question immediately arises as to whether any correlation between the supply and demand curves is to be expected and, if so, whether the correlation between amounts invested and rates of return would differ between men and women.

If there were no correlation between supply and demand curves, any random scattering of equilibrium points for different individuals might be observed, with no systematic relationship between amounts invested and rates of return. If a negative correlation existed between supply and demand conditions, then different people choosing to invest the same amount would receive different rates of return, as at equilibrium points a, c, and d. On the other hand, if the correlations between demand and supply were positive—if, for example, people more able to benefit from human capital investment receive larger subsidies from their families and/or more and larger scholarships and loans—then we might observe a series of equilibrium points such as b, c, and e, where different individuals investing widely differing amounts would receive the same rate of return. A positive correlation between demand and supply will clearly increase the inequality in both investments and earnings.

Given that both demand and supply vary across individuals, we must consider not only the possible correlation between these two factors, but whether or not the variation of one factor outweighs that of the other, and thus dominates the observed results. If supply varies more than does demand, the distribution of equilibrium points will approach that in part A of figure 3.2, and the average observed rate of return will tend to decrease as investment increases. However, if demand is more variable than supply, the average observed rate of return will tend to vary directly with the amount invested, approaching the situation depicted in part B of figure 3.2.

When comparing men and women, we can develop some preliminary insights into possible differences in average amounts invested and average market rates of return by hypothesizing likely average differences in supply and demand curves and likely correlations between them. When dealing with market returns to educational investment, one would expect the average differences in demand curves for men and women to exceed the average differences in supply curves. Free access to public education through high school and considerable public subsidization of higher education make large differences in the distribution of supply curves unlikely, at least until the highest levels of education. On the other hand, shorter years of job experience and discrimination will reduce the average level of women's demand for education relative to men. Therefore, one would on average expect men to invest more and receive a higher rate of return than women. In the case of job training the analysis is more complicated. The supply and demand curves are likely to be highly correlated, because the place of employment in which training is provided is often identical to the place where the returns to that investment must be realized. To the extent that discrimination against women affects access to jobs with training options, demand and supply will be positively correlated, leading men again to invest more without lowering their relative rate of return. On the other hand, if access to training is unrelated to sex, but women choose jobs involving less training, there will be little difference in the distribution of supply. However, men's demand curves will tend to lie above those of women, leading men, on average, to invest more than women, and to receive a higher *market* rate of return. Actual differences in amounts invested and in total rates of return (including nonmarket gains) are likely to be smaller than those predicted on the basis of market returns alone, because of women's greater participation in the nonmarket sector.

When looking at variations in human capital investment within groups of men and women, we would expect an equal distribution of innate abilities, but a much greater variation in demand among women, because of large differences between them in expected labor supply (Heckman and Willis 1977). On the supply side, although there is as great a variation in socioeconomic status for men as there is for women, the variation in opportunities for financing at least some types of investments, and therefore the variation in supply, are likely to be greater for men than for women, because inequality in access to investment financing may affect women other than those who are economically disadvantaged. Thus, when comparing men and women, we might well expect that the correlation between amounts invested and market rates of return would tend to be positive for women (as in figure 3.2B) and negative for men (as in figure 3.2A). Again, these predictions would be modified but not reversed when nonmarket returns are included.

This consideration of variations in the supply of and demand for human capital provides the framework within which we can focus on the crucial question that this chapter addresses: the nature and extent of actual sex differentials in investment in various forms of human capital and the consequences of these differences for rates of return and occupational distribution. Our discussion of sex differentials will focus on educational attainment and on-the-job training, as the two major types of human capital investment having implications for occupational distribution. Each of these investments yields monetary returns in the form of higher wage rates and a lower incidence of unemployment, as well as nonmonetary returns in the form of increased productivity in the nonmarket sector. Both education and job training will be examined within the framework of the general theory as developed above, and empirical evidence on differences between women and men with respect to investments in and returns to these categories of human capital will be presented and analyzed.

Educational Investment

When we turn to statistics and empirical research on human capital, in the hope of obtaining some factual information on sex differentials in investments and rates of return, and eventually relating that information to the substantial observed sex differentials in earnings, we come up against a pronounced asymmetry in the empirical work. The vast bulk of this research has concentrated exclusively on estimating the human capital embodied in, and the rates of return earned by, the male labor force or, even more narrowly, the white, native-born, urban male labor force. Information on the human capital of women, and, to a lesser extent, of minority groups in the labor force is astonishingly scanty, although it has begun to appear recently. Thus human capital theory decends from its theoretical generality to a narrowly applied theory of the distribution of the earnings of full-time male workers.

Most of the . . . theorists who have tackled the problem have confined their attention to the distribution of earnings, especially full-time male earnings.

Indeed, it is somewhat a paradox that what economists think of as "income distribution theory" relates to the distribution of earnings of fully employed males, while what they think of as "income distribution policy" means almost everything else. (Rivlin 1975:8)

In the case of education, one can perhaps understand the desire to standardize for other factors by looking at the effect of educational attainment on earnings within a group as large and homogeneous as possible in all other respects (and hence the penchant for those white, native-born, urban men). But, once as "clean" a return as possible to education *per se* had been estimated, the willingness to remain within fairly narrowly defined limits, and the attendant reluctance to apply human capital theory to the problems of sex differentials in earnings and unemployment rates, appear rather strange. However, once again we must remember that the focus of all these early studies of human capital was on education, and that the large male-female earnings differential has not been accompanied by a corresponding difference in education. In this respect, the sex differential is unlike the white-non-white, the urban-rural, or the native-immigrant differentials. In all those cases, there is at least a crude rank relationship, in that the group with higher earnings also has significantly more education. As T. W. Schultz put it in his presidential address to the American Economic Association:

When farm people take nonfarm jobs they earn substantially less than industrial workers of the same race, age and sex. Similarly nonwhite urban males earn much less than white males even after allowance is made for the effects of differences in unemployment, age, city size and region. Because these differentials in earnings correspond closely to corresponding differentials in education, they strongly suggest that the one is a consequence of the other. Negroes who operate farms, whether as tenants or as owners, earn much less than whites on comparable farms. Fortunately, crops and livestock are not vulnerable to the blight of discrimination. The large differences in earnings seem rather to reflect mainly the differences in health and education. Workers in the South on the average earn appreciably less than in the North or West and they also have on the average less education. . . . To urge that the differences in the amount of human investment may explain these differences in earnings seems elementary. (Schultz 1961:3–4)

Note that the male-female earnings differential is not mentioned, and also that it is the only such differential between groups that is not accompanied by a difference in the average levels of education. This is a paradox that was not successfully grappled with by the human capital economists of the 1960s. In order to put this into perspective, we must take a fairly detailed look at the average level and distribution of educational attainment for men and women, and any changes that have taken place over time. This will be followed by a critical summary of the empirical findings on differential rates of return. Here we will examine market rates of return estimated from the older discounted present value approach and from the earnings function approach, as well as estimates of nonmarket returns.

SEX DIFFERENCES IN EDUCATIONAL ATTAINMENT

What is most striking about the education of men and women is the virtual identity, rather than any significant difference, in median years of school completed. For both the labor force and the population as a whole, female-male differences in average educational attainment had become minimal (one-tenth of a year) by the mid-1960s. This can be clearly seen in the median years of school column in table 3.2, and in figure 3.4, which shows the convergence of the educational levels of men and women.[8] The educational attainment of the total population has risen steadily but the rate of increase leveled off sharply in the middle sixties. Obviously, the increase has been much more pronounced for men than for women. Median education for the female population has remained comparatively stable since 1962, when it reached 12 years, and has advanced only 0.3 years in the past 15 years, whereas the median education of men has grown 0.8 years in the same period of time.

Although both sexes have the same median years of education, the distribution of educational attainment differs between men and women. The probability of graduating from high school has always been somewhat greater for women than for men, but it has been less likely that a woman would complete college, and still less likely that she would enter graduate school. Figure 3.5 presents the distribution of educational attainment by sex in 1952 and 1977. Over time, the distribution of educational attainment has shifted dramatically for both

Table 3.2

Median Years of Educational Attainment of the Population and Percentage Distributions, by Sex, for Selected Years,[a] 1952–1977

Year	Total, 18+[b] (1000's)	Median Years of School	% Distributions						
			Total	Elementary		High School		College	
				<5 yrs.	5–8 yrs.	1–3 yrs.	4 yrs.	1–3 yrs.	4+ yrs.
Male Population									
1952	47,744	10.1	100	9.8	33.1	17.7	21.9	8.2	7.9
1957	50,854	10.7	100	9.2	29.9	18.3	23.7	8.4	8.8
1962	53,889	11.6	100	7.7	26.3	18.5	26.4	10.5	10.6
1967	57,089	12.1	100	5.9	22.5	18.2	29.7	11.9	11.7
1972	67,080	12.2	100	4.1	17.7	21.0	31.0	13.3	13.0
1977	73,587	12.4	100	17.0		19.5	32.3	15.4	15.9
Female Population									
1952	53,596	11.0	100	7.0	30.6	18.4	29.5	8.4	5.5
1957	56,432	11.4	100	7.0	27.2	19.1	32.0	8.0	5.4
1962	60,311	12.0	100	5.9	24.5	18.9	34.1	10.2	6.3
1967	65,140	12.1	100	4.6	20.8	19.2	37.3	11.0	7.1
1972	75,492	12.2	100	3.4	16.4	21.7	38.6	11.7	8.2
1977	82,059	12.3	100	16.0		20.1	38.8	13.9	10.5

SOURCES: 1952: Current Population Reports, Series P-50, no. 49, p. 7, table 1. 1957: Current Population Reports, Series P-50, no. 78, p. 8, table 1. 1962 and 1967: Special Labor Force Reports, nos. 30 and 92, table B. 1972: Special Labor Force Report, no. 148, table B. 1977: "Educational Attainment of Workers, March 1977" *Monthly Labor Review*, Vol. 100, no. 12, December 1977, p. 54, table 1.

[a] Data for 1952 are for October. Data for 1957–1977 are for March.
[b] The data for 1972 and 1977 cover the entire working age population aged sixteen and over.

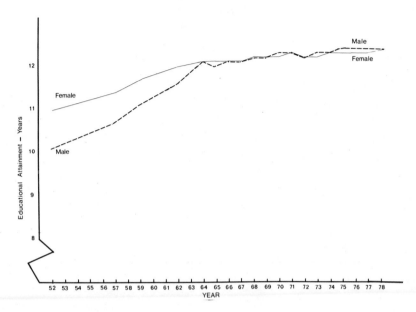

Figure 3.4.   Median Years of Educational Attainment of the Male and Female Population, 1952–1978

SOURCES: 1952: Current Population Reports, Series P-50, no. 49. p. 7, table 1.
1957: Series P-50, no. 78. p. 8, table 1.
1962–76: U.S. Dept. of Labor, BLS, Special Labor Force Reports, nos. 30, 53, 65, 83, 92, 103, 125, 140, 148, 161, 175, 186, and 193, respectively. Table B, pp. A-6, A-7, A-8, respectively.
1977: "Educational Attainment of Workers, March 1977," *Monthly Labor Review* (December 1977), 100(12):54, table 1.
1978: "Educational Attainment of Workers—Some Trends from 1975 to 1978," *Monthly Labor Review*, vol. 102, no. 2 (February 1979), 102(2):55, table 1.

men and women, becoming much more concentrated around the median value. However, women are still more likely to finish high school and less likely to finish college than men.

   One of the most striking and frequently referred to aspects of investment in education through the 1960s is the fact that strong growth in the number and proportion of young people investing in higher education did not adversely affect the rate of return to higher education or the earnings of college graduates relative to less educated workers. One explanation for this is that, due to changes in the industrial mix, the demand for more educated workers was growing

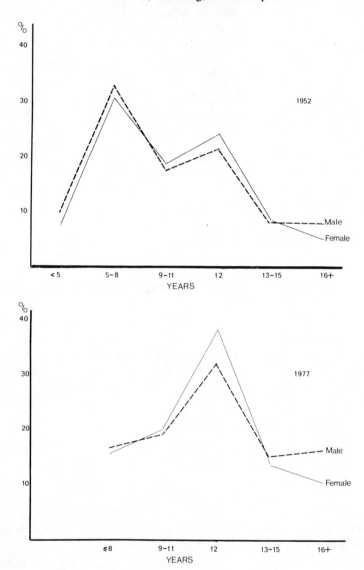

Figure 3.5.   Percentage Distributions of Years of School Completed by Men and Women, 1952 and 1977

SOURCES: 1952: Current Population Reports, Series P-50, no. 49. p. 7, table 1.
1977: U.S. Dept. of Labor, BLS, Special Labor Force Report no. 209. p. A-10, table B.

more rapidly than their supply, as expanded postgraduate enrollments delayed labor force entry (Freeman 1975). However, the job market for college graduates appears to have undergone a downturn during the 1970s, although it is difficult at this point to distinguish any permanent, long-run turnaround from the cyclical effects of the relatively mild 1970–71 and the severe 1974–75 recessions. Of particular interest is the differential effect of slackening growth in demand on male and female college-trained workers.

In documenting the 1969–74 downturn in the college labor market, Freeman emphasizes three major pieces of evidence: a fall in real and relative earnings, slackening growth in the numbers of college-level professional and managerial jobs, and a sharp decline in social and private rates of return to college education.[9] Unfortunately, the data on earnings and rates of return in his study cover only male workers,[10] but the statistics on professional and managerial employment are presented for both men and women, and are suggestive of possible changes in the relative returns to education by sex as a result of differential demand shifts in the professional and managerial job markets during the 1969–74 slowdown. Specifically, it appears that the slowdown in growth was concentrated primarily among men and professionals, with women and managers only relatively moderately affected, and female managerial employment actually rising. As a result, the secular growth in male professional and managerial employment as a proportion of the total labor force was brought to a complete halt, while growth rates in the proportion of females employed in these categories were only slowed slightly.

The CPS data on educational attainment discussed above only give the stock of educated people at different levels for a given year and do not point up the recent changes in the sex distribution of new degree recipients. It is these patterns that are more reflective of future trends. Here, recent data indicate that women made up almost half of college degree recipients in 1974–1975 and also received 45 percent of the master's degrees, and 21 percent of the doctor's degrees (Ph.D., Ed.D., etc.). In 1966–1967, the corresponding percentages were 42 percent, 35 percent, and 12 percent. (National Center for Educational Statistics 1977a:10).

The evidence of declining returns to college for men, and the considerably less clear and mixed evidence for women, are consistent with current trends in college enrollment. Figure 3.6 shows changes in the percent of high school graduates enrolled in college in October of the year of graduation since 1962. Although year-to-year fluctuations have sometimes been substantial, the overall trend in the fraction of male high school graduates enrolling in college has been downward between 1966 and 1976, apparently as a rational supply response to changed market demand conditions. In 1968, 63 percent of male high school graduates were enrolled in college, but this percentage had fallen to 51 percent by 1978. However, the low points in 1974 and 1976, where male enrollment rates dropped below 50 percent, clearly exaggerate the severity of this decline. The percentage of women high school graduates enrolled in college has held its own during the same period, although with some fluctuation corresponding to the business cycle, and is now less than 2 percentage points below that of men. Since the female enrollment rate has been roughly constant since 1975, it temporarily exceeded the abnormally low male rate by 3 percentage points in 1976.

Considerably more pronounced than differences by sex in the distribution of educational attainment are the differences that exist in courses taken and areas of specialization. At all levels, women are heavily represented in education and in the more general cultural fields, such as English, languages, and fine arts. They are only poorly represented in disciplines with a strong vocational emphasis. Table 3.3 presents the distributions by discipline of the bachelor's, master's, and doctor's degrees conferred on men and women in 1966–67 and in 1974–75, the most recent year for which data are available. Five major areas of concentration—education, social science, letters, fine and applied arts and the health professions—still accounted for 64.3 percent of women college graduates in 1974–75, a decline from 77.8 percent of women college graduates in 1966–67.

An index of dissimilarity in fields entered shows that the male and female distributions are quite dissimilar but nowhere nearly as dissimilar as the occupational distributions presented in table 3.1.[11] A recent study also shows that these differences persist even when com-

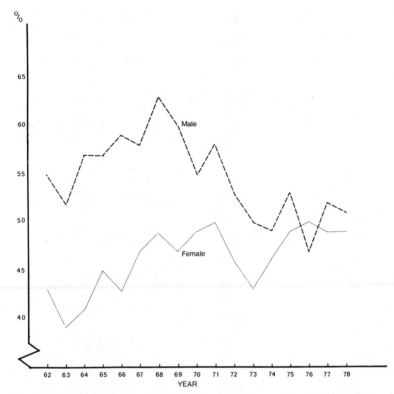

Figure 3.6. Percentage of High School Graduates Enrolled in College in October of Year of Graduation, by Sex, 1962–1978

SOURCES: 1962–1977: U.S. Dept. of Labor, BLS, Special Labor Force Reports, nos. 155, 168, 180, 191, 200, 215.
1978: Unpublished BLS data.

paring men and women with equivalent ability, family background and future career plans (Polachek 1978). For any given year, the degree of dissimilarity is lower the higher the degree, which is not surprising, given that women pursuing higher degrees are more likely to be planning market-oriented careers. The index of dissimilarity in fields entered has declined noticeably at the B.A. level, but the change in the distribution was not statistically significant for either men or women during this eight-year period.[12] This was primarily due to a

Table 3.3

Percentage Distributions of Bachelor's, Master's, and Doctor's Degrees Conferred on Women and Men by Discipline, 1966–1967 and 1974–1975

| | B.A. | | | | M.A. | | | | Ph.D. | | | |
| | 1966–1967 | | 1974–1975 | | 1966–1967 | | 1974–1975 | | 1966–1967 | | 1974–1975 | |
Discipline	women	men	women	men	women	men	women	men	women	men	women	men
Agriculture and natural resources[a]	0.3	2.9	0.6	3.0	0.3	2.0	0.3	1.7	0.7	3.9	0.6	3.6
Architecture and environmental design[b]	0.1	0.8	0.3	1.3	0.1	0.7	0.4	1.4	0.1	0.1	0.1	0.2
Area studies[e]	—	—	0.4	0.3	—	—	0.4	0.4	—	—	0.5	0.5
Biological sciences	3.4	6.4	4.1	6.8	2.3	3.6	1.5	2.8	13.9	10.5	10.2	9.9
Business and management	2.5	19.6	5.3	22.2	0.7	14.0	2.3	20.6	0.7	2.3	0.5	3.6
Communications[e]	—	—	1.8	2.3	—	—	0.9	1.0	—	—	0.6	0.4
Computer and information sciences	0.01	0.1	0.2	0.8	0.1	0.4	0.2	1.2	0.04	0.2	0.2	0.7
Education	38.0	9.3	29.2	8.8	51.0	27.1	56.8	28.1	29.4	15.5	31.6	19.2
Engineering	0.1	11.1	0.3	9.1	0.1	13.4	0.3	9.2	0.4	14.3	0.9	11.4
Fine and applied arts	5.3	2.8	6.0	3.1	4.5	3.2	3.0	2.7	3.8	2.3	2.8	1.7
Foreign languages	5.1	1.5	3.3	0.8	4.3	1.8	1.9	0.8	6.6	2.3	5.5	1.7
Health economics	5.1	1.1	9.1	2.2	3.0	1.7	5.1	2.6	0.7	1.3	2.4	1.6
Home economics	2.6	0.1	3.8	0.1	1.5	0.1	1.3	0.1	1.8	0.1	1.4	0.2
Law	0.02	0.1	0.01	0.08	0.1	0.8	0.1	0.7	0.1	0.1	—	0.1

Letters[c]	12.6	6.6	7.9	4.9	7.8	4.2	5.3	3.0	9.4	4.9	11.7	6.2
Library sciences	0.3	0.1	0.2	0.02	6.5	0.9	4.9	1.1	0.2	0.1	0.3	0.1
Mathematics	3.1	4.3	1.8	2.1	2.3	3.9	1.1	1.8	2.4	4.3	1.5	3.2
Military sciences	—	0.6	—	0.1	—	—	—	—	—	—	—	—
Physical sciences	1.0	4.7	0.9	3.4	1.0	4.7	0.6	3.1	6.6	18.2	4.1	12.4
Psychology	3.3	3.6	6.4	4.8	1.9	2.0	2.3	2.5	9.4	5.5	10.4	6.3
Public affairs & services[e]	—	—	3.1	3.1	—	—	5.3	5.3	—	—	1.0	0.8
Social sciences	15.6	20.8	12.1	16.8	10.6	12.5	3.9	7.3	12.5	12.1	12.1	12.4
Theology	0.6	0.9	0.3	0.7	0.9	1.7	0.8	1.4	0.9	1.6	0.6	3.1
Interdisciplinary studies[d]	1.1	2.5	2.9	3.2	0.9	1.2	1.3	1.3	0.5	0.5	1.0	0.7
Index of Dissimilarity	47.38		41.27		39.6		40.0		33.68		30.1	

SOURCES: 1966–1967: National Center for Education Statistics, *Earned Degrees Conferred*: (OE-54013-67, part A), p. 9, table 6.

1974–1975: National Center for Education Statistics, *Earned Degrees Conferred*: (NCES 77-328), p. 14, table 4.

[a] In 1966–67, this was assumed to be equivalent to agriculture, forestry, and geography.

[b] In 1966–67, this was assumed to be equivalent to architecture and city planning.

[c] In 1966–67, this was assumed to be equivalent to English, journalism, and philosophy.

[d] In 1966–67, this was assumed to be equivalent to trade, industrial training, records management, folklore, and miscellaneous.

[e] These had no comparable equivalents in 1966–1967.

dramatic decline in the percentage of women earning B.A. degrees in education (from 38 percent in 1966–1967 to 29 percent in 1974–1975) and an increase in the percentage of women earning B.A. degrees in business and management, the health professions and psychology. The fact that there has been no significant decline in the degree of dissimilarity for higher degrees can be explained by the high and still growing percentage of women earing M.A.'s and Ph.D.'s in education, which, increased from 51 percent to 56 percent and from 29.4 percent to 31.6 percent, respectively (U.S. Dept. of Labor, Women's Bureau 1969:195–199, and National Center for Education Statistics 1977b:14).

Although large numbers of men major in the social sciences and in education, they are also heavily concentrated in business and engineering, two fields with a vocational emphasis in which women are notable by their absence. These two disciplines accounted for roughly 30 percent of both the bachelor's and master's degrees earned by men in 1974–75, but for only 5.5 percent of the bachelor's and 2.6 percent of the master's degrees earned by women in that same year. Just over 2 percent of all engineering degrees conferred were earned by women. In the area of business and commerce, women earned 8.6 percent of the bachelor's degrees and 2.7 percent of the master's degrees in 1966–67, and these percentages rose sizeably to 16.4 percent and 8.4 percent in 1974–75.

Large percentage increases, but from a much smaller base, can be observed with respect to professional degrees earned by women. Between 1966–67 and 1974–75, the fraction of M.D. degrees earned by women increased from 7.4 percent to 13.2 percent, their shares of veterinary medicine and law degrees from 5.5 percent and 3.8 percent to 15.9 percent and 15.1 percent respectively (U.S. Dept. of Labor, Women's Bureau 1969:195; and National Center for Education Statistics 1977b:19).

There is clear evidence that women have traditionally invested in a different *type* of educational capital than men and that these patterns are only beginning to change. There has been considerable awareness among educators of these patterns, and this in turn has engendered concern over why women make the educational choices they do and how this may affect their future careers. In addition, even though the average *amounts* of such capital accumulated appear to be approximately equal for the two sexes, dispersion in the distribution of educational attainment is much greater for men than women. In order to assess the implications of these sex differences in educational investment, the empirical evidence on the relationship between educational levels and rates of return must be reviewed.

RATES OF RETURN TO EDUCATION

In theory, the rate of return to investment in human capital is defined as that rate which equates the present value of returns on an investment for a given individual to the present value of costs for that same individual. The returns and costs are expected rather than actual and include nonmonetary as well as monetary components. In practice, rates of return to education have been estimated by using cross-sectional data on the actual earnings of individuals, differing from one another not only in age and education, but in other characteristics as well. One technique, called the *discounted present value approach*, calculates a rate of return by discounting the average differences in earnings between two education groups at each age and finding the rate that sets the discounted differences equal to zero. The other technique, called the *earnings function approach*, estimates a rate of return to schooling as the coefficient of a variable measuring years of schooling in a multiple regression equation, where earnings is the dependent variable. Neither of these approaches has yet been used extensively to develop comparative measures of male and female rates of return, for reasons that we will discuss. In addition, serious questions have been raised about the validity of these techniques for measuring rates of return in the proper theoretical sense. In the discussion that follows, we will consider the pros and cons of each approach and present the available evidence to see whether it confirms our expectations on sex differentials in rates of return. Finally, we will bring in evidence on educational returns in the nonmarket sector.

Discounted Present Value Approach

The rates of return calculated with this approach are all based on the equalization of alternative streams of earnings corresponding to different levels of educational attainment. It is usually assumed that any direct costs of education are covered by part-time earnings and, therefore, that total costs are approximately equal to the earnings of the nonenrolled. For any educational level these costs are estimated to be roughly equal to the earnings of the group with one year less education at the age at which the additional education is undertaken. The opportunity costs are assumed to be zero for those in elementary school. Actually, of course, this estimated "rate of return to schooling" is not really a rate of return to schooling at all, but a weighted average of returns to schooling and any other additional investments in human capital made by the more educated group (Mincer 1974a). However, if it is assumed that the rate of return to schooling is the same as the rate of return to other investments in human capital, the calculated rate of return can be said to be equal to the rate of return to schooling, at least in the case of white, native-born, urban males. In other words, this technique does not allow in practice for adjustments in earnings differences between individuals because of systematic differences in experience and other factors which affect earnings, which means that it is most accurate when dealing with a group that is homogeneous with respect to job experience and other earnings-related factors. This helps to explain the relative absence of rate of return studies for women, at least until the early 1970s.

Although the analysis of racial and/or regional differences was quite commonplace in the rate of return to education studies of the 1960s, sex differentials were virtually ignored.[13] Estimates of rates of return for men varied widely, but tended to show an inverse relationship between the rate of return and the level of education.[14] This would imply that, at least for men, inequality in opportunity exceeds inequality in ability, and that figure 3.2A provides the best approximate representation of the male human capital market.

Since 1970, there have been four major studies using the discounted present value approach to measure rates of return to education differentiated by sex. Table 3.4 presents the rates of return to high school and higher education derived from these first four studies. It is immediately obvious that any generalization on the basis of these

Table 3.4

Rates of Return to Education by Sex and Race Estimated by Discounted Present Value Approach

High School Graduation Relative to 8th Grade

	white men	nonwhite men	white women	nonwhite women
A. Niemi (1975)[a]				
1960	6.25	5.50	7.25	8.00
			(5.75)	(6.50)
1970	5.75	6.75	6.50	8.25
			(5.25)	(6.75)
Carnoy and Marenbach (1975)[b]				
1969	14.0	19.9	15.1	19.1

High School Graduation Relative to Partial High School Completion

	white men	nonwhite men	white women	nonwhite women
Hines et al. (1970)[c]				
1960	14.5	24.6	56.2	32.8

1–3 Years College Relative to High School Graduation

	white men	nonwhite men	white women	nonwhite women
Hines et al. (1970)				
1960	12.1	2.2	6.9	16.7
Hoffer (1973)[d]				
North				
Lifestyle 1			3.4	9.2
Lifestyle 2			1.5	5.6
Lifestyle 3	7.1	—	0.0	3.6
Lifestyle 4			0.8	4.9
South				
Lifestyle 1			3.2	8.1
Lifestyle 2			1.6	1.9
Lifestyle 3	9.3	—	0.1	0.5
Lifestyle 4			0.9	1.4

Table 3.4   (continued)

College Graduation Relative to High School Graduation

	white men	nonwhite men	white women	nonwhite women
A. Niemi (1975)				
1960	7.75	4.75	5.25	8.25
			(5.50)	(8.00)
1970	8.00	6.00	6.50	8.50
			(7.25)	(8.50)
Carnoy and Marenbach (1975)				
1969	16.2	13.6	14.9	19.4

College Graduation Relative to Partial College Completion

	white men	nonwhite men	white women	nonwhite women
Hines et al. (1970)				
1960	15.1	10.1	13.4	41.4
Hoffer (1973)				
North				
Lifestyle 1			11.7	17.5
Lifestyle 2			7.5	11.3
Lifestyle 3	9.6	—	5.3	8.9
Lifestyle 4			7.4	11.6
South				
Lifestyle 1			11.6	17.3
Lifestyle 2			7.4	10.9
Lifestyle 3	10.1	—	5.3	8.3
Lifestyle 4			7.4	11.0

SOURCES: [a] U.S. Census, Subject Report, *Employment Status and Work Experience*, 1960 and 1970.

The lower labor force participation rates of women are not allowed for, in that only those who earned any income are included. However, the effects of women's lower average annual hours are included when this technique is used. The numbers in parentheses are rates of return calculated on the basis of adjusted income data obtained by weighting female income in each age-education cell by the ratio of male and female hours worked annually. These can be interpreted as the potential rate of return to education for full-time female workers. Because this adjustment was made within each of the two racial groups, the adjusted rates of return for white and nonwhite women are not directly comparable. The income streams are adjusted for taxes and mortality, but not for secular earnings growth or ability. The absence of the latter adjustments was not considered to bias the results because of the offsetting effects found by Hines et al. (see note below). Total private costs of high school were estimated as 75 percent of the mean income of 18- to 24-year-olds who entered the labor force with eight years of education. Total private costs of college included an estimate of direct costs (tuition and fees, from the U.S. Office of Education) and 75 percent of the mean earnings of high school graduates between the ages of 18 and 24.

[b] U.S. Census, 1970, Special Report, *Occupation and Earnings*.

Rates of return are based on mean earnings data for all those 18 years and older in the experienced labor force. The experienced civilian labor force is somewhat smaller than the total civilian labor force because of some people looking for first jobs who would not be included among the experienced labor force. The earnings streams are adjusted for mortality and, in the case of males, for taxes, but not for secular earnings growth or ability. Annual cost estimates are based entirely on foregone earnings and are assumed to equal 75 percent of a full year's salary of a person of the same race, sex and age, with the level of schooling completed below that being taken by the observed individual. Carnoy and Marenbach also estimated changes in rates of return from 1939 to 1969 on the basis of income differences. However, these results are not included here because differences in education are expected to be more closely related to earnings differences than to income differences.

[c] 1960 Census 1:1000 Sample.

The rates of return found here are implicitly adjusted for the lower rates of labor force participation and hours of work of women, in that the entire population aged 14 and over and not enrolled in school, including those with zero wages, salaries, and self-employment income, is used in deriving age-earnings profiles for the four race-sex groups, based on mean wages and salaries plus self-employment income. The rates of return in the table are not adjusted for secular earnings growth, ability, mortality or taxes. When such adjustments were made to the rates of return for white males, the effect was greatest for secondary schooling, where the private rate of return was lowered 19 percent and the social rate of return was lowered 29 percent. The aggregate of the adjustments was quite small for college education, because the upward adjustment resulting from secular growth in earnings was offset by the downward adjustment for ability differences. Total private costs are taken to be equal to earnings forgone while in school, which are estimated as equal to the earnings of people of the same age and schooling level but not enrolled in school.

[d] 1967 Survey of Economic Opportunity.

Comparable rates of return for white males by region from Hanoch's study were included for purposes of comparison. Labor force participation and hours of work are taken into account by constructing hypothetical "lifestyles," each embodying different assumptions concerning lifetime labor force behavior. Lifestyle 1 assumes 2,000 hours of work per year for every year between leaving school and retirement at age 65. This pattern approximates full-time continuous participation, a pattern similar to that of most men, and is most directly comparable to the adjusted data for women in

Table 3.4   (continued)

Niemi's study (see note a above). Lifestyles 2, 3, and 4 all assume zero hours worked annually when children under the age of 6 are present, but differ in the hours worked annually for those years women are assumed to actually be in the labor force. Lifestyle 2 assumes 2,000 hours per year for every year in the labor force. Lifestyle 3 assumes 2,000 hours per year from initial labor force entry to the birth of the first child, and 1,000 hours per year after reentry into the labor force. Lifestyle 4 uses 2,000 hours per year before marriage and average annual hours worked for women for every year in the labor force after marriage. The earnings streams are not adjusted for ability, secular economic growth, or taxes. The average direct costs of attending college were estimated to be $850. Foregone earnings were taken into account by entering only the amount actually earned by college students into their earnings streams for those years spent in college.

studies is difficult. Each of them uses a different data base and makes (or does not make) different adjustments for other factors, such as economic growth, taxes, mortality, ability, and hours of work, as described in the source notes following the table. Given sex differentials in mortality and hours of work, as well as expected differences between the sexes in the impact of taxes on human capital investment (to be discussed in chapter 6), these methodological differences between studies make comparisons extremely difficult.

However, even more important than the differences in data and methodology are certain methodological difficulties common to each of the studies. The discounted present value approach does not permit other earnings-related characteristics, which differ systematically between the sexes, to be fully controlled for when measuring the relationship between education and earnings. For men at all education levels, age and years of job experience are extremely well correlated, but for women they are not, and the relationship between age and job experience varies according to the level of education. Therefore, for women, the calculated rate of return is not clearly attributable to education. In addition, there are other potential biases, in that other personal characteristics affecting earnings, such as ability or motivation, are unlikely to be randomly distributed across education groups.

Therefore, the rate of return calculated in this manner is an *ex post* measure of the relative economic advantage of each level of educational attainment compared with the next lowest group, and not by any means a rate of return in the theoretical sense, where education is seen to vary, with all other factors remaining unchanged.

In addition, because of the rapid rise in female labor force partici-pation, the typical cross-sectional picture of female labor force partici-pation, as we saw in chapter 2, does not represent the experience of any actual cohort of women in recent history. Therefore, because of systematic differences between cohorts in labor market experience, rates of return calculated on the basis of cross-sectional data may have little or no bearing on the average rate of return to be expected by a group of female college entrants today. On the other hand, when rates of return for men have been calculated from both cross-sectional data and approximate cohort data from a series of census years, the esti-mates have been roughly similar, because of the relatively consistent labor force behavior of men over a period of time (Carnoy and Marenbach 1975:315). Although the direction of any net bias is unclear, the problems inherent in this approach are myriad. The rapidly growing literature on the distribution of income and the life cycle relationship between human capital investment and earnings provides an alternative approach to the estimation of rates of return and a more comprehensive approach to human capital investment, by focusing simultaneously on schooling and postschool job training.

Earnings Function Approach

The human capital approach views educational investment as a productive process through which productivity is enhanced and sub-sequent earnings are increased. An individual's current earnings (Y_s) should be composed of some initial level of earnings (Y_o) plus some linear function of the dollar value of the amounts invested in education in past years, on the assumption that no further investments are taking place.

$$(1) \qquad Y_s = Y_o + r_s \sum_{t=0}^{S} C_t$$

If the amount invested in education is expressed as a fraction of potential earnings for the year t (K_t), then earnings in year S can be expressed as

(2) $\qquad Y_s = Y_o \prod_{t=1}^{S} (1 + K_t r_s)$ or $\ln Y_s \simeq \ln Y_o + r_s \sum_{t=0}^{S} K_t$

If it is assumed that 100 percent of potential earnings are invested in education each year (assuming part-time earnings in school offset direct costs), then $K = 1$ and

(3) $\qquad\qquad \ln Y_s = \ln Y_o + r_s S$

where S equals the number of years of school completed. This is the basic earnings function, developed initially by Becker and Chiswick (1966), which expresses the log of current earnings as a linear function of years of schooling. This procedure has several advantages over the discounted present value approach. First, no information on education costs is required. Second, because other important earnings-related characteristics, such as job experience, can be held constant in the estimating equation, rich sources of individual microdata can be fully exploited. This has recently permitted the estimation of rates of return to education for women using data sets in which full information on *actual* years of job experience are available.

Although this method of estimating educational rates of return has advantages, it has come under increasingly sharp criticism. The coefficient of years of schooling (r) may not be a correct measure of the rate of return, because years of schooling are not a good proxy for the money costs of investment. One study found that the intensity of investment (the fraction of potential earnings invested in education) increases with education level, which suggests rates of return estimated in this fashion are biased upward (Leibowitz 1976). There are also questions about the bias introduced by omitting a measure of ability (Griliches 1977). Assuming ability to be positively correlated with schooling, this would also create an upward bias in estimates of rates of return. In addition, this estimating form requires that rates of return be equalized at the margin, because only one average rate of return is generated (Blaug 1976). However, since there is no evidence that the importance of these biases differs for women and men, we will compare sex differences in these rates of return to obtain a sense of their relative size.

All four earnings function studies which have derived schooling coefficients by sex suggest that the women's average rates of return are, if anything, higher than men's, as can be seen in table 3.5. This contrasts with the results from discounted present value studies presented above, which showed white women, at least above the high school level, having consistently lower rates of return than men. Each of these four studies is based on a microdata set and uses wage rates, for working women only, rather than annual earnings as the dependent variable. The studies in table 3.4, on the other hand, all used some measure of annual earnings, and, as the notes to that table indicate, some include nonworking women in their samples. Those rates of return in table 3.4 that fully adjust market returns for the lower participation rates and hours of women can be seen as lower-limit estimates of their total rates of return, based on the assumption that returns to education are realized only in market work. On the other hand, the results in table 3.5 can be interpreted as upper-limit estimates of the same rates of return, involving the implicit assumption that the hourly wage rate is a measure of both market and non-market productivity at the margin, and is thus a better variable than annual earnings to use in estimating sex differentials in rates of return to education. In other words, these rates are estimates of the full rate of return and not just a rate of return experienced through market work alone. These results could suggest the possibility that rates of return to nonmarket work are differentially important to women because, on the basis of market rates of return alone, it had been predicted that men's returns would exceed women's. It is also possible that education is a particularly important credential for at least some women in gaining access to the kind of job experience that leads to wage growth over time.

However, the fact that women's rates of return in table 3.5 are actually higher than those of men is probably the result of selectivity bias. As we saw in chapter 2, working and nonworking women with similar observable characteristics will still tend to differ in unmeasured tastes and productivities. Thus the equality of market and nonmarket productivities at the margin for an individual in no way

Table 3.5

Rates of Return to Education by Sex Estimated from Earnings
Functions (the dependent variable is the wage rate in all four studies).

	Women	Men
Mincer and Polacheck (1974)[a]		
Single	7.7	n.a.
Married	6.3	7.1
Landes (1977)[b]	9.7	9.3
Corcoran & Duncan (1978)[c]		
Black	7.9	6.2
White	7.6	6.0
Madden (1978)[d]		
Black	7.5	5.0
White	9.3	4.6

SOURCES: [a] Data from the NLS for white women aged 30–44 who were working in 1966 were used, and the other variables controlled for in the regression included estimated total work experience, current job tenure, home time following birth of first child, and other home time. For white married men of the same age, the Survey of Economic Opportunity (SEO) data for the same year were used. Only years of work experience since school completion were controlled for in the male regressions.

[b] This study was based on the SEO and was restricted to employed white males and females aged 14–65. Individual data were aggregated into ninety-six occupations across which regressions were run. Variables included in the regression included average number of years since completion of formal schooling ("potential" work experience), average hours per week, percent of men or women in occupation working full time, percent who reported that current job differed from longest job held in 1966, variance in weeks worked in 1966, and a proxy for occupation-specific earnings growth.

[c] The data used here are from the Ninth Wave of the MID, covering all working household heads and spouses aged 18–64 in 1975. Other independent variables include seven different work history measures, such as years of experience before present employer, years of training on current job and proportion of total years worked full time, six measures of labor force attachment, and other demographic variables.

[d] This study was based on data from the NLS for young men and women. The sample included only working men and women aged 18–25 in 1969. Independent variables included potential experience, weeks worked, health and geographic variables, family background variables, and IQ.

implies that working and nonworking women are equally productive. The assumptions imbedded in the estimation techniques used in these earnings function studies make it inevitable that the rates of return to education presented in table 3.5 are biased upward, and can be interpreted *only* as upper limits.

Both Mincer and Polachek (1974) and Madden (1978) looked as well at differences in rates of return between different levels of education. Mincer and Polachek found that rates of return increased with level of education for women in the 30- to 44-year-old group. Madden compared high school and college returns for both men and women and found that while college graduation had a higher pay-off than high school graduation, the difference was considerably greater for women than for men. This pattern is consistent with theoretical expectations developed earlier in the chapter, and cannot be attributed to differential labor force participation rates between education groups. If anything, in this case, selectivity bias would lead to a greater overestimation of returns at lower education levels.

The results of these studies, although they must be interpreted with caution, suggest both the differential importance of educational investment for women and the possible importance of education in the nonmarket sector. However, before examining sex differentials in other forms of training in the job market, we will discuss some independent evidence on women's nonmarket educational returns.

Nonmarket Returns

The rate of return studies only tell one part of the story about returns to educational investment. If education is a productivity-enhancing experience, we would expect it to affect productivity in all activities—not just in the labor market. Activities such as cooking, voting, child rearing and volunteering are some examples of nonmarket activities which are probably enhanced by general educational investment. To the extent that individuals benefit in this way from these investments, we would like to take account of this in our calculation of total private rates of return.

Although measurement problems in this area can create great and even insurmountable difficulties, it is obvious that these considerations are of importance when it comes to evaluating the returns to education. This is particularly so in the case of women, many of whom spend a significant portion of their adult lives in nonmarket activities. Exclusive concentration on market returns, as in the results in table 3.4, should bias downward any estimates of the gains from education, and this bias should be greater for women than for men. However, we have also seen that an opposite upward bias, due to selectivity, is created when total returns to all women are estimated from data on the wage rates of working women only. Thus, in exploring this area, it is important to avoid the trap of circular reasoning. Just because women's measured market returns to education appear lower than men's does not necessarily mean that their nonmarket returns are higher than men's by the same amount. This requires the assumption that educational returns across individuals are equalized at the margin, and this is not the case. The nonmeasurability of nonmarket returns makes this an easy trap to slip into, but a dangerous one, given the value-laden assumption on which it is based.

Becker (1964) was the first to suggest that college is a marriage market, and not just a training ground for the labor market. However, he never suggested that men might gain through marrying a more educated woman but only that "women go to college, partly to increase the probability of marrying a more desirable man" (p. 101). In support of this proposition, he presents data on *family* income of men and women classified by education. The income differentials between high school and college graduates are still much smaller for women than for men, and Becker concludes that even when income gains through marriage are taken into consideration, the rate of return to a college education is lower for women than for men, which is consistent with the fact that a smaller proportion of female than of male high school graduates goes on to college.

This same line of reasoning has recently resurfaced in Freeman's study (1976:174–75). He suggests that in crude dollar terms, the difference in income between high school and college women is much smaller than the difference in income between the husbands of college and of high school women, suggesting a greater gain to college from marriage than from working. This difference was found to be primarily due to the increased probability of a college-educated woman finding a college-educated husband. However, his evidence for younger women suggests that the gains to college from working are rising in relation to the gains from marrying.

Benham (1974, 1975) has reexamined the observed positive relationship between wives' educational attainment and husbands' earnings, first mentioned by Becker, and in effect has turned the marriage market hypothesis on its head. Although he acknowledges that this relation is clearly consistent with the idea of assortative mating, where college-educated women marry more productive men, he proposes and tests the hypothesis that men who marry more educated women become more productive in the labor market because their productivity is affected by the knowledge and ability of their wives. His estimates indicate that the husband's earnings increase about 6.5 percent for each year of his own schooling and 3.5 percent for each year of his wife's schooling. It also appears that the effect of the wife's schooling increases with the length of marriage, for up to twenty to thirty years, and that whether the wife acquired her education before or after marriage does not change the influence of that education on her husband's earnings. These latter two findings tend to support the productivity hypothesis advanced by Benham, as opposed to the selective mating hypothesis. The examination of human capital returns within a family framework would suggest that the husband would also reap nonmarket returns from assortative mating, but this relationship has not been tested.

Child rearing is an important category of nonmarket work. There has been increasing recognition of the importance to children of early learning in the home for their later education and career success (Leibowitz 1974). More educated parents can transfer human capital to their children, and thus individual investments in education have the potential for creating intergenerational returns. Although these returns do not accrue specifically to the individual making such investments, they are important to the family and to society.

Leibowitz (1975) uses data from time budget studies to relate time spent in child care to educational attainment. More educated women are found to devote less time to household production throughout the life cycle, but more time to child care. This is true even though their children also receive more time from their fathers and other adults.

These findings imply a high income elasticity for spending time in child care, or increased productivity in child care due to higher education, or both. Using longitudinal data on the life histories of a group of unusually bright children, she also found that both parents' educational levels had a significant impact on the level of schooling attained by children (Leibowitz 1974b). However, because the mother's education is positively related to the child's IQ and the father's education is not, differential home investments are assumed. In more recent research, Leibowitz (1977) has tested this relationship further with data for preschool children, finding that the level of the mother's education has a positive effect on her child's verbal development, whereas the father's education has no effect.

Nonmarket returns to educational investment certainly exist, but no research to date has been able to document their relative magnitude or their differential importance for men and women. A presumption exists that women gain relatively more in this area than men, but such a presumption is not a sufficient reason to assume away any evidence of women's lower market returns to educational investment.

Job Training

Years of education, type of education (in terms of quality and specialization), and degrees conferred are all important entry credentials into the market for job training. Education is only the beginning of the story in terms of differential human capital investments and market outcomes, but it is a particularly crucial beginning in the case of sex differentials because of the previously observed differences between more and less educated women in labor force participation behavior and rates of return. Given many women's patterns of discontinuous labor force participation, education and degrees conferred become particularly important credentials for a woman seeking to distinguish herself from the average woman, as being more career-oriented and willing to make further job training investments. In this section, we will discuss the roles of the employee and the employer in the training process and likely implications for sex differentials in the acquisition of and return to job training. Then, as in the previous section, we will look at actual differences between the sexes in training received and job experience, and compare the limited evidence available on rates of return.

One of the major distinctions usually made between investments in education and job training is their degree of generality. In most cases, skills learned in high school and college enhance productivity in many contexts, both within the market and outside it; therefore, education is usually described as a form of *general* training. On the other hand, training received in connection with the job is more often specific to the occupation and industry for which it is learned and, therefore, it is less easily transferable outside of that context. Job training that increases productivity more in firms providing it than in other firms is defined as *specific* training (Becker 1964). Although it is perfectly true that some educational programs develop very specific skills and some job training is very general, this is a useful analytical distinction to make when comparing education and job training.

In order to understand the distinction just made between the nature of educational and job training investment, it is important to understand the theoretical distinction between *general* and *specific* training. Like the concepts of perfect competition and pure monopoly, general and completely specific training are extreme forms or ideal types at either end of a spectrum. All actual training has elements of both.

Given perfectly competitive markets and worker mobility, general training will be financed by the worker receiving it. Perfectly general training would result in an increase in productivity and wages in all firms, not just the one where it was received. Therefore, there would be no way for the firm, if it were to pay some of the training costs, to capture a return on this type of investment by keeping the worker's wage below his posttraining marginal product because, under such circumstances, the worker would leave. In the case of general on-the-job training, direct costs as well as opportunity costs are incorporated into the earnings streams and take the form of earnings foregone during the training period. This can be seen in figure 3.7. Untrained workers, who are assumed to make no further investment in human capital after leaving school, receive OU dollars per time period throughout their working lives, and have the horizontal age-earnings profile UU'. Generally-trained workers receive lower earnings during the training

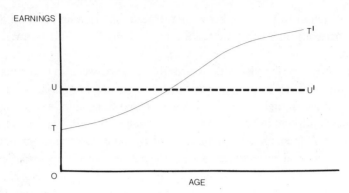

Figure 3.7. The Relation of Earnings to Age for Generally Trained and Untrained Workers

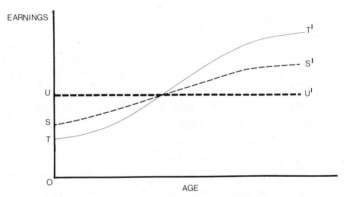

Figure 3.8. The Relation of Productivity and Earnings to Age for Generally Trained, Specifically Trained, and Untrained Workers

period because training is paid for by them, and higher earnings at later ages, when they are collecting the return on their investment in training. Age-earnings profile TT' represents the variation of both productivity and earnings over time for the generally-trained worker.

If training is completely specific, however, the value of market opportunities available to a worker outside the firm in which the training was received is not commensurate with that same worker's productivity within the firm. This would be the case even in a competitive market because of the specific nature of the skills acquired, but would also be the case for almost all training received by workers in monopsonistic and/or segmented labor markets, as a result of their immobility. In fact, such market imperfections blur the distinction between general and specific training; it may well pay an employer to invest in the apparently general training of relatively immobile workers. Whoever actually invests in specific training, the payoff continues only as long as the worker remains in the employ of the firm where the training was obtained. Thus the willingness of either the firm or the worker to make these investments is inversely related to expectations of turnover. Firms could finance the training investment by capturing a sufficiently large return from those staying with the firm to cover the losses from those who leave. However, by recognizing that turnover itself is related to wages, firms can actually reduce turnover by sharing the return from the investment with workers by paying them higher wages. Finally, by requiring workers to share some of the cost of investment, the demand for specific training opportunities can be adjusted to meet the supply available (Becker 1964:22).

This shared investment provides mutual benefits in the form of insurance against future turnover, since both parties have invested and would suffer a capital loss from the separation of worker and firm. Although the marginal productivity of the specifically-trained worker follows the time path TT' (which is also the age-earnings profile of a worker with the same amount of general training) in figure 3.8, his or her age-earnings profile will be a curve like SS' because the firm pays part of costs and collects part of the returns from specific training.

General training is irrelevant to turnover, since the worker bears the entire cost of investment, and takes that investment along wherever he or she goes. Specific training, however, should provide an incentive to minimize turnover, and both quit rates and layoff rates should be inversely related to the amount of specific training. The more segmented the labor market, and the less worker mobility there is, the more important specific training will be. This leads to the general prediction of an inverse correlation between the level of training and turnover, and consequently unemployment.

Since Becker's first theoretical analysis of job training as a human capital investment (1964), it has been expected that women would have less incentive to make specialized investments and more incentive to acquire general human capital, both in school and on the job. In this regard, Becker draws an analogy between "unspecialized" women and tourists.

Women spend less time in the labor force than men and, therefore, have less incentive to invest in market skills; tourists spend little time in any one area and have less incentive than residents of the area to invest in knowledge of specific consumption opportunities. . . . Women, tourists, and the like have to find investments that increase productivity in several activities. A woman wants her investment to be useful both as a housewife and as a participant in the labor force, or a frequent traveler wants to be knowledgeable in many environments. (pp. 51–52)

To the extent that job training is costly, men and women will differ from each other in their incentive to seek jobs involving training, if they differ in their expectations of years in the labor force. In addition, if women expect their market participation to be intermittent, specific training, which is largely useful only in the firm where it was acquired, will be even less attractive than general training, which increases productivity in many firms. Likewise, employers will be affected in their hiring decisions by their expectations of higher average turnover for women, particularly married women. An employer will prefer to hire male workers for jobs requiring specific training if he believes women to be less reliable or less likely to be long-term employees than men. As a result, we would expect that women would receive, on average, less training than men.

TRAINING INVESTMENT

While some postschool job investment takes place within the framework of formal apprenticeship or job training programs, the bulk of job training is more informal and is simply acquired through the accumulation of experience. There is thus the obvious difficulty that no direct measure of years of, or amounts invested in, on-the-job training, comparable to data on educational attainment, exists. Until the recent advent of longitudinal data, the amount of job training received by workers had to be estimated indirectly. In the absence of direct information, Jacob Mincer (1962b) developed an imaginative technique for estimating the amount of on-the-job training from cross-sectional age-earnings profiles for men with different amounts of education. However, the analysis of the costs and returns to on-the-job training in terms of life-cycle earnings only provides an estimate of that portion of the training investment financed by the individual rather than the firm. In other words, in figure 3.8, the measured costs and returns would be estimated by comparing SS' to UU' but the real productivity costs and gains would be measured by comparing TT' and UU'.

After the completion of formal schooling, an individual's net earnings (Y_{s+1}) in the first year of work experience $(t = s + 1)$ will be equal to his or her initial earnings capacity (Y_s) minus any direct or indirect costs associated with training (C_{s+1})

$$(4) \qquad Y_{s+1} = Y_s - C_{s+1}$$

In the subsequent year, net earnings will be augmented by the return on the initial year's investment and diminished by further investments. More generally, actual earnings in year j

$$(5) \qquad Y_j = Y_s + \sum_{t=s+1}^{j-1} r_t C_t - C_j$$

At the peak of the earnings profile (Y_p)

$$(6) \qquad Y_p = Y_s + r \sum_{t=0}^{P} C_t$$

and the total volume of postschool investment can be estimated as

$$(7) \qquad \sum_{t=0}^{P} C_t = \frac{Y_p - Y_s}{r}$$

or equivalently, the incremental volume of postschool investment associated with additional schooling can be estimated as

$$(8) \qquad \sum_{t=s_1}^{s_2} C_t = \frac{Y_{s_1} - Y_{s_2}}{r_s}$$

where Y_{s_1} and Y_{s_2} equal initial postschool earnings capacity related to two different levels of schooling.[15]

If one can derive r_s and determine the value of Y_s, then the dollar volume of postschool investment can be calculated. Mincer calculated r, using the discounted present value approach described previously, and estimated Y_s to be the observed earnings for each schooling group with ten years of job experience.[16]

Using two alternative estimation techniques (eq. 4 and eq. 7–8), Mincer (1962b, 1974a), estimated substantial dollar investments in on-the-job training for men. For the male labor force, on-the-job training is at least as important as formal education when measured in terms of costs. Using the relatively flat age-earnings profiles for women in 1949, Mincer estimated that women invested roughly one-tenth as much as men in job training (1962b). This estimate obviously assumes that the shape of the earnings profile is solely a reflection of the degree of training investment.

In fact, given the lack of comparable evidence on men's and women's investments in job training, the number of years of job experience and the shape of the age-earnings profile can be used as indirect evidence of differential investment. However, the latter procedure inevitably involves circular reasoning. The observed age-earnings profiles may be consistent with several alternative interpretations, in the absence of information on the true causal relationship. Typical age-earnings profiles for men are upward sloping over much of the life cycle and concave in shape, as can be seen in figure 3.9. Human capital theory interprets this as evidence of worker investment patterns, with positive annual net investment (C_j) which is either diminishing or increasing at a rate lower than the rate of return (Mincer 1974a:13). There are several reasons to expect diminishing investments over time. First, given a finite life span, later investments yield returns for a shorter period than do earlier ones, and thus tend to produce a smaller total net gain. Second, the investment process itself raises the value of the individual's time, and this increases the cost of later investments, which use more expensive time than do earlier ones.[17] Finally, the embodiment of human capital in the person doing the investing results in increasing marginal costs within each period, as diminishing returns set in, and thus forces some spreading out of capital accumulation over time.

The age-earnings profiles observed for men would also be consistent with pure aging effects, which bring costless learning, but are

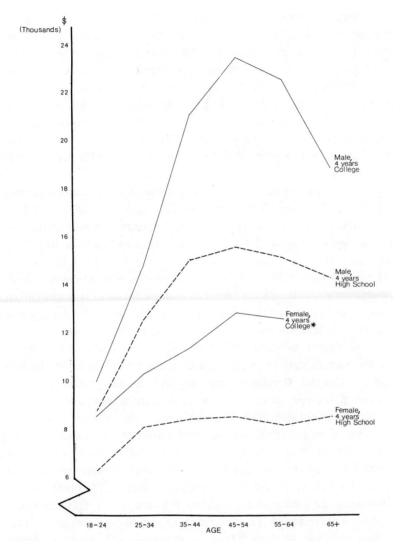

Figure 3.9.   Median Year-Round Income by Age, Sex, and Level of Education, 1976

SOURCE: Current Population Reports, Series P-60, no. 114, pp. 192–201, table 47.

* NOTE: Data not available for females with four years of college education, aged
sixty-five years or more: base is less than 75,000.

eventually overtaken, near the end of the life cycle, by depreciation and obsolescence. However, the relatively flat earnings profiles for women suggest some systematic differences between the sexes above and beyond the aging process, which is common to both. Although the cross-section earnings picture does not give the true profile for any cohort of women, it does not differ drastically, as will be seen in chapter 4. These observed differences in shape of the profiles for men and women, therefore, may indicate the importance of differential training between men and women as one of the possible determinants of earnings differences.

The only other indirect evidence of job training which is comparable for men and women is retrospective information on the number of years and type of job experience. Such information is available for men and women aged 18–64 who were interviewed in 1976, as part of the Panel Study of Income Dynamics conducted by the University of Michigan. Figure 3.10 and table 3.6 present the average years of work experience since age 18 for men and women by race. It is clear from these data that women have less experience than men at every age and that these differences widen over the life cycle. However, it is also true that the degree of variation among women in years of experience greatly exceeds that among men after the age of 25, both in absolute terms (standard deviation) and relative to the mean years of experience (coefficient of variation). Therefore, although the averages for women are significantly lower than for men, they are a very bad predictor of the job experience accumulated by any individual woman.

It is important to note, however, that the information presented in figure 3.10 and table 3.6 covers the entire MID sample, and not just those who were employed at the time of the survey. Thus male-female differences are greater than would be the case if only those currently working were included. The differences in experience between the total sample and those working 500 hours or more in 1975 are insignificant for men, but currently employed women of both races had greater than average work experience.[18] Whether all women or working women only constitute the appropriate sample from which to estimate average years of experience depends, to a large extent, on evidence concerning the homogeneity or heterogeneity of the female population with respect to labor force attachment. The evidence of considerable

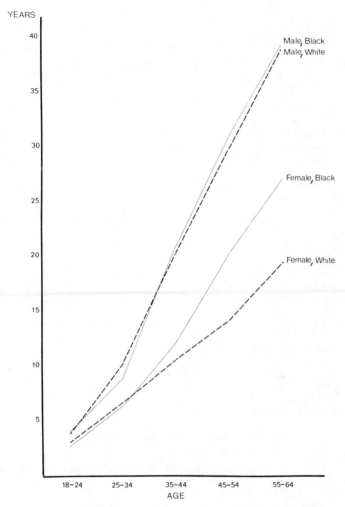

Figure 3.10.   Average Work Experience by Age, Sex and Race, 1975
SOURCE: Corcoran (1978:93).

heterogeneity and possible selectivity bias presented in chapter 2 suggests that figure 3.10 and table 3.6 underestimate the measure of female experience that would be relevant to an explanation of differences by sex in wages and unemployment.

Although we can assert with confidence that male workers of a

Table 3.6

Average Work Experience by Age, Sex, and Race in 1975

Age	White Men	Black Men	White Women	Black Women
18–24				
Weighted Mean	3.95	4.03	3.02	2.76
Standard Deviation	1.59	4.00	1.86	1.78
Coefficient of Variation	.40	.99	.54	.64
25–34				
Weighted Mean	10.44	8.99	6.79	6.55
Standard Deviation	3.37	3.07	3.81	4.22
Coefficient of Variation	.32	.34	.56	.64
35–44				
Weighted Mean	20.42	20.66	10.57	12.30
Stardard Deviation	3.80	3.40	6.95	7.17
Coefficient of Variation	.19	.16	.66	.58
45–54				
Weighted Mean	29.95	31.10	14.17	20.41
Standard Deviation	3.91	3.81	9.67	10.39
Coefficient of Variation	.13	.13	.68	.51
55–64				
Weighted Mean	38.88	39.45	19.54	27.09
Standard Deviation	5.82	5.62	13.76	13.25
Coefficient of Variation	.15	.14	.70	.49

SOURCE: University of Michigan Survey of Income Dynamics—Ninth Wave. Courtesy of Professor Mary Corcoran, unpublished data.
NOTE: The sample includes all household heads and spouses, whether currently working or not.

given age have more years of experience, on the average, than their female counterparts, information on the trend over time in the size of the sex differential in experience does not exist, and this is the very information that would be most useful in relation to an analysis of how relative earnings and unemployment rates have changed. At any point in time, the experience accumulated by a worker depends on three factors: age, educational attainment, and continuity of labor force attachment since entering the labor force. If labor force participation has been continuous since leaving school, *potential* experience, which equals age – education – 6, accurately measures actual experience. As we saw in chapter 2, average age has declined by about 3 years for both men and women workers over the past 20 years. During the same period, median years of education rose from 11.3 to 12.6 for the male civilian labor force, and from 12.1 to 12.6 for the female civilian labor force. As a result, our estimate of average potential experience fell from 23.4 to 19.1 years for men, and from 21.4 to 17.8 years for women, declines of 4.3 and 3.6 years, respectively.

For men, this assumption of continuous participation is fairly accurate, and there is no reason to believe that our estimate of a decrease of 4.3 years in average experience between 1957 and 1977 is biased. For women, on the other hand, the measure of potential experience is an overestimate of actual experience in both years. The crucial question is whether the degree of such overestimation has changed over time, and thus whether the estimate of a 3.6-year decrease in average female work experience is biased. Continuously rising female labor force participation rates and declining inter-labor force turnover throughout this period indicate that women are interrupting their work experience for fewer and shorter periods today than was the case twenty years ago. Thus potential experience overestimated actual experience more in 1957 than in 1977, and the actual decline in average experience in women workers was probably less than 3.6 years. It appears that the work experience differential between the sexes has narrowed in the past twenty years.

Job tenure is a particularly important dimension of job experience because it measures the length of specific job experience with an individual employer. To the extent that specific training takes place, it will be related to job tenure, because specific training affects a worker's productivity only in the current job, and thus its profitability depends on the duration of the job. Therefore, it is important to examine male-female differences in job tenure as a possible source of differences in training. Figure 3.11 shows the median years of job tenure for men and women by age for 1973 (the most recent year for which detailed data is available). Differences by sex in job tenure appear after the age of 25, and the gap between men and women widens through age 60, after which it decreases slightly. As can be seen in table 3.7, the dif-

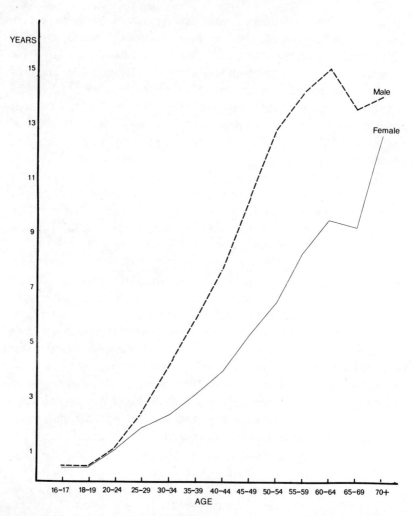

Figure 3.11. Median Years of Tenure on Current Job, by Age and Sex, January 1973

SOURCE: U.S. Dept. of Labor, BLS, Special Labor Force Report, no. 172, p. A-8, table A.

Table 3.7

Job Tenure Trends by Sex and Age, 1951–1978

Years of Job Tenure

	1951	1963	1966	1968	1973	1978
Total 14 +[a]						
Men	3.9	5.7	5.2	4.8	4.6	4.5
Women	2.2	3.0	2.8	2.4	2.8	2.6
Gap	1.7	2.7	2.4	2.4	1.8	1.9
Age 20–24						
Men	1.2	1.0	1.0	0.8	1.2	.9
Women	1.4	1.1	1.1	0.9	1.2	.9
Gap	−0.2	−0.1	−0.1	−0.1	0.0	0.0
Age 25–34						
Men	2.8	3.5	3.2	2.8	3.2	2.7
Women	1.8	2.0	1.9	1.6	2.2	1.6
Gap	1.0	1.5	1.3	1.2	1.0	1.1
Age 35–44						
Men	4.5	7.6	7.8	6.9	6.7	6.9
Women	3.1	3.6	3.5	2.9	3.6	3.6
Gap	1.4	4.0	4.2	4.0	3.1	3.3
Age 45–54						
Men	7.6	11.4	11.5	11.3	11.5	11.0
Women	4.0	6.1	5.7	5.1	5.9	5.9
Gap	3.6	5.3	5.8	6.2	5.6	5.1
Age 55–64						
Men	9.3	14.7	15.8	14.8	14.5	14.6
Women	4.5	7.8	9.0	8.7	8.8	8.5
Gap	4.8	6.9	6.8	6.1	5.7	6.1
Age 65 +						
Men	10+	16.6	15.5	13.5	13.9	13.5
Women	4.9	8.8	11.2	10.0	10.9	8.4
Gap	5+	7.8	4.3	3.5	3.0	5.1

SOURCES: 1951: Bureau of the Census Current Population
Reports, Series P-60, No. 36 (Washington D.C.: 1951).
1963–73: BLS Special Labor Force Reports Nos. 36, 77, 112
and 172 (Washington, D.C.: various years).
1978: Unpublished BLS data.

[a] The figures in 1968, 1973, and 1978 are for age 16 and over.

ference between men and women in average job tenure widened during the 1950s and early 60s, but narrowed after 1968. Since 1973, average job tenure and the male-female gap have remained roughly constant.

More direct evidence on training has recently been collected from the Ninth Wave of the MID. One question designed to get at a direct measure of specific training was phrased as follows: "On a job like yours, how long would it take the average person to become fully trained and qualified?" (Duncan and Hoffman 1978). In a sample of working household heads and spouses aged 18–64, there were large differences in this measure betwen white males and other race-sex groups, with white males holding jobs which required 2.25 years on the average to become fully trained, while the other groups were in jobs requiring an average of less than a year of training. Within broad occupational classifications, these differences persist, and suggest that a finer breakdown of occupations would show women to be concentrated in jobs requiring less training. So, however on-the-job training is measured, either directly or indirectly, it appears that women do systematically receive less of both its specific and general components.

RATES OF RETURN TO JOB TRAINING

Because the costs of training are not directly observable, the estimation of a return to training requires assumptions about the relationship between years of experience and dollars invested. If total training costs are taken as a percentage of gross earnings, then this proportion can be assumed to measure the fraction of the year devoted to training. In the estimation of empirical earnings functions originally developed by Jacob Mincer (1974a), it is assumed that earnings increase with years of experience, but at a diminishing rate, because of the assumed monotonic decline in the fraction of time devoted to training as experience progresses.

(9) $ln\ Y = \alpha + \beta_1 S + \beta_2 T - \beta_3 T^2 + u$

Where T measures total years of job experience, β_2 measures the initial percentage gain in earnings with a year of job experience which cannot be viewed as a rate of return to training, because it combines in one number the return to a unit of training times the fraction of total job experience devoted to training.

When data on years of experience are not directly available, they can be reasonably estimated for men by assuming that labor force participation is continuous after the completion of schooling. However, for women, continuous work experience cannot be assumed. Recently, data available from the NLS and the MID have permitted detailed analysis of the relationship between earnings and work experience for women through the examination of individual work histories. Using the NLS data for women aged 30–44, Mincer and Polachek (1974) adapted the earnings function described above to intermittent work experience, breaking up postschool investment into successive segments of participation and nonparticipation, as these occur chronologically. In this case, five intervals are used—three periods of work experience (prechildbearing, intermittent after the first child and current) and two periods of nonmarket activity. The positive coefficients of the work experience segments and the negative coefficients of the home time segments may suggest net investment in and net depreciation of human capital, respectively. When comparing these married and single women with married men in the same age group from the SEO, interesting differences emerge in both the amounts of experience and the relationship between experience and wage levels. Average experience for men was 19.4 years, for single women 15.6 years and for married women 9.6 years. An additional year of experience leads to a 1.2 percent increase in wages for married women, a 2.6 percent increase for single women and a 3.4 percent increase for married men. It could be argued that, because women anticipate discontinuous participation, they choose to allocate a smaller proportion of time on the job to investment in training and, therefore, job experience for them does not augment wages to the same extent as for men. However, even single women with relatively continuous work histories find that experience increases their earnings less than it does for men.

Corcoran (1978), using the MID, found similar differences between men and women in the payoff to job experience when no distinction was made between types of experience. However, when work experience was divided into different segments, both Corcoran (1978) and Duncan and Hoffman (1978) found that men's and women's

returns became similar. The four experience categories used by
Corcoran were: (1) postinterruption experience prior to working with
one's present employer; (2) experience with one's present employer
prior to one's present position; (3) training completed in present position; and (4) years of posttraining tenure. Returns to these four distinct experience segments were remarkably similar between men and
women, but not all segments were equally valuable. An additional
year of training raised wages by 6–9 percent, while an additional year
of postinterruption experience raised wages by only 2 percent. It seems
that women have spent less time than white men in those experience
segments that have the highest payoff in terms of earnings. In addition, Corcoran found little direct evidence that labor market interruption lowered earnings for women, other than through its indirect effect
on the length of job tenure.

   With major differences between men and women in both actual
years of on-the-job training received and types of job experience, it
becomes important to understand the process by which these differences arise. It is obvious that occupational selection plays a key
role in this process, because differences in training requirements are
very much associated with occupations. The final section of this
chapter discusses occupational selection and job mobility as an
integrating framework for understanding the differences in education
and training between men and women already discussed.

Occupational Selection and Job Mobility

   The amount of labor supplied to the market, the level and type of
education received and the intensity and specificity of the job training
acquired would all be the simultaneous outcomes of an individual's
career or occupational decision if there were completely free personal
choice. Conventional neoclassical life cycle models assume such
freedom of choice and normally use the maximization of individual
lifetime earnings as the motivating assumption. More recently,
neoclassical models of intertemporal decision-making are introducing
more realistic assumptions about motivation, but have not changed
the basic underlying assumption of free choice. Utility-maximization

is replacing earnings-maximization as an operative assumptive, as the importance of nonmarket production and the nonpecuniary aspects of jobs are increasingly recognized. In addition, the family is being recognized as an appropriate locus for analysis, because for many individuals the choice of job and occupation may involve the weighing of individual gains (losses) against family losses (gains).

However, to the extent that educational opportunities and access to jobs involving training are not open to all, the sequence of events itself becomes a crucial determinant of the final occupational outcome. The amount and quality of education previously acquired directly affects an individual's subsequent access to jobs with training options. Likewise, an individual's labor force commitment, which is, to some degree at least, determined by differential job opportunities, constrains occupational selection, because of its implications for occupational and job mobility.

When comparing men and women, we are particularly interested in the process by which education and training are tied into occupational selection. As was noted at the beginning of this chapter, the occupational distributions of men and women remain sharply dissimilar despite the rapid increase in women's labor force participation and attachment, as well as the strong increase in their share of college and graduate degrees. There is no data on trends in the acquisition of training by sex[19] but human capital theory would lead one to predict that women would choose to invest more in job training (as would their employers) as the payoff period in the labor market lengthens. However, the lack of change in occupational dissimilarity suggests that women have not been successful in translating gains in participation and education into occupational gains. Discrimination in access to training opportunities is one obvious explanation, but a more complex explanation may also include some lag in the effect of changing levels of education and training on the female occupational distribution, because of concurrent changes in the structure of demand.

The absence of any change in the degree of occupational dissimilarity between men and women between 1970 and 1977 does not, however, suggest a static occupational structure by any means. Over those seven years there were significant changes for both men and women in their distribution across occupations.[20] This reflects changes in the underlying occupational structure of demand in a dynamic economy, as well as changes in occupational selection. If the occupational structure had not changed over the seven-year period, there would have been slightly more improvement in the degree of occupational dissimilarity.[21] Because the most dynamically growing occupations are the very ones which have traditionally been strongly male- (e.g., doctors, lawyers) or female- (e.g., secretaries, service workers) dominated, the result has been an accentuation of occupational differences. If these trends had not been mitigated by some shift in occupational selection patterns there would have been a slight deterioration in the degree of occupational dissimlarity.[22]

To date, there have been only a few studies which have attempted to explain empirically differences in the distribution of men and women between occupations at a point in time in terms of systematic differences between the sexes in labor supply and human capital investment (Zellner 1975; Boskin 1974a; Polachek 1979). The problem with this approach is that it requires the assumption that an individual is associated with only one occupation over his or her working life. The assumption is that each individual chooses a lifetime occupation that maximizes his or her income stream, which leads to the prediction that women planning to work less over the life cycle will choose occupations requiring less training, so as to minimize the penalty for labor force withdrawal and maximize present wages. Zellner found that female-dominated occupations were characterized by flatter participation-wage rate profiles. Using longitudinal data, Polachek has estimated an "atrophy" rate for each occupation, based on the average decline in annual earnings experienced for each year out of the labor market by women currently employed in each of five extremely broad occupational categories. He found that the fraction of time spent in the labor force after completion of school is positively related to the atrophy rate associated with a woman's present occupation. However, the causal relationship is unclear. Do women choose occupations so as to optimize expected earnings streams or do women's occupations discourage continuous participation because of their relatively flat wage-experience profiles?

Boskin's study may shed some light on this question. He used eleven crude occupational categories to estimate a function predicting the probability of entering a particular occupation, based on three characteristics of each occupation. These were: (1) the present value of expected lifetime full income (assumed to involve 2,000 hours of work per year for both males and females); (2) the ratio of estimated training costs to net worth; and (3) the present value of lifetime earnings lost due to unemployment. The most striking result is that white males place relatively greater weight in their occupational choice decision on expected lifetime earnings, whereas black men and all women placed relatively greater weight on relative training costs and potential losses due to unemployment. This is consistent with the hypothesis of differential access to financing of training and education costs; it appears that women and minority groups may be differentially constrained in the maximization of earnings by the barrier of high training costs.

Recent data from the MID reveal average differences across occupations in the time individual workers estimate is necessary to become fully trained and qualified (Duncan and Hoffman 1978). When these average years of training are correlated with the percentage of women in each occupation, there is a strong negative association, indicating that the longer the training period, the smaller women's representation in the occupation. Table 3.8 shows both these correlations and the average differences between men and women, within each occupation, in the number of years of training required. The sharp differences between men and women within occupations in years of training may simply reflect the fact that the occupational classification is not fine enough, or, alternatively, could reflect differential access to training provided to white males within occupations, which may be an important determinant of job and occupational mobility over the life cycle.

A comparison of cross-sectional data on the occupational distribution at two points in time or an analysis of differences in life cycle characteristics between members of different occupations cannot convey the dynamic paths of individual careers, which are made up of a series of occupational changes. In fact, the accumulation of human capital over the life cycle and the development of skills will naturally lead to occupational mobility as well as job mobility. Although occupations may appear mutually exclusive at a point in time in terms of skill, over time an individual can acquire the skills to move from one

Table 3.8

Sex Composition and Training Requirements for Selected Occupations

Occupation	% Female in Occupation 1970[a] (1)	% Female in Occupation 1977[b] (2)	No. of Years Needed to Become Fully Trained[c]				
			Average (3)	White men (4)	Black men (5)	White women (6)	Black women (7)
Physicians, dentists	3.57	9.48	5.21	5.21[d]	—	—	—
Other medical	81.8	74.5	1.95	3.84[d]	—	1.60	—
Accountants	25.3	27.5	2.40	2.94	—	1.32[d]	—
Teachers, primary & secondary	69.5	68.7	2.57	2.88	—	2.38	3.23
Teachers, college	28.5	31.7	3.29	3.59	—	2.80[d]	—
Engineers, architects, chemists	2.5	3.7	2.89	2.95	—	—	—
Technicians	23.3	32.5	1.96	2.48	—	1.18	—
Judges, lawyers	5.1	9.5	2.51	2.51	—	—	—
Other professional	43.1	40.4	2.32	2.36	—	—	—

Secretaries	97.7	99.1	.80	—	—	0.79	0.32
Other clerical	67.8	73.5	.81	1.19	0.89	0.72	0.43
Sales workers	39.4	43.3	1.40	1.93	0.50[d]	0.58	0.14[d]
Foremen	8.0	9.0	3.13	3.41	2.06[d]	—	—
Other craftsmen	4.3	7.1	2.54	2.62	1.97	0.98[d]	—
Police, firemen	3.0	2.7	2.25	2.46	0.39	—	—
Transport equipment operatives	4.5	6.8	.52	.54	0.42	—	—
Other operatives	38.4	39.6	.71	.96	0.62	0.48	0.20
Private household workers	96.9	97.0	.52	—	—	0.38[d]	0.62
Other service workers	61.6	58.3	.60	.92	0.36	0.53	0.60
Farmers	4.8	6.4	2.86	2.84	—	—	—
Correlation coefficient with average training	−.509	−.509					

SOURCES: [a] 1970 Census.
[b] *Employment and Earnings*, January 1978.
[c] Duncan and Hoffman (1978).
[d] Result based on fewer than 25 observations.
— Fewer than 10 observations.

to another. The mix of specific and general training acquired will play a role in determining job mobility, but occupational mobility will result even when workers remain in the same firm, because the accumulation of skills involves upward movement through various occupational categories.

There is evidence to suggest that not only do women impose limitations on themselves in terms of mobility, but additional constraints are imposed by their employers. Among the unemployed, women of all ages have indicated much less willingness than men to accept a job in another area (Niemi 1974). In the recent MID survey, women were twice as likely as men to indicate that self-imposed limitations in job location or work hours were factors in taking their present job (Hill 1978). However, it is interesting to note that in the Michigan data, women were no more likely than men to say that there would be better jobs available elsewhere if they were willing to move. On the employer side, Duncan and Hoffman's study (1978) of training found that job experience before present employer and with present employer had a high payoff in terms of the probability of receiving training on current job for white men, whereas neither type of prior experience had much effect on women's chances of receiving training. This suggests an institutional view of promotion practices which would be expected to limit occupational mobility for women within firms, as well as job mobility between firms, because of their relatively low payoff. Actual data confirm that the proportion changing jobs at least once a year is lower for women than men. Of those who do move, fewer women than men change occupations, which is the usual process for achieving upward mobility (Niemi 1974). Recent NLS data have permitted a more comprehensive definition of job mobility (the total separation rate minus the labor force withdrawal rate), which also shows higher rates of mobility for men at all tenure levels (see table 3.9).

Job mobility and occupational mobility often involve geographic mobility as well. As a form of investment in human capital, geographic mobility has special characteristics, and differs from other such investments in that it affects the entire household, not just the individual making the investment. If a family member attends school or engages in on-the-job training, other family members are not dragged into the classroom or workpace along with him or her. But a

Table 3.9

Job Mobility Rates

Years of Tenure	Married Women Aged 35–49 by 1969 Tenure	Men Aged 45–59 (averages for 1967–1969 & 1969–1971)
0–2	26.3	25.1
2–4	5.4	17.5
4–6	7.1	11.0
6–8	8.6	12.4
8–10	4.4	6.3
10–12	3.9	7.0
12–14	3.9	3.8
14–18	2.2	4.5
18+	1.6	3.8

SOURCE: Mincer (1978), estimated from National Longitudinal Surveys.

migration decision will generally require that the entire household move, if it is to remain a family unit. With two or more members in the family, the decision-making process and the computation of the net gain from migration becomes more complicated as the costs and returns of all family members must be summed up and discounted over time to determine the net loss or gain to the household from a particular move. Therefore, a move that would be profitable (unprofitable) to the individual worker may involve a net loss (gain) to the family as a whole and thus will not (will) be made (Mincer 1978).

Because of both longer work-life expectancy and higher wages, a man typically has potentially more to gain or lose from a particular job move than an woman. Therefore, in most situations, the gains (losses) for the husband will outweigh the losses (gains) for the wife, leading to sharp sex differentials in geographic mobility as an investment in human captial. Consequently, it is expected that most men who move will enjoy economic gains both for themselves and their families, whereas many women who move may in fact suffer personal economic losses, such as lower earnings, unemployment, and job discontinuity. In such cases a woman is called a "tied mover" (Mincer 1978). Not only do a woman's family responsibilities reduce her potential rate of return to human capital investment, but the optimal pattern of skill accumulation for her husband may reduce her rate of return to human capital investment still further, not only in the case of family migration, but also in some cases where the family stays in the same location despite personal job gains to the wife from moving, in which case she would be referred to as a "tied stayer."

Several recent studies have found that the wife's employment inhibits family migration (Mincer 1978; Polachek and Horvath 1977; Sandell 1975), but for those couples that do move, the wives of migrants suffer differentially more unemployment (Mincer 1978), and/or decreases in income (Polachek and Horvath 1977). Thus, both the lower rate of job mobility for women who are tied stayers, and the shorter job tenure and more subsequent unemployment for women who are tied movers, imply lesser occupational progress for women than men.

Conclusion

Substantial sex differences exist in every dimension of human capital investment except in the level of educational attainment. Over time, the gap between men and women's educational attainment has been eliminated and, among young cohorts, it appears that women's propensity to enroll in college is roughly similar to men's. On the other hand, there is little evidence that the type of education women receive has changed much, as was seen in the analysis of major subjects in college. Trends in both labor force continuity and job tenure suggest that the gap between men and women in work experience is narrowing, particularly in the young cohorts. However, an analysis of longitudinal data from the MID shows strong evidence that the quality of working experience in terms of the amount of training received differs substantially between men and women as recently as 1976.

It is unlikely that women's occupational distribution will even approach that of men until the quality and type of training women receive changes. Although a portion of these differences can probably be explained by differences between men and women in their life cycle time allocation choices, different investment opportunities are clearly an important part of the story. At this point in time, it seems apparent that educational opportunities are fairly similar for men and women, at least through the college degree, but job training opportunities are not. Promotion within firms and movement between firms are the means by which individuals achieve occupational mobility over the life cycle. Certain occupations cannot even be entered without prior training opportunities. Some evidence suggests that work experience does not enhance the probability of upward mobility for women in the same way it does for men. However, for both men and women, education is very important in gaining access to good training opportunities. It is clear that education and training go hand in hand in explaining the occupational distribution.

We must next examine the movement of men and women with their embodied human capital into labor markets, and the interaction of stocks and rates of growth of human capital with other factors, to determine earnings and rates of unemployment. In chapter 4, we take our first step in this direction by following the predictions of the human capital model to their logical conclusion in terms of wage and unemployment differentials between the sexes. The failure of this model to provide all the answers, particularly in the context of dynamic change, is starkly highlighted by this approach. Although human capital theory is correct in establishing that education and training are important correlates of earnings, it seems wrong to rely entirely on individual utility-maximizing behavior as the driving force behind changes in occupational distributions, wages, and unemployment. Chapter 5 goes on to pull the dynamics of the story together, by focusing on the functioning of the job market as an allocator of jobs. Such factors as discrimination, employment investment in training, and differences between occupations and industries in cyclical fluctuations and rates of growth are all important parts of the vicious circle linking labor supply and training with differential market reward structures for men and women.

NOTES

1.   This index is calculated by taking the absolute value of the difference, for each of the occupations listed, between the percentage of the female experienced civilian labor

force and the percentage of the male experienced civilian labor force in the occupation, summing these absolute differences across all occupations, and then dividing by two. The value of this index would equal zero if men and women had identical distributions across occupations. At the other extreme, if men and women were completely occupationally segregated, so that they were never in the same occupation, the index would have a value of one.

2.   Human capital theory was not unknown in earlier years, but was left undeveloped as a concept. See A. Smith (1776), and Marshall (1938).

3.   This assumes that wages and productivity are highly correlated with each other. A brief discussion of the marginal productivity theory of wages is found in chapter 4.

4.   Charles Brown on the University of Maryland has suggested that in some cases, the psychic costs for schooling investment are negative. "Being in school allows one to postpone the psychic trauma of entering the real world" (personal communication).

5.   One problem with using the internal rate of return as a criterion for investment decisions is that, in certain cases, there will be more than one value that solves the equation. If the earnings trajectory of H crosses the L trajectory more than once, this would be a problem. However, in the case of human capital decisions, this is unlikely to be the case because earnings profiles are usually monotonic. Even when comparing two earnings profiles, one of which includes a period out of the labor market for nonmarket work, it is highly unlikely that, after reentry, the profile will rise above the alternative earnings profile. See Hirschleifer (1958) for a full discussion of these points.

6.   There are several reasons for believing that rates of return decline as the amount invested increases. Because of the importance of an individual's own time in producing human capital, it is impossible to accumulate the desired amount of human capital instantaneously and, therefore, the larger the desired amount, the longer the period of time over which it must be accumulated. Investments made later in life rather than earlier are likely to have smaller total benefits and involve higher total costs. Later investments cannot produce returns over as long a period of time as earlier investments and, in addition, will have a lower present value merely because the receipt of these returns is postponed. As human capital is accumulated, the value of an individual's time increases, as does the marginal cost of further human capital accumulation. However, if an individual's productivity in the production of human capital rises as rapidly as the value of time, the marginal cost of accumulating human capital will not rise (Becker 1967:6–8). Also, "The rates of return to any person depend, however, not only on his investments but also on those by others and on the derived demand for persons with different kinds of human capital. For example, a college education might yield a very high payoff if few persons manage to get one and if those who do are in great demand" (Becker and Chiswick 1966:360).

7.   "Ability" is placed in quotation marks because it does not mean simply innate ability, but the ability to reap the returns to human capital investment, which will be constrained for women through discrimination in job opportunities.

8.   Mean years of schooling can only be estimated by guessing at the average education within each schooling interval. For the cohort born between 1940 and 1944 who were aged 33 to 37 in 1977, Jencks (1972:21) reported slightly higher mean years of schooling for men (12.39) than for women (11.99).

9.   However, evidence presented by Welch and Smith (1979) indicates that, when the

earnings of high school and college graduates with equivalent experience are compared, there is no drop in the *relative* earnings of college graduates during this period.

10.   Freeman estimates that the rate of return to investing in college for men fell from 11 to 12 percent in the early 1960s to about 8 percent in the early 1970s.

11.   The construction of this index was explained in footnote 1. These same patterns of dissimilarity were found in an analysis of several microdata sets, one for females attending college in 1959 and one for the same group in 1973 (Polachek 1978).

12.   Chi-square tests were performed to test for significant change between the two periods in the distribution of both men's and women's fields at the B.A., M.A. and Ph.D. levels. None of the chi-square statistics exceeded the critical value at the 95 percent level of significance.

13.   The one exception is Renshaw (1960). However, his figures were not adjusted for differential rates of labor force participation and are therefore biased. Some of the notable estimates for males include Becker (1960), Hansen (1963), Becker (1964), Miller (1965), Hanoch (1967), and Weisbrod (1966).

14.   E.g., Becker (1964), Hanoch (1967), and Hansen (1963).

15. $Y_{s_1} = Y_o + r \sum_{t=0}^{s} C_j$

$Y_{s_2} = Y_o + r \sum_{t=0}^{s_2} C_j$

$Y_{s_2} - Y_{s_1} = r \sum_{t=s_1}^{s_2} C_j$

$\sum_{t=s_1}^{s_2} C_j = \dfrac{Y_{s_2} - Y_{s_1}}{r}$

16.   From equation 5, $Y_j = Y_s$ when $r \sum_{t=s+1}^{j-1} C_t = C_j$.

If training costs in each year are equal, then $rjC_j = C_j$ or $j = 1/r$, the "cross-over point" which corresponds to the number of years it takes for earnings to reach the level they would have been with no job training investment.

17.   However, this effect could be mitigated or eliminated if productivity in learning grew as fast as productivity in earning (Mincer 1974a:13).

18.   Years of experience by sex and race for the total sample and for "workers" (i.e., those who worked 500 or more hours in 1975) were as follows:

	White Men	Black Men	White Women	Black Women
Total	20.32	18.54	10.63	12.90
"Workers"	20.01	18.34	13.74	16.04

SOURCE: Corcoran 1978: p. 54, table 2.2.

Although we do not have any direct evidence on the shape of the *distribution* of years of experience among women who worked 500 or more hours in 1975, it seems safe to predict that there would be less variation than across the total group of women.

19.   In a recent paper by Edward Lazear (1979), indirect evidence of increased

investment in on-the-job training was found. The rate of wage growth for young women between 1968 and 1973 has increased, suggesting the possibility of increased investments in job training.

20. We ran a chi-square test for both men and women, to test the hypothesis that there was no significant change in their occupational distributions between 1970 and 1977. That hypothesis was strongly rejected at the 99 percent confidence level for both men and women.

21. When the index of occupational dissimilarity is recalculated for 1977, holding the sex composition of each individual occupation constant (at the 1970 level), but allowing the overall occupational structure to vary, there is a slight increase of 0.7 percent in the dissimilarity index between 1970 and 1977. For technique, see Blau and Hendricks (1979).

22. When the index of occupational dissimilarity is recalculated for 1977, holding the overall occupational structure constant (at the 1970 level), but allowing the sex composition of occupations to vary, there is a slight decrease of 0.5 percent in the index of occupational dissimilarity.

Chapter 4

Labor Markets: Earnings and Unemployment

The preceding two chapters have reviewed the determinants of both the quantity and quality of labor supplied by women and men. We must next consider the implications of these supply differences for sex differentials in earnings and unemployment. This chapter will begin by examining the major differentials in earnings and unemployment predicted on the basis of the supply differences previously discussed, an approach which is dictated by orthodox theory. Then these predicted differentials will be compared both to observed patterns and trends and to predictions based on segmented labor market theories. The following chapter will explore the nature of discrimination and its role in the dynamics of the vicious circle which reinforces sex differentials in market outcomes over time, despite important changes in the nature of labor supply.

Clearly the outcome of wage and employment determination is substantially different for women than for men. Tables 4.1 and 4.2 provide the basic summary data on earnings and unemployment rates for both sexes—two complementary indicators of labor market inequality. The pattern of lower earnings and higher unemployment rates among women is familiar, but the underlying causes are still far from being adequately understood. Factors relating both to differences in productivity and to sex discrimination must be taken into account, and their respective contributions to the earnings and unemployment differentials carefully analyzed.

Even more disturbing than the existence of these sizable differentials is the fact that both gaps appear to have widened over time. Table 4.1 reveals that the annual earnings of full-time year-round female

Table 4.1

Median Earnings of Full-Time Year-Round Workers by Sex,
1955–1977

Year	Median Earnings Women	Men	Women's Median Earnings as a Percent of Men's
1955	$2,719	$ 4,252	63.9
1956	2,827	4,466	63.3
1957	3,008	4.713	63.8
1958	3,102	4,927	63.0
1959	3.193	5,209	61.3
1960	3,293	5,417	60.8
1961	3,351	5,644	59.4
1962	3,446	5,974	59.5
1963	3,561	5,978	59.6
1964	3,690	6,195	59.6
1965	3,823	6,375	60.0
1966	3,973	6,848	58.0
1967	4,150	7,182	57.8
1968	4,457	7,664	58.2
1969	4,977	8,227	60.5
1970	5,323	8,966	59.4
1971	5,593	9,399	59.5
1972	5,903	10,202	57.9
1973	6,335	11,186	56.6
1974	6,772	11,835	57.2
1974(r)	6,970	11,889	58.6
1975	7,504	12,758	58.8
1976	8,099	13,455	60.2
1977	8,616	14,626	58.9

SOURCES: 1955–1974: *Fact Sheet on the Earnings Gap*, U.S. Dept. of Labor, Employment Standards Administration, Women's Bureau.
1975 and revised 1974 figures: U.S. Dept. of Commerce, Bureau of the Census, Series P-60, no. 103, p. 27, table 12. The method of calculating the median earnings was revised in 1975, and thus these figures are not strictly comparable to those for earlier years. For purposes of comparison, both sets of figures are given for 1974.
1976: U.S. Dept. of Commerce, Bureau of the Census, Series P-60, no. 107, p. 17, table 11.
1977: U.S. Dept. of Commerce, Bureau of the Census, Series P-60, no. 116, p. 17, table 11.

Table 4.2

Unemployment Rates by Sex, 1947–1978

Year	Total	Male	Female	D = F − M	R = F/M
1947	3.9	4.0	3.7	−0.3	0.93
1948	3.8	3.6	4.1	0.5	1.14
1949	5.9	5.9	6.0	0.1	1.02
1950	5.3	5.1	5.7	0.6	1.12
1951	3.3	2.8	4.4	1.6	1.57
1952	3.0	2.8	3.6	0.8	1.29
1953	2.9	2.8	3.3	0.5	1.18
1954	5.5	5.3	6.0	0.7	1.13
1955	4.4	4.2	4.9	0.7	1.17
1956	4.1	3.8	4.8	1.0	1.26
1957	4.3	4.1	4.7	0.6	1.15
1958	6.8	6.8	6.8	0.0	1.00
1959	5.5	5.3	5.9	0.6	1.11
1960	5.5	5.4	5.9	0.5	1.09
1961	6.7	6.4	7.2	0.8	1.13
1962	5.5	5.2	6.2	1.0	1.19
1963	5.7	5.2	6.5	1.3	1.25
1964	5.2	4.6	6.2	1.6	1.35
1965	4.5	4.0	5.5	1.5	1.37
1966	3.8	3.2	4.8	1.6	1.50
1967	3.8	3.1	5.2	2.1	1.68
1968	3.6	2.9	4.8	1.9	1.65
1969	3.5	2.8	4.7	1.9	1.68
1970	4.9	4.4	5.9	1.5	1.34
1971	5.9	5.3	6.9	1.6	1.30
1972	5.6	4.9	6.6	1.7	1.35
1973	4.9	4.1	6.0	1.9	1.46
1974	5.6	4.8	6.7	1.9	1.39
1975	8.5	7.9	9.3	1.4	1.18
1976	7.7	7.0	8.6	1.6	1.23
1977	7.0	6.2	8.2	2.0	1.32
1978	6.0	5.2	7.2	2.0	1.38

SOURCE: *Employment and Earnings*, January 1979, pp. 154–155, tables 1 and 2.

workers are a smaller fraction of the earnings of their male counterparts than was the case twenty years ago. Although the unemployment gap exhibits substantial cyclical fluctuation, and therefore any
trend is less immediately obvious, table 4.2 shows that the male unemployment rate is now a smaller fraction of the female unemployment
rate than was the case in the 1950s. There may be many possible
explanations for this apparent worsening of women's relative position
in the labor market, and we will examine several of these in detail.
However, the consistency of the patterns for both earnings and unemployment rates makes it difficult to dismiss these changes as insignificant, and places the burden of proof upon those who hold that these
changes in the relative economic position of women workers are
apparent rather than real.

We will begin with an analysis of labor markets, combining the supply implications of sex differentials already discussed in chapters 2 and
3 with a simple theory of labor demand based on productivity alone
and unrelated to sex. In such markets, observed unemployment and
wage differentials between men and women would be a function of differences between the sexes in the quantity and quality of labor supplied. Alternative assumptions about the structure and functioning of
markets will also be explored within the context of the orthodox
framework. Wage and unemployment differentials predicted on the
basis of this orthodox approach will then be compared with actual differentials over the postwar period. Finally, models of labor market
segmentation will be explored as a possible source of alternative or
complementary explanations for postwar trends. It may appear to
some that this approach to the interpretation of earnings and unemployment differentials gives undue weight to individual choice as the
primary determinant of labor market outcomes. In reality, as we shall
see, existing wage and unemployment differentials are the result of the
dynamic interaction between individual choice and market structure.
By starting the discussion with supply factors, we are following an
established tradition. However, our motive is not to be orthodox, but
to be strategic in our attempt to highlight both the strengths and
weaknesses of this dominant approach as it confronts the challenge of
explaining these differentials.

The Orthodox Approach to Labor Markets: Theory and Implications

The theory of the demand for labor under perfectly competitive labor market conditions and profit maximization is based on the marginal productivity principle, which states that, other things being equal, the wage rate and the level of employment are inversely related. At the micro level, each profit-maximizing employer will try to adjust employment so that the value of the marginal product of labor equals the wage rate,[1] and, at the macro level, the wage rate adjusts to provide employment for the available labor supply. This inverse relationship—the downward-sloping demand curve for labor—derives from both diminishing marginal returns to labor in the productive process and the fact that the quantity sold of the final product obeys the law of demand and is inversely related to its selling price. The demand for labor as an input into the productive process is derived from the demand for the output of that process.

As long as the labor market operates under perfectly competitive conditions, including *full information*, neoclassical theory predicts that wages will adjust to labor supply and there will be no unemployment. Under such conditions, since there would be no leeway on the demand side of the market to generate unequal compensation for equal work, any observed sex differences in earnings, which are the product of wage rates and hours of work, would have to be rooted in the supply side of the market, stemming from variations in the amount and/or skill level of the labor supplied. Even in the case of monopsony—a single buyer of labor—demand is not differentiated by sex, and differences in supply elasticity between men and women will determine relative wages. However, in the case of monopsony, the employer pays his employees less than the value of their marginal product and, by recognizing differences between groups of workers in their alternative wage opportunities, he is able to pay different wage rates to equally productive groups of workers. It is only when we drop the assumption of perfect information that we would also predict the existence of unemployment differentials, due to differences in the likelihood of and return to job search between men and women. Each of these three cases—pure competition, monopsony, and search under imperfect information—will be examined in turn, in order to develop predictions of patterns and trends in wage and unemployment differentials between the sexes which would be expected if systematic differences in labor supply were the only determinants of sex differences in earnings.

PURE COMPETITION

In the simple case of perfectly competitive labor markets and full information, average wage differentials between the sexes will result from systematic differences in average skill level and occupational distribution. We have seen in chapters 2 and 3 that substantial female-male differences persist in both the average quantity and skill composition of labor supplied to the market. Women's market labor supply remains lower than men's and more responsive to labor market conditions, although the gap has narrowed. On the average, women still participate in the labor force less frequently, less continuously and for shorter hours and fewer weeks per year than men. Therefore, they are less likely to invest in job-related types of education and more likely to enter occupations which do not require extensive investments in on-the-job training. However, women differ substantially from one another, with many women working most of their lives and following career paths, while others work only occasionally or not at all. Therefore, wage differentials predicted for the average woman will not apply to women in different education and occupation groups. This heterogeneity in labor supply behavior, previously discussed in chapter 2, makes it essential to distinguish between different groups of women when we make predictions based on this approach.

On the average, we would expect the gap between the earnings of men and women to grow with age, as men assimilate more productivity-enhancing job experience than women. However, one would expect the extent to which the earnings gap widens with age to have become less pronounced over time, as the proportion of women experiencing continuous patterns of labor force participation grows. Recent increases in labor force participation rates among young women have been seen to be part of a cohort phenomenon, with young cohorts of women displaying greater labor force attachment at every age than their older counterparts.

Across education groups, we would expect sex differentials in earnings to diminish with progressively higher levels of educational attainment, because of the strong positive correlation between education and labor force participation among women. Although the earnings gap would be expected to widen with age within each education group, the gap would not be as large or widen as much for the more educated. If all training were general, and therefore employee-financed through a reduction in the net wage, we would expect that, at the time of entry into the labor force, women's earnings would exceed men's within education groups,[2] because we have previously observed that women receive less training and experience lower average job tenure than men. However, even in the case of perfect competition, employer-financed specific training is likely to be of some importance. If employers finance a larger proportion of the training men receive than the training received by women because men are believed to have lower turnover rates (Landes 1977), the net effect of differential investment in training on sex differences in wages at the time of labor force entry is unclear. This is because, for a given amount of training, men would receive a higher net wage than women, thus mitigating or possibly reversing the effect of women's lesser investment in themselves on net entry wages.

Because black women have traditionally had higher labor force participation rates than white women and black men have had lower labor force participation rates than white men, we would expect the earnings gap by sex between blacks to be narrower than between whites. However, rapid increases in labor force participation among white women and relatively stable patterns of labor force participation among black women make predictions about trends in their earnings differentials problematic. The rapid increases in labor force participation among young white women at the start of their careers should narrow the gap between the earnings of black and white women, at least in the short run, but, on the other hand, the simultaneous growth in labor force attachment among white women should work in the other direction, although perhaps with some time lag.

MONOPSONY

As was indicated above, monopsony—the situation where the employer has monopoly power in the labor market and thus faces an upward-sloping supply curve of labor—leads to a situation in which workers may be paid less than the value of their marginal product and equally productive workers may be paid unequally. The monopsonist who practices either perfect wage discrimination among workers, or a less complete degree of wage discrimination, will end up paying different wages to men and women. The first model is most applicable to professional/managerial labor markets, where salaries are often negotiated on an individual basis, while the second model applies to most other occupations, where a standard rate is defined for a broad category of workers. An employer with monopsony power need not be prejudiced to practice discrimination. Under certain market conditions, wage discrimination "pays" in that it maximizes profits. Although a case of pure monopsony would be difficult or impossible to find, certain elements of monopsony power are seen to exist in many labor markets, often enhanced by the development of customary labor practices, such as pensions and seniority systems, to be discussed in the final section of this chapter.[3]

In the general monopsony case, given the upward-sloping labor supply curve, the marginal cost of hiring another worker (marginal cost of labor = MCL) exceeds the wage that worker must be paid, because it also includes the cost of bringing the wages of all workers already hired up to the new level. Thus, as can be seen in figure 4.1, the MCL lies above the labor supply curve and rises more rapidly as employment expands. This naturally gives the monopsonist a strong incentive to restrict employment and thus keep costs down. Hiring will take place only up to the point where the MCL equals the value of the marginal product (VMP), which is the point where MCL intersects the demand for labor. This is to the left of the point where supply and demand intersect under perfectly competitive conditions. If the labor market in figure 4.1 were competitive, OL_2 workers would be hired and paid a wage rate OW_2. Under monopsony, however, only OL_1 workers are hired and they are paid only OW_1; both employment and wages are depressed as a result of labor market monopsony. This out-

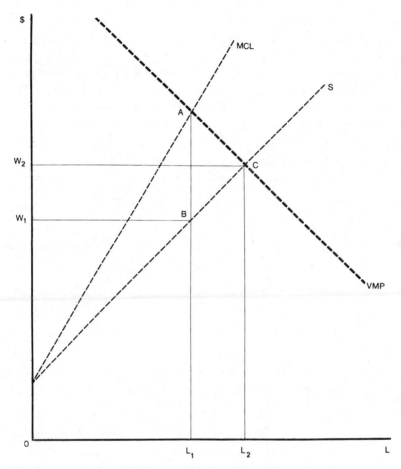

Figure 4.1.   Wage and Employment Determination under Monopsony.

come is frequently characterized as monopsonistic exploitation, in that each worker is paid less than his or her contribution to total receipts.

Just as it pays a monopolist in the product market to practice price discrimination if he is able to separate his buyers into two or more distinct groups with different demand elasticities, so it pays a monopsonist to practice wage discrimination by separating his labor force into distinguishable groups with different labor supply elasticities. An obvious characteristic by which groups of workers may be distinguished is sex. If the supply functions of men and women differ, the monopsonist can pay them different wage rates. More specifically, the group with the lower labor supply elasticity will be paid a lower wage. This is illustrated in figure 4.2, where groups A and B are depicted as having different supply functions to the monopsonistic employer. (We will avoid labeling these two groups men and women at this point, until we have gone into the question of which sex is likely to have the less elastic labor supply.) Group A's willingness to work for the firm is less affected by alternative wage offers than that of B (i.e., labor supply function A is less elastic), and the monopsonistic employer is able to

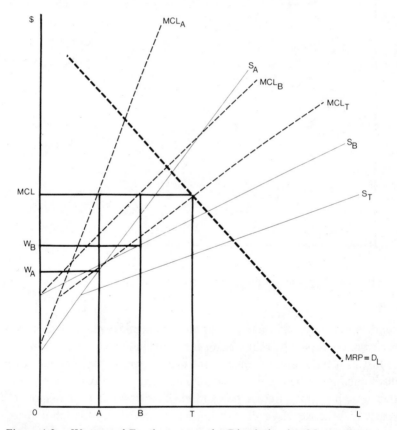

Figure 4.2.   Wages and Employment under Discriminating Monopsony
NOTE: $OA = BT$, and $OA + OB = OT$.

pay workers in group A a lower rate than those in group B simply because of their relative immobility. Note, however, that all workers are subject to monopsonistic exploitation, in that they are paid less than their marginal revenue product.

For monopsony power to provide a possible explanation of observed sex differentials in earnings, the female labor supply function facing the employer must be less elastic than the male labor supply function. In terms of the above examples, women must correspond to group A and men to group B. If the male labor supply function were the less elastic, the observed wage differential between equally productive men and women would be an underestimate of the extent of sex discrimination, and, instead of helping to explain this differential, the existence of monopsony power in labor markets would imply an even wider earnings gap to be explained.

What evidence do we have that the female labor supply function is less elastic than that of men? At first glance, based on the evidence presented in chapter 2, the opposite would appear to be the case. All studies of labor supply indicate that the female labor force is considerably more responsive to changes in wage rates than is the male labor force. However, what is relevant for monopsonistic behavior is not the elasticity of *aggregate* labor supply, but rather the elasticity of labor supply to a particular employer, occupation, or industry. Although these firm-specific supply elasticities have not been directly estimated for men and women,[4] certain readily observable differences between men and women can be seen as strong signals that women's firm-specific labor supply elasticity is likely to be less than that of men. First, there is considerable evidence, already discussed in chapter 3, that women are less mobile than men within the labor force, both geographically and occupationally. Second, only roughly 16 percent of working women are unionized, as opposed to 28 percent of working men.[5] A union changes the nature of labor supply by setting a reservation wage for the group, thus making the supply curve perfectly horizontal at the union's reservation wage. This prevents the employer from exploiting individual differences in the setting of group wages. In occupations or industries where men are more highly unionized than women, this should reinforce the effect of differential mobility in making women's firm-specific supply elasticity lower than that of men.

General research on job mobility would seem to reinforce the predictions made earlier. Younger workers are more likely to move between jobs than older workers, and married workers, particularly women, are less likely to move than single workers. Therefore, as workers age, it would be expected that employers with monopsony power would be able to hold down women's wages relatively more than men's, because women are more likely to be tied to a particular job or location. This would be another reason to expect the earnings gap between men and women to widen with age, and to be greatest between married people.

SEARCH

Because both workers and jobs are heterogeneous, and information is imperfect and available only at some cost, the search process by both workers and employers is a significant factor in labor market adjustments, influencing both earnings and unemployment rates. In the two simple labor market models previously analyzed, unemployment was nonexistent. The introduction of the search process provides the conceptual link between unemployment and earnings.

Search theory has revitalized neoclassical market models by explaining in an individualistic and optimizing framework such phenomena as differing wages for "identical" workers and persistent positive levels of unemployment. To date, most of the search literature has focused on the optimal duration of job search, given the decision to search.[6] Therefore, empirical implications relate largely to wage rates and the duration of unemployment, rather than to the incidence of unemployment. To derive predictions relating to unemployment rates, it is necessary to extend the theory to include the decision to search as well as the optimal duration of search.

Any useful analysis of these phenomena must of course begin with a clear understanding of the labor force concepts described in chapter 2. All those who made any effort to find work during the preceding four weeks, but did not have a job and were available for work during the survey, are classified as unemployed, as are persons on layoff waiting for recall and those waiting to start a new job within the next thirty days. The unemployment rate, which tells us what percentage of the labor force is unemployed in a given week, is derived by dividing the number of unemployed by the total labor force, which is defined as the sum of the employed and the unemployed. The average annual unemployment rate is the product of the average number of unemployment spells per worker per week times the average number of weeks per spell.[7] Therefore, the unemployment rate could increase either because more workers experience a spell of unemployment or because the average length of a spell increases.

The Incidence of Unemployment Spells

Search activity is not synonymous with the state of unemployment. Some unemployed workers—those on temporary layoff awaiting recall—are included in the unemployment statistics even though they may not be involved in search activity because they continue to be tied to a particular job. On the other hand, among those engaged in job search in a particular week, not all would be categorized as unemployed. A worker can choose to search full-time and be counted as an unemployed member of the labor force, or if currently employed, can search part-time while remaining on the job. It has been estimated that at least 50 to 60 percent of all quits move from job to job without ever experiencing unemployment (Mattila 1974). Therefore, it is mainly labor force entrants and laid-off workers without the possibility of recall who engage in search as a full-time activity. The key to sex differentials in the incidence of unemployment spells must lie in the differential incidence of labor force entry and layoff for men and women, and differences between them in the percentage of voluntary job quits that are followed by full-time search activity.[8]

At any point over the business cycle, women make up a larger proportion of labor force entrants than men. In 1974–75, 63 percent of entrants were women (Lloyd and Niemi 1976). The fact that women have a much greater rate of inter-labor force mobility (movement in and out of the labor force) than men has already been discussed in chapter 2. The rate of inter-labor force turnover for women is three to five times as great as that for men, but has shown a downward trend over time, as female labor force participation and permanency of labor force attachment have increased. As can be seen in table 4.3, data on the sources of unemployment (job loss, quitting, and labor force entry and reentry) reveal that the incidence of unemployment due to entry or reentry alone was 2 to 4 times as high for women as men between 1967 and 1978. The higher entry and reentry rates for women should increase their incidence of unemployment spells relative to men.

Table 4.3

Rates for Different Sources of Unemployment for Men and Women, 1964–1978

Date		Males 20+				Females 20+		
	Total	Job Loser	Job Leaver	Entry	Total	Job Loser	Job Leaver	Entry
June 1964	3.6	2.3	0.5	0.8	5.2	2.2	0.9	2.0
Dec. 1964	3.8	2.5	0.4	0.8	4.1	1.7	0.8	1.6
June 1965	2.9	1.8	0.4	0.7	4.8	2.1	0.9	1.8
Nov. 1965	2.5	1.6	0.4	0.5	4.3	1.4	0.9	2.0
Jan. 1966	3.4	2.3	0.5	0.6	4.2	1.7	0.8	1.7
June 1966	2.3	1.2	0.4	0.7	3.9	1.1	1.0	1.8
1967	2.3	1.5	0.4	0.5	4.3	1.6	0.7	2.0
1968	2.2	1.3	0.4	0.4	3.8	1.3	0.6	1.8
1969	2.1	1.2	0.4	0.6	3.7	1.2	0.6	1.9
1970	3.5	2.2	0.4	0.8	4.8	1.9	0.8	2.1
1971	4.4	2.9	0.5	1.0	5.7	2.4	0.8	2.5
1972	4.0	2.5	0.5	1.0	5.4	2.2	0.9	2.4
1973	3.2	1.9	0.5	0.8	4.8	1.6	0.9	2.3
1974	3.8	2.5	0.5	0.8	5.5	2.1	1.0	2.4
1975	6.7	5.1	0.6	1.1	8.0	4.0	1.1	2.9
1976	5.9	4.1	0.6	1.2	7.4	3.2	1.2	3.0
1977	5.2	3.4	0.6	1.2	7.0	2.8	1.2	3.0
1978	4.2	2.6	0.6	1.1	6.0	2.3	1.0	2.8

SOURCES: 1964–1966: Kathryn D. Hoyle, "Why the Unemployed Look for World", *Monthly Labor Review* (February 1967), 90(2): 35.
1967–1974: U.S. Dept. of Labor, *Employment and Training Report of the President, 1976*, p. 238, table A-25.
1975–1977: U.S. Dept. of Labor, *Employment and Training Report of the President, 1978*, p. 218, table A-25.
1978: *Employment and Earnings*, January 1979, p. 166, table 13.

Women's geographic and occupational immobility increases the percent of "voluntary" job quits for married women which are followed by a period of unemployment because of family migration in response to husbands' job opportunities.[9] For reasons discussed in chapter 3, wives are more likely to be "tied movers" than husbands because of the greater likelihood that husbands' gains from migration will be absolutely greater in size than any losses experienced by wives. Women's shorter expected duration of continuous labor force participation is of particular importance in this respect. Data on unemployment rates by mobility status confirm these expectations by showing that, for males, interstate mobility has the effect of decreasing their unemployment rate, whereas for females, the opposite is true (Niemi 1975). The greater likelihood that women's voluntary quits will be followed by unemployment should also increase their incidence of unemployment relative to men.

On the other hand, the figures in table 4.3 also reveal that in most years men are more likely to experience layoff than women and these differences are greatest during the downturn of the business cycle. Men are heavily employed in industries, such as construction and heavy manufacturing, which are strongly affected by seasonal and cyclical swings in demand. Because of occupational segregation, women's respresentation in these industries is small, and therefore, economy-wide, they experience a lower incidence of layoff despite the fact that, within firms, their relative lack of specific training tends to make them more vulnerable to layoff.

Although differential search probabilities stem from many sources, relatively high inter-labor force mobility among women, in addition to their greater likelihood of engaging in job search following a "voluntary" job quit, suggest a higher incidence of unemployment spells among women. A balancing of these considerations would suggest that the incidence of women's unemployment is most likely to exceed men's within the married group and least likely to exceed men's within the single group. However, the effect of these factors on the relative incidence of unemployment spells may be mitigated by the greater likelihood of layoff among men. Over time, as women's inter-labor force mobility decreases and their career attachment increases, we would expect that the sex differential in incidence of unemployment spells per average labor force participant—to the extent that it exists—would narrow.

The Duration of Unemployment

In the simple search models, where the relevant time horizon is assumed to be infinite and the available wage distribution is known, the period of unemployment depends on the distribution of wage offers and the cost of search per unit of time. Each individual is assumed to have a *reservation wage*, below which no job offers will be accepted. This is illustrated in figure 4.3, which shows both the reservation wage and a hypothetical expected wage offer curve, which is derived from the (known) distribution of wage offers. The wage offer curve shows a diminishing rate of increase per unit of time, because the likelihood of sampling a significantly higher wage than offers already received diminishes as more wage offers are sampled. The reservation wage is defined as equal to the wage offer which

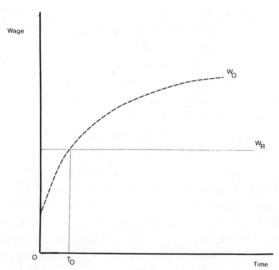

Figure 4.3.   The Wage Offer Curve and Reservation Wage.

NOTE: W_O = wage offered.
        W_R = reservation wage.
        T_O = optimal duration of search.

equalizes the marginal gain from and cost of additional search. Therefore, the reservation wage is expected to be higher, the lower the cost of search, other things being equal.

Variations on the simple search model include the introduction of such modifications as a finite time horizon and a wage distribution that is unknown and/or changing over time. In each of these cases, the reservation wage itself will change as the search process proceeds. A search is terminated when an individual either accepts a job, or drops out of the labor force because the wage offers sampled fall below his or her minimum reservation wage. For an employed job hunter, this would be his current wage, whereas for an unemployed job hunter, this would be the value of his or her marginal product in the nonmarket sector. On average, return from job search for women would be expected to be lower than that for men because of their shorter work-life expectancy. However, women's search costs may be either higher or lower than men's; this will depend on average differences, between unemployed men and women, in market and/or home productivity. Therefore, it is difficult to predict *a priori* which group would find satisfactory wage offers more quickly.[10] However, women are more likely to terminate their search by dropping out of the labor force than men, given the higher value of their nonmarket time. On balance, it is not possible to predict whether the average duration of unemployment for women would be shorter or longer than for men.

Wage Differentials

Search models also have implications for wage differentials between the sexes which, if anything, reinforce the predictions already made with simpler models based on perfect information. The search process is most likely to reinforce the wage differentials previously discussed in the case of joint job search by married working couples (Frank 1978). With the increase in the percentage of husband-wife families with two earners from 36.1 percent in 1950 to 48.7 percent in 1975 (Hayghe 1976), the implications of joint search models should have increasing predictive power over time. For couples, the search for a pair of jobs is constrained geographically and it is, therefore, extremely unlikely that the best wage offer for the wife will be found in the same geographic region as the best wage offer for the husband. One or both of the spouses must compromise or they must separate. The compromise will be most costly for the spouse who works more hours and who has the largest stock of market-related human capital. If family income maximization is assumed, the wife will be more likely to compromise, thus widening the already existing wage gap between men and women. This consideration will reinforce the prediction that the wage gap between married men and women should be significantly wider than that between single men and women.

Each of the three simple labor market models discussed relies on differentials in labor supply between men and women to predict patterns in wage differentials. Supply behavior is most sharply differentiated in the case of married men and women, and, therefore, the wage gap would be expected to be greater for them than for other groups. On the other hand, the wage gap should be smallest for highly educated men and women, whose labor supply behavior is least differentiated by sex. The last model, which includes search behavior, has implications for the incidence and duration of unemployment as well. Although women are expected to have more unemployment spells than men, search theory does not provide unambiguous predictions on relative unemployment duration. Thus no definite expectation regarding unemployment differentials emerges from the theory.

In each case, the narrowing gap in labor force participation and attachment between men and women over time would be expected to lead to a narrowing of the gap in wage rates, unemployment spells and average unemployment duration. Although the differentials between earnings and unemployment rates for men and women in tables 4.1 and 4.2 are not inconsistent with the theory discussed above, the trends in these differentials appear to be. In the next two sections of this chapter, these actual differentials will be explored in more detail, in order to compare the theoretical predictions just discussed with the actual data, and to isolate sources of inconsistency. Although none of the within-group differentials we will examine in earnings or unemployment rates have been adjusted to control for all the possible differences between groups that might affect these differentials, we are confident that the systematic patterns that do emerge will tell a consistent story. Education will be seen to be a key variable in identifying sources of inconsistency between theoretical predictions and actual experience.

Earnings Differentials

The average earnings of men and women are most directly comparable when the sample is restricted to full-time year-round workers. Although, even within this restricted sample, men's and women's average hours of work differ slightly, this restriction permits us to examine patterns in relative compensation which are not primarily the result of either variations in annual labor supply, as discussed in chapter 2, or unemployment differentials, which will be discussed subsequently. It is evident from the examination of the data which follow that the aggregate differential in table 4.1 remains striking when men and women are compared within racial, occupational or education subgroups, or by age. Certain observed patterns and trends in the differentials do not conform to the theoretical predictions derived above, and raise questions concerning both the strict comparability of the available data and the adequacy of a purely choice-theoretic approach. We will begin by examining patterns in age-earnings profiles for 1975 and then look at trends over time in the earnings gap.

We have already discussed in chapter 3 the use of age-earnings profiles as indirect evidence of life cycle paths in human capital investment. Therefore, we would be engaging in circular reasoning if we were to use these profiles in and of themselves as support for the theory we would now like to test. Fortunately, more direct evidence of sex differentials in years of work experience and job training from the MID no longer requires such an indirect approach. Sex differentials in years of work experience and job training have been established as primary factors in an explanation of sex differences in earnings. However, it is unclear whether these differences themselves result primarily from sex differences in participation and career choice or from external constraints imposed by the market.

As predicted in the human capital model (but also consistent with alternative models), the gap between male and female earnings grows with age over the life cycle within all education, racial and marital groups. The growth of the gap is slightly less for blacks than whites, and substantially less for single individuals than for those in other marital groups (Fuchs 1971), as would be predicted by the theory. However, when comparing education groups, patterns of earnings differentials do not conform to predictions, as can be seen in figure 3.9. In 1975, for high school graduates, women's earnings were 73.7 percent of men's at ages 18–24 and 53.8 percent of men's at ages 45–54. For college graduates, women's earnings were 82.2 percent of men's at ages 18–24 and 52.7 percent of men's at ages 45–54, indicating a much greater deterioration with age. It had been predicted that, at higher levels of education, the gap between male and female earnings should widen less precipitously, because more educated women work more over the life cycle and make greater investments on the job as they age.

Indeed, some of the most interesting patterns in earnings differentials are those between education groups. Particularly dramatic is the fact that female college graduates earn less than male high school graduates at all points in the life cycle. Although all age-earnings profiles show some evidence of training, women with only a high school education or less apparently receive very little such training. Within education groups, the male profiles are steeper in the early years, and exceed female earnings even upon entry into the labor force (18–24), suggesting the differential importance for men of firm-specific training financed by the employer, and therefore the possible importance of discrimination against women in access to training. This unequal access would become more important the higher the education group, because education and training are highly complementary.

As we already know from an examination of table 4.1, the earnings gap has widened over time despite the theory's predictions to the contrary. If we examine the trends in the earnings gap by race (see table 4.4) we find that, although it has widened from 35 percent to 42 percent for whites, it has narrowed significantly, from 45 to 25 percent, for nonwhites. This may seem surprising at first glance because, while white women have shown dramatic increases in labor force participation since 1955, nonwhites have only shown some increase in the last decade. This may be partially explained by a con-

Table 4.4

Median Income of Full-Time Year-Round Workers by Race and Sex,
1955–1977.

Year	Male White	Female White	Female/Male Earnings Ratio (%)	Male Nonwhite	Female Nonwhite	Female/Male Earnings Ratio (%)
1955	$ 4,377	$2,858	65.3	$ 2,665	$1,468	55.1
1956	4,628	2,937	63.5	2,767	1,634	59.1
1957	4,874	3,096	63.5	2,983	1,810	60.7
1958	5,102	3,194	62.6	3,209	1,877	58.5
1959	5,391	3,300	61.2	3,150	2,125	67.5
1960	5,572	3,377	60.6	3,683	2,289	62.2
1961	5,817	3,429	58.9	3,692	2,264	61.3
1962	5,994	3,582	59.8	3,577	2,186	61.1
1963	6,245	3,687	59.0	4,019	2,280	56.7
1964	6,457	3,835	59.4	4,234	2,663	62.9
1965	6,802	3,935	57.9	4,272	2,672	62.6
1966	7,179	4,142	57.7	4,508	2,934	65.1
1967	7,518	4,380	58.3	5,015	3,336	64.3
1968	8,047	4,685	58.2	5,518	3,489	63.2
1969	8,953	5,182	57.9	6,104	4,251	69.6
1970	9.447	5,536	58.6	6,638	4,664	70.3
1971	9,902	5,767	58.2	7,006	5,194	74.1
1972	10,918	6,172	56.5	7,576	5,341	70.5
1973	11,800	6,598	55.9	8,298	5,724	69.0
1974	12,434	7,021	56.5	9,061	6,541	72.2
1974(r)	12,399	7,235	58.4	9,320	6,805	73.0
1975	13,233	7,737	57.5	10,151	7,598	74.5
1976	14,212	8,376	58.7	10,478	7,884	75.2
1977	15,378	8,870	57.7	11,037	8,447	76.5

SOURCES: U. S. Bureau of the Census: Current Population Reports, series
P–60, no. 118, pp. 247–249, table 61.
NOTE: This method of calculating the median income was revised in 1975 and
thus these figures are not strictly comparable to those for earlier years. For purposes of comparison both sets of figures are given for 1974.

vergence between the characteristics of white and nonwhite working
women, with average education levels among nonwhite working
women rising dramatically (J. P. Smith 1979). However, this leaves
the widening wage gap among whites unexplained, for the average
educational attainment of men and women has been rising at roughly
the same rate for the past ten to fifteen years.

Figure 4.4 shows changes over time in the age-income profiles for men and women.[11] Those of women not only lie below those of men in every case, but are considerably flatter. In both 1955 and 1965, the profiles for women are almost horizontal between the ages of 20 and 64, a configuration consistent with little or no on-the-job training. The

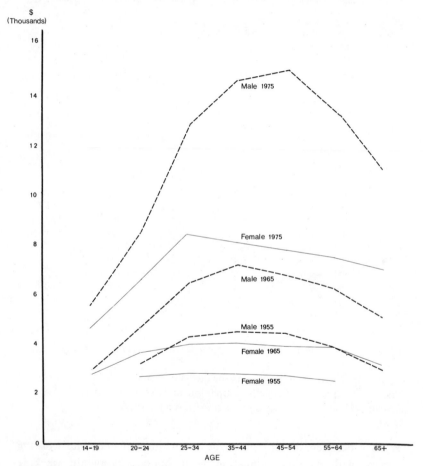

Figure 4.4. Age-Income Profiles for Full-Time Year-Round Workers by Sex, 1955, 1965 and 1975

SOURCE: 1955: Current Population Reports, series P-60, no. 23, p. 13, table 3.
1965: Series P-60, no. 51, p. 33, table 20.
1975: Series P-60, no. 105, p. 190, table 46.

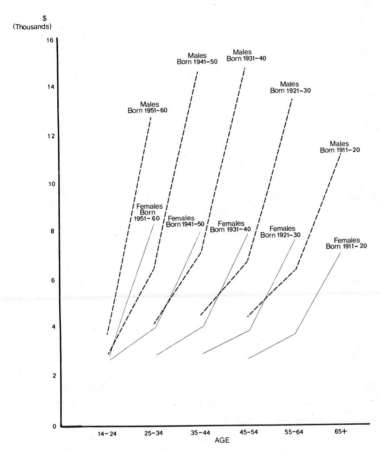

Figure 4.5.   Age-Income Profiles for Cohorts of Men and Women.

SOURCE: 1955: Current Population Reports, series P-60, no. 23, p. 13, table 3.
1965: Series P-60, no. 51, p. 33, table 20.
1975: Series P-60, no. 105, p. 190, table 46.

male profiles, on the other hand, are upward-sloping until ages 35–44
in all three years. In 1975, the profile for women exhibits evidence of
investment in on-the-job training for the first time, and closely resem-
bles the male age-earnings profile ten years earl ɾr. Over time, the
relationship between age and earnings has become more strongly positive up to age 44 for both men and women. However, even in 1975, the
profile for men still rises more rapidly and peaks later than that for

women. In fact, female/male earnings ratios have widened over time within every age group except for those 65 and over.

We must be careful not to interpret these age-earnings profiles too literally, because they are based on cross-sectional data for women and men from different cohorts. When we examine the experience of any cohort over time, as in figure 4.5, although the profiles look very different from the cross-sectional ones, because of the unusual importance of inflation in the 1970s and the continuous rise in earnings over time, we find that the deterioration in the earnings ratio with age is similar to that suggested to figure 4.4. For example, 14- to 24-year olds in 1955 had a female-male earnings ratio of 83.9 percent. In 1975, this same cohort was aged 35–44 and had an earnings ratio of 54.9 percent, representing a decline of 29 percentage points. This reflects, in fact, an even greater relative deterioration than we would estimate from the 1975 cross-sectional profiles, which show a decline of only 23.6 percentage points in the earnings ratio betwen 14 to 24 and 35 to 44 years of age. It seems particularly interesting to find that, while cohort age-participation profiles for women are rising more dramatically than cross-section profiles (as shown in chapter 2), cohort earnings ratios are simultaneously declining even more rapidly than cross-sectional profiles would suggest. This is exactly the opposite of what human captial theory would predict, and again suggests the possibility of some alternative explanation.

Tables 4.5 and 4.6 reveal that the earnings gap[12] between men and women is not simply the result of a skill differential, as defined by differing occupational levels or educational attainment, for it exists within all major occupations and education groups. What is striking is that women's earnings constitute a similar fraction of men's earnings within all these groups, and that this relative earnings position of women has shown little if any change over time.

Two aspects of the patterns revealed in table 4.5 are of particular interest. In 1960, female clerical workers were in the best position relative to their male counterparts, but this advantage eroded steadily between 1960 and 1975, as the earnings gap in this occupation grew from less than 33 percent to over 40 percent. This was due to the fact that the earnings of female clerical workers grew more slowly than those of any other group, which in turn is no doubt related to the ris-

Table 4.5

Median Earnings of Full-Time Year-Round Workers by Sex and Selected Major Occupation Groups, 1960, 1970, 1975

Major occupation Group	1960 Median Earnings Men	Women	Women's Earnings as a % of men's	1970 Median Earnings Men	Women	%	1975 Median Earnings Men	Women	%
Professional and technical workers	$7,115	$4,358	61.2	$11,806	$7,878	66.7	$16,133	$10,639	65.9
Nonfarm managers, officials, and proprietors	6,648	3,514	52.9	12,117	6,834	56.4	16,093	9,125	56.7
Clerical workers	5,291	3,575	67.6	8,617	5,551	64.4	12,152	7,562	62.2
Sales workers	5,842	2,389	40.9	9,790	4,188	42.8	14,025	5,460	38.9
Operatives	4,997	2,969	59.4	7,623	4,510	59.2	11,142	6,251	56.1
Service workers (except private household)	4,088	2,340	57.2	6,955	3,953	56.8	9,488	5,414	57.1

SOURCES: 1960: Current Population Reports, series P-60, no. 37, table 27, p. 47.
1970: *Fact Sheet on the Earnings Gap, 1974*, U.S. Dept. of Labor, Employment Standards Administration, Women's Bureau.
1975: Current Population Reports, series P-60, no. 105, table 52, p. 229

Table 4.6

Median Income of Full-Time Year-Round Workers by Sex and Years of School Completed, 1967, 1970, 1975 (persons 25 years of age and over)

Years of School Completed	1967 Median Income Men	Women	Women's Median Income as % of men's	1970 Median Income Men	Women	%	1975 Median Income Men	Women	%
Elementary school:									
less than 8 years	$ 4,831	$2,820	58.4	$ 6,043	$3,798	62.8	$ 8,647	$ 5,109	59.1
8 years	6,133	3,343	54.5	7,535	4,181	55.5	10,600	5,691	53.7
High school:									
1–3 years	6,891	3,704	53.8	8,514	4,655	54.7	11,511	6,355	55.2
4 years	7,732	4,499	58.2	9,567	5,580	58.3	13,542	7,777	57.4
College:									
1–3 years	8,816	5,253	59.6	11,183	6,604	59.1	14,989	9,126	60.9
4 years	10,909	6,372	58.4	13,264	8,156	61.5	17,477	10,349	59.2
5 years or more	12,510	7,823	62.5	14,747	9,581	65.0	19,658	13,138	66.8

SOURCES: 1967: Current Population Reports, series P-60, table 4.
1970: *Fact Sheet on the Earnings Gap*, U.S. Dept. of Labor, Employment Standards Administration, Women's Bureau.
1975: Current Population Reports, series P-60, no. 105, table 47.

ing female labor force participation rate during this period, and the fact that disproportionate numbers of these labor force entrants and reentrants went into clerical occupations. Sales workers stand out dramatically in all three years covered in table 4.5 as the one occupation in which the earnings gap is significantly greater than the average, being close to 60 percent of male earnings in each sample year. This appears to be the result of substantial occupational segregation by sex *within* this broad occupational category, with men more often found in high-paying commissioned, nonretail jobs, and women concentrated primarily in retail trade.

An examination of cohort profiles and earnings differentials by education suggests the possibility that, at least for women, greater job experience is not always translated into earnings gains to the same extent as for men. In chapter 3, this was primarily attributed to the different types of occupations in which men and women are predominately found.

Unemployment Differentials

The most familiar male-female differential is undoubtedly the earnings gap, and much of the attention given to economic inequality between the sexes has concentrated on this painfully obvious dimension. However, a complete understanding of the economic disadvantages to which women are subject requires that equal attention be given to the sex differential in unemployment rates. Not only do women earn substantially less than men, but they have a consistently higher rate of unemployment as well.

Table 4.2 and figure 4.6 show clearly three basic facts concerning the sex differential in unemployment: (1) the female unemployment rate has exceeded the male rate since 1948; (2) this gap between the two rates has varied procyclically and has been greatest at business cycle peaks; (2) recently the differential also appears to be increasing over time, although not at a steady rate. More specifically, female-male differences in unemployment rates since 1962 have tended to be significantly greater, in both absolute and relative terms, than those prior to that year.[13]

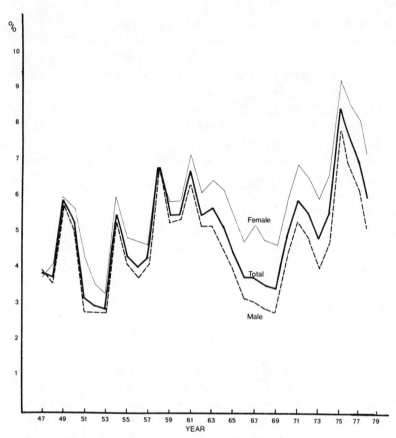

Figure 4.6.   Unemployment Rates, 1947–1978

SOURCE: *Employment and Earnings*, January 1979, pp. 154–55, tables 1 and 2.

These relationships between the two unemployment rates have also held for three major subgroups—men and women aged 25 and over, married men and women, and white men and women. It is interesting to note that the relationship between sex and unemployment among married people is reversed among single people and those in the "other" (widowed, divorced, or separated) category. However, the unemployment of married women is lower than the unemployment rates of all the other sex and marital status groups except married men. Within each sex, married people have the lowest, and single people the highest, rate of unemployment. Some of the unemployment differentials by marital status can be explained by average age differences among marital status groups. The relatively high unemployment among single people can be attributed to the fact that younger workers tend to be concentrated in this category, and thus marital status serves in part as a proxy for age. In particular, detailed Census data on unemployment among women cross-classified by both age and marital status indicate that the observed lower unemployment rate of married relative to single women is the result of the differing age distributions of these two groups. For example, in 1960, single women had a lower rate of unemployment than married women within every age group, but the unemployment rate for all married women was lower than that for all single women (Niemi 1970). This is consistent with prior theory which predicted that, within age groups, single women of a given age would have a lower incidence of unemployment than married women, because most of the reasons suggested for the relatively high unemployment experienced by married women relate to their status as a secondary earners, and apply with less force or not at all to the case of single women, particularly older single women.

Within three groups—nonwhites, teenagers, and those aged 20–24 —pre-1962 unemployment rates did not follow the general pattern of a higher rate for females than for males. However, this situation changed when the 1962–1969 expansion began. Since then the female unemployment rates have been higher than the corresponding rates for males among nonwhites, and until the 1975 recession, the same relationship was true for teenagers. Women aged 20–24 also had a higher rate of unemployment than did men in the same age group during most of the period since 1962. It appears that the 1962 reversal of the relative incidence of unemployment for men and women within these three groups is a specific and striking example of a more general phenomenon—the worsening of the relative unemployment position of women in recent years. For the bulk of the labor force, this deterioration took the less dramatic form of a widening of the already existing gap between the unemployment rates of women and men.

The fact that women's unemployment rates exceed men's is not inconsistent with labor supply theory; however, it is impossible to predict *a priori* the relative importance of sex differentials in spells and duration in the determination of this result. Table 4.7 presents data on average number of spells per labor force participant for men and women, which show a slightly greater incidence of unemployment spells among women in recent years, in contrast to the early 1960s. The indices of inter-labor force turnover presented in chapter 2 do not suggest that female inter-labor force mobility can provide sufficient

Table 4.7

Mean Annual Number of Unemployment Spells per Labor Force Participant, by Sex, 1959–1977

	Men	Women
1959	0.2880	0.2501
1960	0.3174	0.2839
1961	0.3318	0.3044
1962	0.3329	0.3191
1963	0.2957	0.2955
1964	0.2855	0.2993
1965	0.2450	0.2531
1966	0.2103	0.2399
1967	0.2083	0.2318
1968	0.1897	0.2299
1969	0.2037	0.2210
1970	0.2552	0.2548
1971	0.2662	0.2709
1972	0.2460	0.2615
1973	0.2222	0.2551
1974	0.2814	0.3023
1975	0.3113	0.3245
1976	0.3012	0.3115
1977	0.2756	0.2975

SOURCES: Computed from BLS, Special Labor Force Reports nos. 11, 19, 25, 38, 48, 62, 91, 107, 115, 127, 141, 162, 171, 181, 192, and 201, (Washington, D.C., various years).

NOTE: The following assumptions were made in estimating average spells per labor force participant: (1) those with three or more spells were estimated as having three spells; (2) those without work experience who were looking for work were estimated as having only one spell. Both assumptions will lead to an underestimate of spells, but it is not clear that this will systematically bias the sex differential.

explanation for the reversal of the gap between men and women in the incidence of unemployment spells. Although the importance of high inter-labor force turnover in raising the likelihood of female unemployment at any point in time is well documented (Niemi 1975), the data suggest that this turnover has been decreasing over time, thus leading us to expect a narrowing of the unemployment differential, not the reverse.

No doubt the leveling off of the growth in the labor force participation rates of older married women and the rapid growth in the participation of those under 35 have contributed to widening the gap between the unemployment rates of women and men. The younger group does have substantially higher rates of inter-labor force turnover and unemployment than those aged 35–64. However, the female-male differential in unemployment rates has widened within each age group, at the same time as female labor force turnover has fallen both in the aggregate and within each age group. Therefore, the changing age distribution of the female labor force can at best explain only part of the worsening unemployment situation of women.[14]

Table 4.8 presents three different estimates of average duration of unemployment in weeks. Both of the estimates of completed duration from the work experience survey show women's duration exceeding men's, a result that is perfectly consistent with search theory but which has not typically been recognized, given the usual CPS data on *interrupted* spells, which shows women's unemployment duration to be less than men's.[15] However, these estimates of average duration may disguise sharp differences between men and women in the distribution of weeks of unemployment, with men's duration showing a greater variance because of their greater likelihood of experiencing temporary layoff on the one hand, and their greater likelihood of remaining in the labor force for a long search on the other hand. The upward drift in unemployment rates for both sexes may be due to some increase in average duration but, unfortunately, work experience data have not been available for long enough to discern clear trends. The widening gap between the unemployment rates of men and women, however, is more likely to be due to the apparent reversal of the sex differential in the incidence of unemployment spells.

To some extent at least, these observed differences between the

Table 4.8

Average Duration of Unemployment in Weeks, by Sex, 1961-1977.

	Interrupted Spells		Estimates of Completed Spells[a]		Estimated Duration[b]	
	(1)	(2)	(3)	(4)	(5)	(6)
Year	Male	Female	Male	Female	Male	Female
1961	16.9	13.1	10.3	11.0	10.0	12.3
1962	16.3	12.1	9.9	10.0	8.1	10.1
1963	15.5	11.7	9.7	10.6	9.1	11.4
1964	14.5	11.6	9.1	9.7	8.4	10.8
1965	12.9	10.3	8.0	12.1	8.5	11.3
1966	11.6	8.5	7.1	7.7	7.9	10.4
1967	9.5[c]	7.5[c]	7.1	7.9	7.7	11.7
1968	9.4	7.5	6.8	7.9	7.9	10.9
1969	8.5	7.3	6.9	7.7	7.1	11.1
1970	9.5	7.9	9.1	9.2	9.0	12.0
1971	12.3	10.1	10.5	11.1	10.3	13.2
1972	13.4	10.6	10.0	10.5	10.3	13.1
1973	11.2	8.8	8.8	9.3	9.6	12.2
1974	10.9	8.4	9.1	9.3	8.9	11.5
1975	15.3	12.6	12.7	12.4	13.2	14.9
1976	17.3	14.0	12.3	11.6	12.1	14.3
1977	15.9	12.5	10.9	11.0	11.3	14.3

SOURCES: Cols. (1)–(2), 1961-1969: unpublished BLS data. 1970-1977: *Employment and Earnings*, January issues, 1971-1978. Col. (3)–(6): computed from BLS Special Labor Force Reports, nos. 11, 19, 25, 38, 48, 62, 91, 107, 115, 127, 141, 162, 171, 181, 192, and 201 (Washington, D.C., various years).

[a] Total weeks of unemployment were computed from the frequency distributions of duration, and divided by total number of spells of unemployment to give weeks per spell, or the average duration of a completed spell. To the extent that spells began before the year of the survey and lasted beyond the year of the survey, some interrupted spells are included.

[b] Estimated from the known relationship between unemployment rates and spells (see note 7).

$$DUR_{est} = (U/L) \frac{L \cdot 52}{N \cdot S} = \frac{52 \cdot U}{N \cdot S}$$

[c] Data available for second half of 1967 only.

earnings and unemployment rates of men and women obviously result from productivity differences between men and women, that is, differences in the quantity and quality of labor supplied, along the lines discussed in chapters 2 and 3. However, disturbing trends in relative earnings and unemployment rates and unexpected differentials in earnings within education groups suggest the need for a fuller explanation of these phenomena, incorporating not only factors affecting individual decisions on the supply side, but also important dimensions of the structure of labor markets and how they may impact differently on men and on women. Even before we look at discrimination as an additional explanatory factor in the differentiation of men and women in the market, we must be familar with some of the forces which cause the segmentation and internalization of labor markets. In the next section we will introduce some key concepts from the dual labor market literature and discuss some of their implications for sex differentials in earnings and unemployment. We will see that dual labor market theory is not a substitute for human capital and labor supply theory, but rather its complement in providing a fuller explanation of market outcomes.

Segmented Labor Markets

Although segmented labor market (SLM) theory encompasses a range of views about the important characteristics of market structure, it can be distinguished from the orthodox approach previously discussed by the importance attached to the characteristics of jobs and the process by which they are allocated.[16] Orthodox theory, although it recognizes the importance of demand fluctuations in the explanation of changes in market outcomes over the business cycle, emphasizes the importance of supply factors in the long-run determination of wages and employment. Market structure is not explicitly discussed as an independent factor governing market outcomes. As long as there is sufficient competition between employers and between workers, and as long as the structure of labor markets does not change systematically over time, these assumptions are reasonable. However, SLM theories are based on the recognition that, over time, technological change has dichotomized labor markets by creating a "primary" sphere, where skills are important in the production process, and a "secondary" sphere, where they are not.

The principal factor distinguishing jobs in the primary sector is the requirement of stability or low turnover. For historical reasons, some jobs have become technologically more sophisticated than others. These jobs must be filled by stable workers, because the relatively high costs of training and recruitment make turnover costly and a long-term relationship between the firm and the worker desirable. Jobs in the secondary sector are distinguished by menial or low-skilled work, little opportunity for advancement, and employment instability. The primary sector is characterized by high wages and low turnover, whereas the secondary sector is characterized by low wages and high turnover.

At first glance, it appears that this description of the workings of labor markets is entirely consistent with the orthodox approach, which predicts that individual differences in labor supply and human capital investment determine differences in wages, employment and occupational distribution. In other words, workers with a strong attachment to the labor force could invest in training by entering the primary sector, and could earn higher wages and be less vulnerable to unemployment. On the other hand, those with a low level of labor market commitment could choose not to invest in training, and could enter the secondary labor market, where they would earn lower wages and be more vulnerable to unemployment. However, this interpretation overlooks one of the major distinctions between the two approaches: whereas orthodox theory sees productivity differences between workers as being primarily related to differences between them in individual characteristics, SLM theory sees these differences as being related to the nature of their specific jobs as well. The firm's wage and personnel practices are seen to have an important independent effect on the determination of worker quality, in that the behavioral traits of workers associated with jobs in each sector are reinforced by the job experience itself and by the existence, or the absence, of performance-related rewards. Specifically, the quit rate will be negatively related to the firm's wage policy. This theory emphasizes the independent importance of firms' job allocation mechanisms in the explanation of individual differences in wages and employment stability. If turnover costs differ between firms, then wage differentials will persist even within groups of workers who are homogeneous in terms of initial productivity (Salop 1973).

Over time, duality in the labor market has intensified because of the growing importance of specific skills in the production process, as well as because of institutional changes, such as the unequal distribution of union strength across industries and the growing importance of minimum wages. The development of internal labor market theory (Doeringer and Piore 1971), partly in response to these changes, recognized the growing proportion of jobs which are allocated within large firms and organizations. An internal labor market is defined as "an administration unit . . . within which pricing and allocation of labor is governed by a set of administrative rules and procedures" (Doeringer and Piore 1971:1–2). The evolution of internal labor markets is closely tied to the growing importance of on-the-job training. Technological change has caused significant increases in the specificity of skills required within firms, and has thus increased not only the total cost of job training, but also the percentage of training costs borne by the employer. The development of internal labor markets has also been affected by the development of customary law, such as seniority rules, which have been reinforced by the growth of unions. Internal wage structures and promotion patterns that persist over time tend to become customary, and thus to be considered right, fair, and equitable.

In a world of internal labor markets, the market for entry-level jobs becomes the market for specific training options. Employers' and/or unions' differential estimates of the relative costs and returns from training alternative job applicants will determine the access of individuals to internal labor markets and their job assignments within the internal structure (Thurow 1975). Employers will base estimates of the costs of training on various background characteristics, such as education and IQ, which are correlated with adaptability to training. Differential expectations of turnover will also affect estimates of returns. Within internal labor markets, workers already hired are allocated to jobs according to experience and training, as well as expected stability. Thus competition is more limited higher on the promotion ladder, and those who do not make it into jobs with training opportunities will be relegated to the secondary labor market, where the jobs are characterized by limited training and advancement opportunities. This leads to occupational crowding of those groups that are discriminated against, which exacerbates those wage differentials created by differential access to training.

Dual labor market theory was initially developed in the 1960s to deal with problems of urban poverty, racial discrimination and the persistence of income inequality, but many of its constructs have important implications for the analysis of sex differentials in wages and employment.[17] Its concentration on the problems of disadvantaged workers, however, led to the neglect of some distinctions among primary jobs which are particularly important in the case of sex.[18] Even within internal labor markets, the job promotion paths may be very different for men and women with similar entry credentials. It may not be simply a question of slower promotion, but rather of completely different job tracking, with job stability among men rewarded by promotion through the managerial ranks, while women with similar entry level characteristics are promoted through a much shorter series of steps in the clerical category. Differences between men and women in job tracking within internal labor markets can have an important independent effect on job stability.

The structure of organizations plays a powerful role in creating work behavior. Women in low-mobility organizational situations develop attitudes and orientations that are sometimes said to be characteristic of those people as individuals or "women as a group," but that can more profitably be viewed as more universal *human* responses to blocked opportunities. (Kanter 1977:159).

The large representation of women within internal labor markets requires that the simple notion of two nonoverlapping labor markets be expanded to include a larger number of segmented labor markets, each of which is distinguished by a different combination of wages and turnover costs.

Without introducing overt wage discrimination, which involves paying equally productive workers different wage rates, and which will be discussed in chapter 5, SLM theory shows how restrictive hiring practices in the high-wage sectors can result in systematic wage differentials between the sexes, despite the equalization of wages and productivity on the individual level, and despite equal pay for all workers within each job category. Restrictive hiring practices are usually based on "statistical discrimination," which excludes individuals from consideration for high-wage jobs on a probabilistic basis, because they are members of groups which are viewed as being less stable *on average*. The concept of statistical discrimination is closely related to the concept of efficient search by employers. As prospective employees are searching for jobs, employers are searching for employees to fill job vacancies. In filling a particular job slot that has a wage attached to it, employers searching for new employees face a distribution of marginal products among the potential candidates for the job. However, individual marginal products are unknown and the employer must compare the cost of gathering information about individual productivity to the expected return in terms of increases in productivity of the worker eventually hired. The model of employer search is a variant of the search model previously discussed with marginal products replacing wages (Lippman and McCall 1976: part 1). In the search for information about productivity, employers can subdivide the pool of potential workers on the basis of readily observable characteristics, such as age, race, and sex, which are thought to be correlated in some crude way with productivity and/or stability. The employer can then discriminate between these groups on a statistical basis by restricting his search to the group that is believed to have the highest average productivity, or the group whose productivity is least expensive to ascertain.[19]

Phelps (1972), describes statistical discrimination in the case of women as follows:

The employer who seeks to maximize expected profit will discriminate against . . . women if he believes them to be less qualified, reliable, long-term, etc., on the average than . . . men, . . . and if the cost of gaining information about the individual applicants is excessive. . . . (S)ex is taken as a proxy for relevant data not sampled. (p. 659)

Statistical discrimination not only excludes women from job promotion ladders within internal labor markets but crowds their growing numbers into the more competitive secondary sector, where wages are lower.[20] Even if employers respond to women's growing labor force participation by moving more jobs into this sector, women's wages will remain relatively low.

In some respects, the predictions of SLM theories regarding patterns of wage and unemployment differentials between the sexes are similar to those of orthodox theory. For example, SLM theory would predict wage differentials between the sexes, which would widen with age because of the exclusion of women from primary jobs with promotion ladders. SLM theory would also predict that women would have higher unemployment rates than men for the same reasons. In addition, however, observed patterns and trends not predicted by the orthodox theory are also consistent with the SLM approach. The sharply widening gaps between men and women in wages and unemployment rates suggests the existence and growing importance of market constraints in the determination of market outcomes. Crowding will occur in the low-wage sectors if the demand for labor grows less rapidly than the supply of workers. The lack of change in the occupational dissimilarity index, along with the rapid growth in women's labor force participation, has meant that a growing fraction of the female labor force is concentrated in jobs in which women are overrepresented.[21] Within segmented labor markets, a rise in the labor force participation of women should increase the incidence of unemployment spells for women relative to men. Changes in unemployment duration will depend on the speed with which vacancies are filled. Overcrowding would also cause a widening of the wage gap as the productivity of jobs in the secondary or female sectors is depressed relative to the productivity in the primary or male sectors.

The existence of segmented labor markets and statistical discrimination has implications for cyclical variations, as well as patterns and trends, in employment and earnings by sex. In periods of sustained prosperity, the number of qualified men searching for employment falls, and the pool of unemployed men comes to be dominated by the least productive. Under these circumstances, even if the employers' initial belief that the average male marginal product exceeded the average female marginal product had been correct, it will now no longer be effective to use sex as a simple screening device. At this point, employers begin to search among the pool of unemployed women. This model of adaptive search behavior suggests the interesting implication that female employment and earnings would be more responsive to cyclical fluctuations than would male employment and earnings, at least initially. Some empirical results consistent with this theory have been obtained for nonwhite versus white workers (Kosters and Welch 1972; Wohlstetter and Coleman 1972), but it has not yet been applied directly to women and men.

We do not view SLM theory as an alternative to the orthodox theory discussed above. Rather, it complements that theory by adding to it a necessary institutional and historical context. In both theories, differences in training between individuals are the key to individual differences in wages and employment. Both theories assume profit maximization and an equalization of productivities and wages, although in the case of SLM theory, this equalization takes place on average across individuals within a job category, rather than over time for a given individual. The major difference between the theories is one of emphasis, with orthodox theory highlighting the implications of individual choice and SLM theory describing the structural factors constraining choice, which may differentially impact on different groups.

In chapter 5, we will continue our discussion of demand by looking at discrimination explicitly as an independent force affecting differentials in market outcomes. We will next examine the empirical literature on wage and unemployment differentials to discover what evidence exists concerning the relative contributions of supply and demand variables to these market outcomes. Finally, all these factors will be brought together in a dynamic context in order to explain the persistence of sex differentials in occupational distribution, wages and unemployment, despite a rapid increase in women's labor force participation and career aspirations.

NOTES

1. In the case of monopoly in the product market, the marginal revenue product would be equated to the wage rate.

2. This prediction requires the additional assumption that, within education groups, there are no differences in productivity.

3. Madden (1975) has developed an elaborate rationalization for the usefulness of the monopsony approach in the case of sex, despite the existence of many employers. This is based on three conditions: (1) the existence of male market power; (2) the differentiability of the labor market by sex; and (3) the perception of employers that female workers are less responsive to wage changes than male workers. Although general and imprecise, this approach highlights an important dimension of sex differences in earnings.

4. Some preliminary testing of the hypothesis of differing supply elasticities for men and women in individual labor markets is found in Cardwell and Rosenzweig (1975).

5. As women's labor force participation rates have increased, the percentage in unions has actually declined over the last ten years (Wertheimer 1976).

6. Lippman and McCall (1976) is the most recent and comprehensive review of this literature.

7. $U = SPELLS \times DURATION/52$

> where SPELLS = total number of spells of unemployment experienced during the year
> DURATION = average number of weeks per spell
> U = total number of unemployed per week
> Therefore $U/L = (SPELLS/L \times 52)(DURATION)$

8. "A shift from outside the labor force into paid employment or *vice versa* can be viewed as an inter-industry job change. There are two possible ways of making any job shift. The first is to engage in job search as a full-time activity until an acceptable job is found, after first leaving one's old job. Either an intra-labor force move or an inter-labor force move made in this fashion involves a transitional period of unemployment while the search is taking place. The more usual method of job changing, however, is to engage in search as a part-time activity, leaving one's old job only after a new one has been obtained. In the case of a shift from one market job to another or from the market to the nonmarket sector, this second method does not involve transitional unemployment, for having a job takes precedence over seeking work in the BLS definitions of employment and unemployment. On the other hand, a housewife or student who is seeking work in the market is defined as unemployed, with the search for a job taking precedence over any nonmarket activity. Thus a given level of inter-labor force turnover will be associated with a higher unemployment rate than the same level of intra-labor force turnover" (Niemi 1977:22).

9. In fact, some of the very factors which affect sex differentials in search behavior are the same factors which would limit the elasticity of female supply to the individual firm in the case of monopsony.

10. On the one hand, it could be expected that women's search costs would be higher than men's because of more viable nonmarket opportunities, and their returns would be lower because discrimination reduces the number and level of wage offers received per unit of time spent searching. This would lead to shorter average duration for women. On the other hand, it could be argued that, if search is not a full-time activity for women but can be seen as complementary to nonmarket work, then

women's costs of search could be lower. In this case, their geographic immobility and inflexible job requirements might lead them to search longer on the average than men (Barrett and Morgenstern 1974).

11. Note that the data in figures 4.4 and 4.5 are for median income, rather than median earnings, as in table 4.1. The latter would ideally be preferable, but is unavailable by age. Therefore, we must make the not unreasonable assumption that, *among year-round full-time workers*, almost all annual income is actually derived from earnings, and thus the age-*income* profiles approximate age-*earnings* profiles and are a fairly unbiased representation of the variation in earning power with age. This same *caveat* applies to figure 3.9, and to the time-series data on income by race and sex in table 4.4.

12. The earnings gap, a handy summary statistic for indicating the relative positions of men and women, is defined as the percentage (of male earnings) by which male earnings (M) exceed female earnings (F); i.e., $1 - F/M$ or $(M-F)/M$.

13. Niemi (1977) regressed the female-male unemployment differential on measures of cycle and trend for 1950–1972 and found that the upward trend in labor force participation for women resulted in a statistically significant increase in their absolute and relative unemployment over time.

14. See Niemi (1977) for further evidence on and discussion of these points.

15. Search theory makes predictions about the length of a completed spell of unemployment. However, CPS data on unemployment duration only measure the average length of spells in progress up to the date of the sample survey. It is unclear whether the CPS sample statistic on unemployment duration is an under- or overestimate of the length of completed spells. On the one hand, under stable economic conditions, measured spells are on the average halfway through their full length at the time of the survey, leading to a downward "interruption bias." On the other hand, it is spells with longer than average full lengths that are more likely to be in progress at the time of the survey, leading to an upward "length bias." Salant (1977) has shown that the length bias dominates, giving the duration data an upward bias; however, the extent of the overestimate will differ among demographic groups. We would expect that men's duration is more overestimated than women's because of women's somewhat greater tendency to leave the labor force. Evidence from the Work Experience Survey (WES) on completed spells suggests that this bias has had the effect of making women's average unemployment duration look shorter than men's, when in fact the opposite is the case.

16. Much of this discussion is taken from two reviews of the orthodox and SLM approaches—one written from an orthodox point of view (Cain 1976) and one from a radical point of view (Gordon 1972).

17. A good application of SLM approach to sex differentials can be found in Blau 1977, ch. 2.

18. Piore (1975) broadens dual labor market theory to include different tiers within the primary sector, but he explicitly states that his categorization applies to men but not to women (p. 134).

19. For example, if test scores are more reliable for one group than another, it will be cheaper to search among the group with more reliable scores.

20. Labor market barriers cause the supply of female labor to be greater in feminine occupations (including nonmarket work in the home) and smaller in masculine ocupa-

tions than would be the case if the market were free to adjust. Consequently, marginal productivity and wages are depressed in the overcrowded female occupations (Bergmann 1974:103–10).

21. In 1960, women in occupations in which women were overrepresented (45 percent or more of occupation) made up 23.9 percent of the labor force. By 1970, the proportion of women in these occupations had advanced to 27.4 percent (Bergmann and Adelman 1973:511).

Chapter 5

Discrimination and the Dynamic Determinants of Wages and Unemployment

Discrimination in the labor market occurs whenever workers who are equally productive on average are treated differently, either in hiring, wage rates, job assignment, promotion or firing. Prejudice against any group (in this case, working women) can be defined as discrimination *in intent*, or direct discrimination. Custom, institutions and historical circumstances may interact in such a way as to cause discrimination *in practice* as well, even though prejudice as such is not a factor. Discrimination against women, regardless of its initiating cause, will result in higher unemployment rates, as well as lower earnings, than would be the case without discrimination. To date, theoretical models of sex and race discrimination have concentrated on the resulting wage differentials and neglected the possibility of differential unemployment rates. This is because wage flexibility and supply inelasticity have been implicitly or explicitly assumed. However, in the presence of imperfect information and wage rigidities, the preference for discrimination cannot be completely satisfied via differential wage rates (Gilman 1965). Unemployment differentials will result as well. Thus, to the extent that social custom, legal and/or union minimum wages, pressures for equal pay, and similar forces tend to make wage rates relatively inflexible downward, theories of discrimination are equally relevant to both phenomena. A great deal of wage inflexibility does exist in reality. In its absence, the gap between the unemployment rates of women and men would be narrowed, but the male-female earnings differential would be even wider than it actually is.

193

The terms "prejudice" and "discrimination" are often used as if they were synonymous, but this is an imprecise usage that should be avoided. Obviously, discrimination may result from prejudice, but it is also possible, under certain conditions, for discrimination to occur in the absence of any prejudice. On the other hand, it may sometimes be impossible for the prejudiced to put their feelings into action by practicing discrimination. Thus we shall use the term "prejudice" to denote negative feelings with regard to women, resulting in the desire to discriminate or to avoid association with women, at least in certain roles. Discrimination actually occurs when women are treated differently than men of equal productivity, either by being paid lower wages on the average or by not being hired for some jobs.

In the first part of the chapter, various theories of discrimination will be critically reviewed and their implications for wage and unemployment differentials derived. This will be followed by a review of the empirical literature on wage and unemployment differentials. As two dimensions of inequality, wages and unemployment have clear conceptual links which have led to similar methodological approaches. Usually, supply differences between men and women are controlled for, and unexplained residuals are interpreted as measures either of discrimination or of excluded and/or unmeasurable differences in supply. An analysis of these results will attempt to point out the strengths and weaknesses of the orthodox approach. Findings from these studies suggest the threads of a dynamic story of the evolution and persistence of sex differentials over time, which will be summarized in the final section of this chapter.

Discrimination

Several theories of discrimination have been developed by economists in the attempt to explain the economic positions of minorities and women, in particular their lower earnings. Frequently an approach to discrimination that was originally developed to deal with racial differentials will later be expanded to apply to sex differentials as well. Although the positions of women and nonwhites are clearly far from completely analogous in many respects, within the relatively narrow confines of the determination of their earnings and unemployment rates in the labor market, the effects of discrimination by race and be sex are quite similar.

The theory of discrimination developed by Becker (1957, 2d ed. 1971) deals explicitly with the implications of direct discrimination or prejudice. It is based on the behavioral assumption that "if an individual has a 'taste for discrimination,' he must act *as if* he were willing to pay something, either directly or in the form of a reduced income, to be associated with some persons instead of others" (2d ed., p. 49). Employers, fellow employees and consumers are all seen as potential discriminators. This model is a particular application of the basic concept of utility maximization in the context of a perfectly competitive economy, and assumes perfect wage flexibility.

Discrimination by employers will create wage differentials over and above those to be expected on the basis of differences in productivity alone. Employers discriminating against women will hire men at higher wages than they would have to pay equally productive women, in order to satisfy a taste for discrimination. These prejudiced employers, when faced with female workers available at the money wage W_w, act *as if* the net wage rate were $W_w (1 + d_i)$, where d_i is the employer's "discrimination coefficient" against women. This discrimination coefficient represents a nonpecuniary cost of contact with women, and $W_w d_i$ is the monetary equivalent of this nonmonetary cost. In the short run, differing tastes for discrimination among employers will be reflected in a market-clearing wage differential that will be a function of the proportion of the labor force composed of the group discriminated against, and of the distribution of tastes for discrimination among employers. One implication of this theory is that, in the long run, market discrimination will tend to be slightly less in competitive industries than in monopolistic ones. Under competitive conditions, employers who do not discriminate make more profits by hiring equally productive but cheaper workers, and are able to grow relative to their discriminating competitors. In fact, under one set of assumptions,[1] one unprejudiced producer in a competitive market could continue growing indefinitely at the expense of his higher-cost rivals, eventually forcing them all out of business and taking over the entire market. Becker's (2d ed., p. 48) finding of a greater ratio of black to white workers in competitive than in monopolistic industries is consistent with the existence of employer discrimination against blacks. Similar data on women have not been developed.

Prejudiced individuals discriminate not only in their role as employers, but as fellow employees and consumers as well. The prejudiced male employee, when offered the money wage W_m for a job which entails working with female coworkers, acts *as if* the net wage rate were $W_m (1-d_j)$, where d_j is his discrimination coefficient against women, and $W_m d_j$ is the monetary equivalent of the nonmonetary cost of association with women. Prejudiced coworkers may refuse to work with females unless they are paid a premium to do so. Like employer discrimination, discrimination by employees is also expected to create wage differentials, but of a different sort. If men are only willing to work alongside of women when they are compensated by a higher wage, then men in integrated work situations would be expected to earn higher wages than equally productive men in segregated surroundings. Therefore, one implication of employee discrimination is that the greater the proportion of women in a particular skill group, the greater the dispersion of earnings of men in that same skill group (Chiswick 1973). Although this implication has not been tested using data on women and men, Chiswick has found this to be true in the case of whites and nonwhites.

Employee discrimination may also explain why the wage gap between the sexes increases with education level. The higher the job level, the more costly it will be for the employer to hire a woman rather than a man with the same skills. Not only will the resistance of male subordinates be greater the higher the job level of the woman to be hired, but the actual costs of compensating them will be greater because larger numbers of workers will fall below that job level in the job hierarchy (Arrow 1972).

Finally, prejudiced consumers may refuse to purchase goods and services from women unless these are less expensive than those obtainable from males. This is most likely to be the case in professional occupations such as doctors and lawyers. Such a consumer, faced with the opportunity to purchase services produced by women at a price P per unit, acts *as if* the net price were $P (1 + d_k)$, where d_k is his discrimination coefficient, and Pd_k is the monetary equivalent of this nonmonetary cost. In a study based on individual data from the 1960 Census, Victor Fuchs (1971) found that the female-male ratio of average hourly earnings was lowest among self-employed workers, and also that a much smaller proportion of female than of male workers were in the self-employed category. In general, compared with wage and salary earners in private industry and with government employees, the self-employed have the most immediate contact with their consumers. Fuchs concludes that the observed patterns of earnings differentials and occupational distribution are consistent with the hypothesis of consumer discrimination. This finding has recently been corroborated in a study using data from the 1970 Census (Brown 1976).

Because of consumer and/or employee discrimination, even unprejudiced employers may refuse to hire women unless they can be paid a wage low enough to compensate for their lower value (due to consumer discrimination) and/or their higher cost (due to coworker discrimination) to the firm. In the presence of wage rigidities, occupational segregation and unemployment differentials are obvious implications of Becker's theory, if tastes for discrimination vary systematically with industry and/or occupation.

Following Becker's pioneering analysis, work by economists in the area of discrimination has developed along two lines, which unfortunately have tended to remain largely independent of and separate from one another. First, there has been further theoretical development and refinement; this has involved both modifications of Becker's original theory and the formulation of alternative theories or hypotheses about how market discrimination takes place. Although a substantial theoretical literature exists, the derivation and direct rigorous testing of its empirical implications has been minimal. The findings of Becker, Chiswick, and Fuchs mentioned above are consistent with some of the hypotheses deduced from discrimination theory, but in no way do they represent a full test of the theory.

The second line of development has been the technique of testing for the existence of discrimination *indirectly*, by testing a nondiscriminatory (human capital) model of wage and/or unemployment differentials, and estimating the extent of discrimination residually as the fraction of the wage of unemployment gap between the sexes unexplained by factors relating to productivity. We will thoroughly review this empirical literature on sex differentials in the next section of this chapter. We first assess the developments in the theory of discrimination that occurred in the 1960s and 1970s.

Kenneth Arrow (1973) further develops Becker's model and attempts to relate it more closely to the theory of general competitive equilibrium. He derives the long-run implication that in Becker's model, if there are no costs of adjustment, wages between men and women or blacks and whites with identical skills will be equalized and perfect segregation will be the result, as employers adjust their work force in search of the cheapest labor, and workers switch employers in search of the highest wages. As a result, Arrow and Thurow, among others, are dubious about the ability of Becker's theory of discrimination in its pure form to explain the persistence of earnings gaps over time between equally skilled workers. In fact, Thurow (1975) argues that

[t]he amount of discrimination in the economic system is not determined by the average discrimination coefficient of whites (or men) but by the marginal discrimination coefficient—the man with the smallest discrimination coefficient. If there were any employers with zero or low discrimination coefficients against black (or female) employees or any capitalists willing to lend money to black (or female) entrepreneurs, it would be possible to set up a business that only employed black (or female) labor at their lower wage rates. Since the firm would be paying lower wage rates it would be making profits and could afford to sell its output for less than firms practicing discrimination and hiring high-cost white (or male) labor. The firm with only black (or female) employees would drive white (or male) firms out of business or force them to quit practicing discrimination. Since there clearly are individuals who do not have discrimination coefficients or who would be willing to lend money to black (or female) entrepreneurs in exchange for large profits, the question arises as to how discrimination has been able to last for decades. The economic pressures of a competititve market should have eliminated it long ago (p. 160).

Although their perceptions of this problem with the theory of discrimination are thus quite similar, Arrow and Thurow explain the persistence of discrimination differently. In fact, Thurow specifically takes issue with and discards Arrow's principal explanation, which is that there are important fixed costs of adjustment which prevent wage differentials from being eliminated even in the long run. For example, if discrimination by coworkers is an important consideration, then marginal adjustments (i.e., adding some women workers to a previously all-male labor force) will increase rather than reduce costs. Thus adjustments to changes in relative wages must be discontinuous in nature, involving, for example, firing the entire male work force and replacing them all with female workers. Given the personnel costs of hiring and/or training which are fixed and the sunk costs for workers already hired, it will not pay to make such a shift unless the wage differential is sufficiently large. The type of labor market situation in which Arrow visualizes sunk personnel costs as being of particular relevance in explaining the persistence of discrimination over time can be readily applied to the case of women workers because of the rapid growth in their labor force participation rates.

If we start from a position where (women) workers enter in an essentially all-(male) world, the discriminatory feelings by employers and by employees, both of the same and of complementary types, will lead to a difference in wages. The forces of competition and the tendency to profit-maximization operate to mitigate these differences. However, the basic fact of a personnel investment prevents these counteracting tendencies from working with full force. In the end, we remain with wage differences coupled with tendencies to segregation. (Arrow 1973:23)

As indicated above, Thurow finds this explanation for the persistence of discrimination unsatisfactory, but his reasons for rejecting it appears to be based, at least in part, on a misinterpretation. Thurow describes Arrow's analysis as resting on "the distinction between a local and a global optimum" (p. 161). He criticizes Arrow for relying on employer ignorance of the point of true profit maximization to explain the persistence of wage gaps over time. However, this analysis actually relies, not on employer ignorance, but on a real (and correctly perceived) difference in the cost of hiring women for an established employer with an originally all-male labor force, as opposed to a new employer just entering the labor market. The latter would clearly maximize profits by hiring women if their wages are lower than those of equally productive men. However, the former employer is in a situation analogous to a firm with obsolete capital equipment which cannot be replaced piecemeal with more modern equipment. Given the "all or nothing" nature of the change-over from old to new production techniques, and the capital loss that the firm would suffer if it scrapped the old equipment, profit-maximization may result in the firm's continuing to replace and even expand its old-fashioned equipment for a substantial period to time, or even indefinitely. Similarly, the employer who keeps his labor force exclusively male, despite the fact that equally productive women are available more cheaply, does not do so because he is ignorant of the "global optimum" involving an all-female labor force. He is well aware of the existence of this point, but he is equally aware that the capital loss he would sustain in firing his entire male labor force would more than offset the increase in profits. The "global optimum" is simply not the point of profit-maximization for the already-established employer; it is fixed personnel costs, rather than ignorance, that cause discriminatory practices, once established, to show a tendency to persist even in the long run.

Despite their disagreement as to the importance of adjustment costs, Arrow and Thurow tend to agree with one another, and with several other theorists in this area, that imperfect information and employer uncertainty concerning the productivity of men and women play a role in generating and perpetuating sex differentials in earnings. This approach encompasses several variations on the theme of "statis-tical discrimination," a concept first introduced in our discussion of internal labor markets in chapter 4.

Statistical discrimination can occur either on the purely erroneous ground of consistent underestimation of female productive capacities or if the *average* productivities of men and women are actually unequal. However, if average productivities of men and women differ, the resulting average wage differentials cannot be attributed to market discrimination as it has been defined here, but must be explained be differentials on the supply side previously discussed. *Individual* women, however, may still be seen as being discriminated against in that they are judged and compensated on the basis of group averages, which underestimate their actual individual productivity.

Aigner and Cain (1977) take the view that erroneous statistical discrimination will be at least as transient as discrimination based on prejudice, under competitive conditions. In the long run, employers will not persist in believing that men are more productive than women, if in fact their productivities are equal.

Indeed . . . a theory of discrimination based on employers' mistakes is even harder to accept than the explanation based on employers' tastes for discrimination, because the "tastes" are at least presumed to provide a source of "psychic gain" (utility) to the discriminator. (Aigner and Cain 1977:177)

Actually, a theory of statistical discrimination based on erroneous estimates of female productivity comes very close to the theory of discrimination based on prejudice. The long-run implications are the same in both cases: the least prejudiced or the least misinformed employers will be enabled to expand relative to the others, and discrimination will tend to be eliminated by competitive pressures. In fact, the line between ignorance and deliberate prejudice is often unclear; as Arrow indicates, productive capacity may be deliberately (although not necessarily consciously) underestimated as a way to provide a more socially acceptable rationalization for what is really an unacknowledged prejudice.

Neither discrimination theory based on prejudice nor discrimination theory based on erroneous information provide any predictions about unemployment rates unless wage rigidities are assumed. However, to the extent that women's wages are rigid in the downward direction, discrimination against women will result in relatively higher unemployment rates for them as well.

Now that we have discussed the theoretical considerations on the supply (labor supply and human capital theory) and demand (SLM theory and discrimination theory) sides which are thought to be relevant to the determination of wages and unemployment for men and women, we will examine the empirical evidence to see whether and how these theories have been tested against the data. Although certain interpretations were suggested by the examination of crude evidence in chapter 4, it is only through regression analysis and other statistical techniques that behavioral relationships can be established with more confidence. In the discussion that follows, we will highlight the major findings and demonstrate the major shortcomings of prevalent methodologies. The findings from these studies will document some of the important links of the vicious circle in which women appear to be trapped.

Empirical Analysis

WAGE DIFFERENTIALS

As was noted above, all the empirical work that has been done on the sex differential in earnings has approached discrimination indirectly, as a residual, by systematically adjusting for all other factors that cause the earnings of women to be less than those of men. Although the existence of the sizeable wage gap that we observe obviously requires explanation, it does not, in and of itself, necessarily imply that there is discrimination by sex; a wage gap would exist in the absence of discrimination if male workers were on the average more productive than female workers. As we have seen, direct market discrimination exists when individuals or groups who are equally productive are paid different wage rates.

We will summarize the major studies that have attempted to decompose the male-female earnings gap by adjusting for all measurable differences between men and women that might be expected to affect differential productivity.[2] Such factors include hours of work, age, marital status, city size, region, seniority, unionization, turnover, absenteeism, education, health, occupation, amount and continuity of job experience, and number of years out of the labor force. These studies are not guided in any rigorous way by a theory of discrimination, but rather depend on the general theory of wage determination via supply and demand in the labor market.

Table A5.1 (in the appendix to this chapter) provides an overview of twenty-one important studies of male-female earnings differences—sixteen dealing with male and female workers generally, and five covering specific professional occupations. This is by no means an exhaustive list, but it does include the most important analyses, and is as detailed and complete as possible without becoming unmanageably cumbersome. Column 1 lists the author(s), and column 2 lists the data sources used and the particular population subgroup studied, The observed earnings ratio, F/M, in column 3, requires some clarification. Conceptually, it is simply the average earnings of women divided by the average earnings of men. Thus a ratio of 1.00 implies that men and women earn the same amount, while a ratio of .50 implies that women earn only half as much as men do. However, as the descriptions in the parentheses indicate, the definition of earnings varies considerably across studies, and therefore these earnings ratios are not directly comparable to one another. Most importantly, some studies use an annual earnings or income measure, while others use an hourly wage rate. The observed female-male earnings ratio is typically higher for hourly than for annual earnings, as the latter type of ratio includes the effects of differences in both wage rates and hours worked, and women on the average work fewer hours per year than men. The effect of differences in hours worked is largely mitigated, but not completely eliminated, by looking at the annual earnings of only year-round, full-time workers. However, even among full-time workers (those working thirty-five or more hours per week), the average work week among women is approximately 10 percent shorter than that for men.[3] The studies using annual earnings figures must include hours of work as an adjustment factor of control influencing earnings, while hourly wage data are of course "preadjusted," or free of the influence of labor supply differences. One should note, however, that annual hours worked may reflect available opportunities or demand variations instead of, or as well as, individual choice or supply variations. We will return to this important and difficult question in relation to all or most of the controls used to account for earnings differences. Supply and demand influences tend to be intermingled, and it is often unclear to what extent "objective" or supposedly nondiscriminatory factors really reflect supply differences alone.

Column 5, the controls used, gives the particular factors from the list above which each study uses to adjust the earnings ratio, and column 4 presents the adjusted earnings ratio $(F/M)^*$, once the influence of the controls listed has been removed. The adjusted ratios are generally higher than the observed ratios, although the difference in some cases is zero or negligible. The percentage of the earnings gap "explained," as presented in column 6, is equal to $\dfrac{(F/M)^* - F/M}{(1 - F/M)}$, the amount by which the gap narrowed as a result of the adjustments divided by the size of the original gap. For example, the first study in the table (Sanborn) found that women earned 58 percent as much as men in 1949, or that the earnings gap was equal to 42 percent of male earnings $(1 - F/M)$. However, after adjusting for age, education, hours of work, urbanness, race, and occupation, Sanborn showed that women earned 76 percent as much as similar men, or that the gap narrowed to 24 percent of male earnings after allowing for the influence of these factors. Thus these factors account for $\dfrac{.76 - .58}{.42}$, or 43 percent of the difference between the earnings of men and women. The remaining 57 percent of the original difference, amounting to 24 percent of male earnings, remains unaccounted for. This residual may be attributed to "discrimination" in some cases, but, as we shall see, such an interpretation can be questioned on a variety of grounds and should be approached with caution.

Table A5.1 makes only too evident the diversity and noncomparability of the results. Since each of these studies has used a different data base, and since, as discussed above, the measure of earnings used has also varied, they have started their analyses with varying measures of the gross (or observed) earnings gap between men and women. These have ranged from about 60 to 20 percent of male earnings, except among young and single people and professional workers, for whom the gap is smaller. The net earnings gap, unexplained after adjustment, was still found to be at least 20 to 25 percent of male earnings in most of these studies, although less than this in those studies that covered academic or professional occupations only. However, even these adjusted earnings gaps are difficult to compare because some studies only adjusted for a few key factors, such as experience and job tenure, while other studies adjusted for a long list of variables, not all of which are closely or uniquely linked to human capital theory.

Given the orthodox model of wage determination, the fact that men earn more than women need not imply that sex discrimination exists. Wage rates will differ if men and women have different amounts of human capital or if they face differing market conditions because of different patterns of occupational choice. Thus these empirical studies attempt to control or adjust for all determinants of wages related to individual productivity or general market conditions. The residual gap between male and female earnings may then be interpreted as an estimate of the quantitative dimension of sex discrimination, but it can be seen as an over- or underestimate, depending not only on the point of view and interpretation of the observer, but also on whether firm-specific or societal discrimination is being measured.

Those who see the unexplained wage gap as an overestimate of the importance of discrimination are more concerned with direct firm-specific discrimination and emphasize the importance of certain productivity differences that are not easily observable and measurable. These include differences in quality of schooling and postschool training which are not captured in a simple one-dimensional measure such as number of years of schooling or experience. This approach looks to differences such as these, rather than to discrimination, in seeking to explain the unexplained portion of the earnings gap.

However, even if we could measure and allow for any and all productivity differences by sex stemming from differing education, training, and work commitment, it is extremely unlikely that we could ever completely account for the entire gap between the earnings of men and women. One can argue with at least equal justification that variables such as occupation and work experience, which are among the most important with respect to sex differentials in earnings, are in part representative of different opportunities rather than different qualifications, and that much of the difference in productivity itself is likely to be the result of indirect discrimination, frequently referred to as role differentiation. Under this interpretation, the unexplained portion of the earnings gap becomes a lower limit or underestimate of the total degree of societal discrimination against women, who are conditioned to expect to spend a substantial proportion of their lives outside the labor force, and are implicitly or explicitly discouraged from investing heavily in market-oriented skills and career preparation. Direct discrimination by individual firms against women in the labor market reinforces this effect, and helps to make this socially conditioned expectation of secondary status a self-fulfilling prophecy.

In fact, as figure 5.1 illustrates, the unexplained portion of the male-female earnings gap is an underestimate of even the direct component of discrimination against women. Because the labor supply curve of women is at least somewhat elastic, the full effect of the discrimination coefficient is not reflected in the equilibrium wage differential. In this figure, D = VMP is the marginal productivity curve for labor (male or female) of a given skill level; it is also the *demand* curve for male labor, against which there is no discrimination. Discrimination against women lowers the demand for female labor to D'; the distance between D and D' represents the nonpecuniary cost of hiring women. Only if the supply curve of female labor is perfectly inelastic (S'), however, will the full impact of tastes for discrimination make itself felt on relative wages. If that were the case, equally productive men and women would earn OW and $OW/(1 + d)$, respectively, implying an earnings gap of AC or $dW/(1 + d)$. In the usual situation, the relevant labor supply will be more like S than S', the female wage will be OW', and the wage gap will be only WW'. However, female employment will be lower (ON' as opposed to ON) because fewer women will be willing to work at the low wages offered by biased employers.

Putting aside for the moment the probably unanswerable question as to whether the residual wage gap significantly over- or underestimates discrimination against women, let us examine the various estimation techniques that have been used in arriving at the array of measures presented in table A5.1. The simplest technique is that of frequency distributions, used by Sanborn, Fuchs, Gwartney and Stroup, Cohen, and Bayer and Astin. For example, if women work fewer hours than men do, this can be adjusted for by multiplying female income by the ratio of male to female hours of work. The ratio of this adjusted female income to male income will be greater than the observed ratio by the same proportion that male hours exceed female hours, and serves as an estimate of what women would earn if they worked as many hours as men do. Successive or simultaneous standardization for other characteristics, such as education, occupation, and age, allows them to predict what women would earn if they had the same level of education, occupational distribution, and age distribution as male workers. Like more sophisticated standardization techniques, this involves the familiar "index number problem" of what

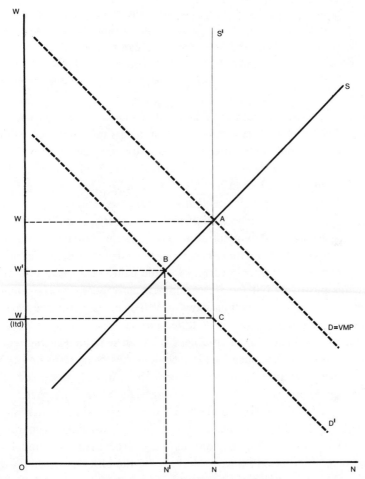

Figure 5.1.   Direct Discrimination and the Wage Gap.

weights to use. The procedure described above predicts what women would earn if they had male characteristics, and compares this adjusted earnings figure to actual male earnings. Alternatively, one could predict what men would earn if they had female characteristics and compare this to actual female earnings. These two procedures may yield different estimates of the residual earnings gap.

The most widely used statistical technique in these studies is multiple regression analysis, which estimates the relationship between earnings as the dependent variable, and the set of characteristics or controls as the independent variables. The portion of the earnings gap attributable to each of the characteristics can then be estimated from the regression coefficients. In its simplest form, this involves a single earnings equation which includes sex as a dummy variable equal to 1 for women and 0 for men. The studies by Cohen and by Gordon, Morton and Braden both employ this technique. If the coefficient of the sex variable is negative and significant, this indicates that women earn less than men even after the effects of other characteristics are accounted for, and this coefficient can be interpreted as a measure of sex discrimination. However, this approach is biased and therefore unsatisfactory. The problem is that the "earnings structure"—the relationship between earnings and various characteristics such as education, experience and marital status—is not the same for men and women. A year of education or experience tends to raise male earnings more than it raises female earnings, while being married affects male earnings positively but female earnings negatively. In more technical terms, significant interactions may exist between sex and the various other characteristics, and can be tested for.

One way to deal with the problem is to run separate earnings equations for men and women.[4] This technique has been employed in all the studies quoted in table A5.1 except those already discussed. The estimated relationships between earnings and various characteristics for men and women can then be used to calculate what women would earn if they had male characteristics or the male earnings structure, or what men would earn if they had female characteristics or the female earnings structure; and thus to decompose the observed earnings differential into its "objective" and "discriminatory" components. The earnings ratio adjusted for differences in objective factors can be estimated either by comparing men's actual wages with what women could earn if they had their own earnings structure but men's characteristics, or alternatively by comparing women's actual wages with what men would earn if they had women's characteristics but their own earnings structure. However, this method has the same index number problem referred to above. In some cases, the choice of weights will make little difference to the results, while in other cases the results may vary considerably.[5]

However, disagreement as to what independent variables are important and should enter the earnings equations, and index number problems as to which weights to use are not, unfortunately, the only estimation difficulties that arise in analyzing male-female earnings differences. It can be argued that, even using separate equations for men and women, ordinary least squares results are inadequate and biased. One refinement is to apply the more complicated technique of two-stage least squares to estimate the determinants of earnings and labor supply simultaneously, because they do mutually influence one another. As Mincer and Polachek express it:

Since lifetime work experience depends, in part, on prior wage levels and expectations, our experience variables are, in part, *determined* as well as *determining*. If so, the residual in our wage equations is correlated with the experience variables, and the estimates of coefficients which we interpreted as investment ratios are biased (Mincer and Polachek 1974:S98).

Although Mincer and Polachek assert that their reestimation of the earnings function by two-stage least squares leaves their conclusions from the ordinary least squares results unchanged, recent reestimates of Mincer and Polachek's regressions by Sandell and Shapiro (1978) suggest that their two-stage least squares estimates were themselves seriously biased, because of the inclusion of children and home time in the first stage equation as exogenous variables. However, reestimates by Sandell and Shapiro (1978) and Mincer and Polachek (1978), in which home time is treated as endogenous, result in conflicting conclusions about the percent of the wage gap explained, with Sandell and Shapiro claiming only 23 percent, and Mincer and Polachek claiming as much as 49 percent. Nonetheless, this question of simultaneity is a very serious one and certainly deserves further attention in future research. To the extent that wages themselves determine lifetime labor supply and human capital investment, the independent effect of productivity on wages is overestimated.

A related technique for dealing with simultaneity problems has been to estimate reduced form and structural equations separately, and to obtain estimates of the importance of discrimination for each.[6] The reduced form equation seeks to explain the wage rate only on the basis of characteristics that are truly exogenous to the individual, rather than simultaneously determined with wage rates. For example, family background variables would be included in the reduced form equation as independent variables, but education and occupation would not. The latter variables would, however, be included in the structural equation. Blinder summarizes the distinction between these two versions of the wage equation as follows:

[W]e present two wage-equation estimates. The reduced form estimates—which are always unbiased— . . . [and t]he structural estimates—which are biased unless the error terms are uncorrelated. . . . Very roughly speaking, the structural estimates can be thought of as the conditional expectation of . . . the wage, given the individual's present socioeconomic condition; and the reduced form can be thought of as the conditional expectation of . . . the wage, given the circumstances of his [sic] birth (Blinder 1973:442).

In table A5.1, the first estimate given for Blinder's study is derived from the reduced form equation, and the second estimate represents the structural equation. Note that none of the male-female wage rate differential is explained by the reduced form, while about one-third of that differential is accounted for by the variables included in the structural equation.

Now let us turn from the question of how to obtain unbiased estimates of the proportions of the sex differential in the earnings attributable to various sources, to the equally important question of how to interpret those estimates once we get them. We are particularly interested in defining "discrimination" unambigously in this context. Unfortunately, this is easier said than done. Estimation and interpretation appear to be equally problematical. The most straightforward and widely accepted interpretation of the decomposition of the earnings differential is described by Blinder (1973) as follows:

R = the raw differential = $E + C + U$; .
E = the portion of the differential attributable to differing endowments (the "characteristics" or objective differential);
C = the portion of the differential attributable to differing coefficients;
U = the unexplained portion of the differential. (This is the portion of the differential due to different constant terms in the male and female earnings equations.)
$D = C + U$ = the portion of the differential attributable to discrimination.

This interpretation has not gone unchallenged, however, The controversy centers around the interpretation of C, while there is general agreement that E is objective and U discriminatory. It has been argued that different coefficients in the male and female earnings equation do not represent, or at least are not entirely the result of, discrimination. For example, Polachek argues that the structural differences in the male-female earnings function can be interpreted as resulting from the division of labor within the household, which yields differences in the labor force and investment behavior of husbands and wives and that "structural differences between males and females need not necessarily be attributed solely to direct market discrimination; for even if the initial husband-wife wage gap is caused by market discrimination, the resulting within family specialization causes differences in market productivity which would overstate the original degree of discrimination" (Polachek 1975a:227). He emphasizes the opposite effects on male and female wages of certain family characteristics—marital status and the number and spacing of children—because of the division of labor by sex. He concludes that Blinder's measure, $D = C + U$, is an overestimate of sex discrimination, because at least part of C is nondiscriminatory.

However, it is not clear that the earnings relationship measured by Polachek even measures the differences between men and women in earnings structures, as he claims. Job experience, not marriage duration and number of children, is the correct measure of market productivity. Because Polachek had no measure of experience (nor, for that matter, did Oaxaca [1973] or Blinder [1973]) but only an estimate of potential years in the labor force since school completion, it is likely that family variables are serving as proxies for differences between men and women in job experience. For a given number of years since school, more years of marriage probably means more job experience for a man and less for a woman. The same would apply to numbers of children. Therefore, unless the structural relationship is correctly specified and includes only those characteristics that can be reasonably assumed to relate to market productivity, it is unclear whether differences in the relationship between men and women result from differences in characteristics or differences in market rewards for the same characteristics. In fact, in a study based on earnings data for a single large publishing company (Osterman 1978), where full information on work histories was available, the positive effect of marriage and children on men's earnings, holding other factors constant, was shown to be a discriminatory wage-setting policy on the part of the firm, which deliberately paid more to married men with a family to support, because of their greater "need." In addition, if one is concerned about measuring not just the initial degree of discrimination, but its overall repercussions, then the evolution of the division of labor between the sexes cannot be viewed as entirely independent of the phenomenon of discrimination itself.

Let us round out this consideration of the large amount of empirical analysis concerning wage differentials by looking more closely at the use and interpretation of several important control variables—occupation, job level, and experience. These variables are of great significance, both because they tend to be important determinants of earnings and because the interpretation of their contribution is fraught with disagreement. This provides a very clear illustration of how the interpretation of supposedly objective findings concerning the relationship between earnings and other variables can easily degenerate into semantic arguments and tautological assertions. The tendency for the beholder to see what he or she wants to see is most evident, and the influence of preconceptions is far from negligible.

The correctness of adjusting for the detailed occupational distributions of male and female earnings as a way of "explaining away" the sex differentials in earnings has been hotly debated. As table A5.1 shows, Sanborn was able to reduce the unexplained earnings gap to only 12 percent of male earnings by the use of narrowly defined occupational classifications as one of his controls—a narrowing of the gap that approaches the adjusted earnings differentials within specific occupations found in part B of table A5.1. However, the occupation or job distribution does not provide an *explanation* of the earnings gap; it simply restates the question in somewhat different form. As Fuchs (1971) so aptly states:

(T)he more detailed the occupational classification the smaller would be the observed sex differential of earnings. Indeed, I am convinced that if one pushes occupational classification far enough one could "explain" nearly all of the differential. In doing so, however, one merely changes the form of the problem. We would then have to explain why occupational distributions differ so much. (p. 14).

By adjusting for occupation, we may simply be providing a measure of discrimination in the form of occupational segregation.

On the other hand, when finely defined occupations or job clusters within broader occupational classes, such as the professional category, are compared, the distribution of men and women across job clusters or detailed occupational categories does not appear to be an important determinant of earnings differentials (Osterman 1978; King 1977). Instead, firm-specific studies (Osterman 1978; Chiplin 1979; Malkiel and Malkiel 1973) show that flatter experience-earnings profiles for women are due to unequal promotion opportunities within specific occupations. In these studies, when job level was included as a variable in the wage equation, the percentage of the wage gap between men and women explained by differences in characteristics was significantly increased. This suggests that discrimination does not just take the form of entry barriers in certain occupations, but also of crowding within occupations at the bottom of the promotion ladder.

As we have seen, intended labor supply, occupational choice, and investment in on-the-job training are closely interrelated. The occupational distribution of women may be so different from that of men because women face barriers to entry into male occupations or because they voluntarily choose those occupations that offer a higher wage at lower and more intermittent levels of labor force participation. Labor supply intentions influence desired investment in training, which in turn influences occupational choice.[7] As either an alternative or an addition to the occupational distribution, work experience and job tenure, as proxies for postschool investments in on-the-job training, are crucial determinants of earnings. Unfortunately, cross-sectional data from the Census and various other samples do not provide information on actual work experience. For those whose labor force participation has been continuous, potential work experience (age minus years of schooling minus six) provides a good estimate of actual experience. However, this estimate tends to be a poor one for women, whose labor force participation has not in general been continuous. The nonavailability of time series data on work experience for men and women represents a significant gap in our knowledge concerning sex differentials. This has allowed very different interpretations of the trends in relative wages and unemployment rates, based on differing conjectures concerning trends in experience, to coexist. As we saw in chapter 3, a decline in average age and a rise in average education have resulted in less work experience for both men and women. However, this effect has probably been greater for men than for women, and thus cannot provide an explanation of the widening gaps in wages and unemployment.

Retrospective information on actual work histories is available from the NLS and the MID, and also in many of the small individual samples covering particular professions. An alternative approach has been to compare the wages of single men and women, whose work experience can reasonably be estimated, using the assumption of continuous participation since school completion (Gwartney and Stroup 1973; Sawhill 1973; King 1978). When work experience is accurately measured, studies uniformly show that men's earnings grow more rapidly with accumulated work experience than women's, and that years out of the labor force cause an actual decline in earnings due to depreciation or atrophy. When panel data are used, it appears that depreciation rates from years of nonparticipation are higher than those estimated using retrospective data—which is subject to much measurement error—(Mincer and Polachek 1978) and that wage growth is accelerating for women in the youngest cohorts as they accumulate more labor market experience (Lazear 1979).

However, certain preconceptions concerning qualitative differences between the sexes in the relationship of experience to earnings continue to cloud the interpretation of results. Polachek's statement that "[t]he quantity of human capital investment per working year differs by sex according to expectations of life cycle labor force commitment" (1975:463) is a perfect example of tautological reasoning. While differences in years of work experience are independently observable, given adequate (i.e., longitudinal) data, differences in intensity of investment per working year can only be estimated from the earnings profiles themselves, and econometric virtuosity cannot dispel the suspicion that a pattern of circular reasoning has been set up. It is argued that women have flatter age-earnings profiles even when we control for actual work experience because they invest less per working year, in expectation of less than continuous future labor force participation, and the fact of this less intense postschool investment can be observed in the relatively flat earnings profiles of women. It could equally well be the case that sex discrimination underlies *all* the observed earnings differential, by creating limited opportunities for investment on the job and consequent discontinuous labor force participation.

This entire residual approach to the estimation of discrimination has been justly criticized for its lack of theoretical underpinning and its inefficiency. As Zellner (1976) puts it:

to test . . . for the existence of discrimination in the labor market by determining whether there is any wage differential left after controlling for all relevant characteristics is somewhat like trying to discover whether you left your watch in the kitchen by looking for it everywhere else first. It would be more efficient to look in the kitchen. It would be better to develop and test directly a theory of discrimination. (pp. 48–49)

An alternative approach to the measurement of wage differentials and the estimation of the size of direct discrimination was first suggested by Reuben Gronau (1974). He argues that actual wage differentials should be measured by differences in wage offers between individuals, rather than actual wages earned. The fact that, at any point in time, roughly 50 percent of women are not working suggests that market wage offers for these women are unacceptable. Wage comparisons only include those actually working and, therefore, suffer from a selectivity bias. The bias introduced by using actual wages to measure differences in wage offers should be greater, the greater the difference between the two groups in labor force participation rates. When comparing men and women, Gronau concludes that "true" wage differentials are larger than those observed, and that there is actually a larger gap to be explained than is implied by the available data. However, Lewis (1974) has pointed out that the direction and size of the selectivity bias depend on certain assumptions about the nature of distributions and the characteristics of groups, and thus, the bias cannot be predicted *a priori*.

Even if the direction of bias is unclear, the direct estimation of wage offer curves suggests a preferable but more difficult approach to the quantification of direct discrimination (Chiplin 1979). In order to apply this approach to the labor market, studies must rely on the personal data of individual firms which include full information on job applicants. The question of promotion, however, may be a more difficult one, because the pool of "applicants" is not always clearly identified. The testing of patterns of discrimination and occupational segregation would require multiple studies, covering different sectors of the economy. Although most of us sense discrimination around us and feel its presence intuitively, we are obviously a long way from quantifying its importance, even in its most direct and overt manifestations. The main conclusion that we can draw from this review is that increased hours of work and work experience will increase women's earnings, but these changes alone will not be sufficient to bring their earnings into line with men's, because even women whose paper credentials are identical to men's do not enjoy the same wage growth with the accumulation of years on the job as men do.

We now turn to a review of empirical research on unemployment differentials. In contrast to the literature on wage differentials, there has been relatively little effort to dissect and quantify the various possible causes of the unemployment differential. To some extent, this may be accounted for by the general concern for explanations of earnings inequality. Although unemployment has a negative effect on earnings, differentials in unemployment rates only explain roughly 17 percent of earnings inequality (Mincer 1975) and, therefore, their importance is significantly dwarfed by wage inequality. However, as the unemployment gap widens and aggregate unemployment rates continue to drift upward over time, policy makers cannot deal effectively with the inflation-unemployment trade-off without knowledge of the actual sources of this contemporary phenomenon.

UNEMPLOYMENT DIFFERENTIALS

Methodologically, economists have approached the sex differential in unemployment rates in a way analogous to the empirical approach described above with respect to wage differentials. That is, the gap is "whittled away" by adjusting for various "economic" characteristics which differ between men and women. Any differences unexplained by factors such as differential mobility may then be interpreted as the result of discrimination. However, the techniques that have been used to analyze the sources of employment differentials have been much cruder. A member of the labor force is either employed or unemployed at a moment in time and, therefore, his or her status cannot be measured along a continuous distribution, as it can in the case of wages. Rather than using individual data, differential unemployment rates are usually explored by using simple techniques, such as cross-tabular comparisons or time-series regressions, in which aggregate changes in unemployment rates by sex are correlated with movements in economy-wide variables expected to affect unemployment.

It should be noted that two factors that are generally systematically related to unemployment, and which account for some of the nonwhite-white unemployment differential, (Gilman 1965)—namely, educational attainment and the occupational distribution—are not responsible for any of the female-male unemployment differential. The educational attainment of male and female workers is essentially identical, as was seen in chapter 3. Unemployment rates show a consistently negative relation to educational levels for both men and women, but female unemployment rates still exceed those for males at each level of educational attainment (Niemi 1974). A more recent study of sex differentials in employment probabilities (Bloch and Smith 1977) found that differences between the sexes in education and potential labor market experience (as well as marital status, city size, union membership, and type of employment) could not explain *any* of the gap in unemployment rates between the sexes. This is the only study to date that has attempted to use regression analysis to divide the gap in employment rates between the sexes into its explained "objective" and residual "discriminatory" components.

Far from accounting for any of the unemployment differential, the differing occupational distributions of men and women result in a lower susceptibility to unemployment due to layoff on the part of women (as discussed in chapter 4) and would lead us to expect a differential in the opposite direction, other things being equal. In fact, if experienced women had the same occupational distribution as experienced men in 1969, their unemployment rate would have increased by 5 percent (Barrett and Morgenstern 1974). This is primarily due to the fact that an equalization of the occupation distribution for men and women would have taken women out of clerical and service occupations, characterized by relatively low unemployment rates, and put them into the skilled blue collar trades, where their unemployment situation is bleak.[8]

However, within occupations and industries, women receive less specific training than men and, therefore, should be more susceptible to cyclical layoff. Past evidence on cyclical variations in *employment* rather than unemployment indicates that women have suffered disproportionately more employment loss than men in recessions (Niemi 1974). Nonetheless, in the most recent severe recession, the converse appeared to be true. Because male-dominated industries were most adversely affected by the 1974–75 recession, women lost 500,000 fewer jobs than they would have lost if the distribution of their industrial employment had been the same as that of men (R. E. Smith 1977). Within industries, they succeeded in maintaining their share of employment, except in durable goods manufacturing, where they suffered disproportionate layoffs. Therefore, if anything, it would appear that recent trends make it even less likely than in the past that women's occupational or skill distribution could explain their higher unemployment rates or the widening gap over time.

At this point, then, we are left with three factors that are believed to raise the unemployment rate of women relative to that of men: (1) the geographic and occupational immobility that results from women's voluntary choices with respect to investment in these forms of human capital; (2) excessive inter-labor force turnover; and (3) discrimination, including occupational segregation. In weighing the relative importance of these three factors, we should remember that we must explain not only the high rate of unemployment among women, but also the widening gap between the unemployment rates of women and men, as female labor force participation has risen over time. Geographic and occupational immobility are more likely to affect the duration of unemployment, and inter-labor force turnover is more likely to affect the number of spells.

It is highly unlikely that geographic immobility has increased over time; the reverse, if anything, has been the case. Thus we are left with inter-labor force mobility, discrimination, or some combination thereof, to provide the primary explanation for both the existence of and the growth in the sex differential in unemployment rates.[9] Although inter-labor force turnover provides a major part of the explanation for the former, it turns out to be inadequate as a consistent explanation for the latter phenomenon.

In earlier study, Niemi (1974) documents the relative importance of inter-labor force and intra-labor force turnover for men and women. In 1960, the average married man moved into or out of the labor force 0.176 times and the average married woman moved into or out of the labor force 0.602 times. On the other hand, in 1955 the average man changed jobs 0.15 times and the average woman changed jobs 0.055 times. On balance, total turnover is higher for women than men and this fact, combined with the fact that inter-labor force turnover is more likely than intra-labor force turnover to result in an unemployment spell, constitutes the primary reason for women's relatively higher unemployment rates. Intra-labor force immobility was also found to contribute somewhat to the female-male unemployment differential. However, indices of inter-labor force turnover presented in table 2.6 do not suggest that female inter-labor force mobility can provide a sufficient explanation for the observed trend in the unemployment rate of women relative to that of men. Although the importance of high inter-labor force turnover in raising the female unemployment rate at any point in time is well documented, additional assumptions are clearly necessary if one is to argue that this frictional component of female unemployment has increased over time. The argument that increasing female labor force participation results in growing inter-labor force turnover and unemployment among women assumes that those women on the margin of the labor force—those currently moving into labor force activity—will tend to have above-average inter-labor force turnover. The shifting of the age distribution of female labor force entrants toward younger ages might be one possible reason for expecting such an effect.

During the 1940s and 1950s, the growth of the female labor force was concentrated among married women over 35 years of age. As a result, the median age of married women workers rose gradually from 38 in 1947 to 42 in 1963 (Perrella 1963). Since 1960, however, the most significant growth in female labor force participation has occurred among married women under 35, who account for virtually all of the continuing rise in labor force participation of married women today. This leveling off of the growth in the labor force participation rates of older married women, and the rapid growth in the participation of those under 35, have contributed somewhat to widening the gap between the unemployment rates of women and men. The younger group does have substantially higher rates of turnover and unemployment than those aged 35–64. However, as we have seen, the average age of male workers fell just as much as that of women. It is also the case that the female-male differential in unemployment rates has widened within each age group as well as in the aggregate, and thus the changing age distribution of the female labor force can at best explain only part of the worsening unemployment situation of women.

Although the correlation between the widening unemployment gap and increasing female labor force participation could be consistent with growing inter-labor force turnover among women, it could also be consistent with the aforementioned overcrowding hypothesis. Direct discrimination against women may thus be a significant factor in their deteriorating unemployment situation.

Niemi (1977) examined the actual effects of the business cycle, the upward trend in female labor force participation, and various other factors on the trend in the female-male unemployment differential. It is clear from these results that the business cycle had the dominant effect on this differential in the younger age groups, while the growth in female labor force participation is of at least equal importance in explaining the worsening of the relative unemployment position of women aged 25–54. After cyclical ups and downs are eliminated, the upward trend in female labor force participation results in increased absolute and relative unemployment for women. This study confirms the hypothesis that the female-male unemployment differential has widened secularly, as well as fluctuating cyclically, but the relative importance of various underlying reasons for this trend cannot be determined from this aggregate data alone.

This positive relationship between female labor force participation and the unemployment gap is disturbing. When these results are viewed in conjunction with the data on inter-labor force turnover over time in table 2.6, it becomes clear that this relationship definitely cannot be explained solely in terms of turnover. Inter-labor force turnover among women has *decreased*, not increased, as female labor force participation has risen over time, both in the aggregate and within each age group. In the past ten years, the annual rate of female labor force turnover has fallen from over 30 percent to about 21 percent. The patterns certainly tend to support the theory that occupational segregation and overcrowding have been a major factor in the worsening unemployment situation of women.

No research to date has been successful in measuring the quantitative significance of discrimination as a factor in explaining wage or unemployment differentials. Nonetheless, the persistence and growth of these gaps between men and women leave no doubt as to the existence of discrimination and occupational segregation and the increasing importance of their constraining influence over time, as more and more women move into the labor market. By calling attention to some of the methodological pitfalls in the empirical analysis of discrimination, we hope to caution economists and other against simplistic answers. Now we will take the available shreds of empirical evidence and piece them together with dynamic theories of the job market to tell the full story of the vicious circle in which women find themselves with respect to occupational distribution, wages and unemployment.

Dynamic Interaction Between Supply and Demand

As we have already seen, discrimination theory in its pure form cannot explain the persistence of discrimination or the widening of the wage and unemployment gaps over time. On the other hand, our review of the empirical literature suggests that, although we cannot measure its exact quantitative importance, discrimination is an important factor in the determination of wage and unemployment differentials. The perpetuation of discrimination in the long run must be linked to some feedback relationship between an original prejudice or misconception and female-male productivity, through the market for job training. Differences between men and women in job experience have been used as a primary explanation of wage differentials on the supply side. Likewise, training and hiring costs have been isolated as a primary cause of persistent differences in the demand for male and female labor.

In the simple models of discrimination reviewed above, predictions of wage differentials were based on a simple production process in which there was only one quality of labor in the market. In a more complex world, each employer hires workers at many different skill levels and wages. If each skill level or job has a wage attached to it, then wage discrimination can be translated into job discrimination, because in order for the employer to pay similar workers different wages he must assign them to different jobs.

In the context, Spence's (1973) model of job signaling provides, at first glance, a theory of dynamic interactions which seems capable of explaining the persistence of wage differentials over time. Spence divides what Thurow refers to as "background characteristics" into two categories: *signals*, such as educational attainment, which can be manipulated or altered at some cost by the individual; and *indices*, such as sex and race, which cannot. A signal, such as the level of education, will be effective in the job market only if the costs of signaling are negatively correlated with productive capacity. If this were not the case, everyone would make the same investment and be indistinguishable in this respect. If this negative correlation exists, it will pay the more productive to invest in education as a way of informing employers that they are more productive. Education becomes a prerequisite for certain high-level jobs, and is productive in this sense for the individual, but it does not increase his or her real marginal product. Education need not be completely unproductive in order to serve as an effective signal. "However, if it is too productive relative to the costs, everyone will invest heavily in education, and education may cease to have a signaling function" (Spence 1973:368).

Initially the problem facing the employer is to distinguish tentatively the productivity levels of his job applicants. One way to do this is to establish an educational signal or credential as a prerequisite for high-wage jobs and unnecessary for low-wage jobs. Given this credential and the offered wage schedule, individuals with differing productivities will each select optimal levels of education. If the low-productivity group finds that their return from investing in the required education credential is too low to justify the investment and if the high-productivity group finds the return from the investment high enough, then the employer's expectations about the productivity differences are confirmed and a stable signaling equilibrium is established.[10] On the other hand, if the credential was set too high or too low, both groups will signal the employer with the same level of education and the employer will not be able to distinguish the groups. If this occurs, the credential can be adjusted until the employer's beliefs are confirmed by the actual productivity differences observed between his high- and low-wage workers.

Equilibrium is defined in the context of a "feedback loop" in which the expectations of employers lead to offered wages that vary according to education group. On the job, the actual relationship between productivity and education is discovered and as a result the employer's expectations are revised. In the meantime, individuals will react to the existing wage differentials by making educational investments. The hiring cycle will be started again and the process will be repeated until employers' expectations are consistent with their actual experience. At that point, equilibrium has been achieved and expectations will become self-perpetuating. There will be multiple levels of education that produce the same equilibrium.

For our purposes, the most interesting aspect of Spence's analysis is the informational impact of indices and the manner in which an index, such as sex, and a signal, such as education, may interact. Assuming that sex and productivity are uncorrelated, sex alone cannot tell the employer anything about productivity. However, because of externalities in the signaling model, the opportunities facing equally productive men and women are not necessarily the same. Because of different relative productivities in the market and nonmarket sectors, men and women who are equally productive in the market are unlikely to invest in education in the same ways. As a result, employers will discover that a certain level of education for women signals on the average a different degree or type of productivity than the same level of education for men. In the next round, employers differentiate the credentials required of men and women for entry into high-wage jobs, and men and women will receive different returns for the same educational investment.

Men and women may well settle into different stable signaling equilibria in the market. If it has been the case in the past that women have accumulated less job experience on the average than men, then highly productive women may have to spend more on education than comparable men to convince employers, who practice statistical discrimination, that they are in the high-productivity group. Thus the return to education is lowered for women, and fewer women than men will find it pays to make the investment. Although it might appear to an observer that women earn less because they choose to invest less in the market for reasons of relative productivity, the actual reason for the wage differential lies within the informational structure of the market itself. Thus women are caught in an informationally based vicious circle in the labor market, or what Spence refers to as "a lower-level equilibrium trap . . . that once achieved persists for reasons endogenous to the model" (1973:374). The possibility of multiple equilibria can thus be translated into arbitrary differences between men and women in their equilibrium-signaling patterns.

The situation becomes even more complex if differences in signaling costs exist for equally productive individuals or groups. If there are no such differences, lower-level equilibrium traps can be eliminated by somehow making it impossible for the employer to take the index (in this case, sex) into account. Spence (1974:41) refers to this as "suppressing potential indices." Suppressing gender as an informational index is obviously difficult or impossible, involving at the very least the elimination of face to face meetings prior to hiring. However, over and above the question of feasibility, there is the fact that, if the source of equilibrium sex differentials lies in different signaling costs, then eliminating sex as an index will result in wage discrimination against women, who have higher signaling costs than men.

Is it reasonable to assume that signaling costs are higher for women than for men? The discussion in chapter 3 tends to indicate that it is. Lower levels of parental and scholarship support, discriminatory admissions policies in certain professions, and psychic costs produced by lack of acceptance, would all tend to produce this result. Thus what is sometimes naively criticized as reverse discrimination, the setting of a lower background prerequisite for those with higher signaling costs, is in fact "equal pay for equal work." Nondiscrimination in rewarding actual productive capacity will imply discrimination at the level of signals (Spence 1974:71), and there is no way to simultaneously avoid discrimination at both levels if signaling costs do differ systematically.

The aspects of the signaling model discussed so far are predicated on the assumption that there is one labor market in which male and female workers with different levels of ability interact with employers. Employers' misconceptions tend to be corrected by experience, and equilibria are established only when these expectations have been adjusted so that they are confirmed by actual events. In the more realistic situation, where there are many different labor markets, the effects of different signaling equilibria will be more profound and far-reaching. In particular, persistent occupational segregation may well be the result if employers' expectations cause entire groups of workers to select themselves out of certain markets. If women never enter a particular market, beliefs about their productivity, whether correct or not, will never be challenged or altered. Such a situation can arise from an original employer misconception based on either prejudice or lack of information, and may continue undisturbed even in the long run. However, while informationally based barriers to mobility are real, they are also unstable, once the pattern of exclusion is disturbed and the vicious circle is broken at some point. Then it is possible for the system to move fairly rapidly to a new and different set of equilibria.

The crucial ingredient missing in Spence's model is job training. In his model, productivity growth that takes place on the job is not emphasized at all,[11] and no distinction is made between individual self-investment in job training and employer-specific investment. Thurow (1975) has developed a model of job competition which emphasizes that most cognitive job skills are not acquired before a worker enters the labor market but only in the course of performing a job. In his model, the labor market is not a place where fully trained workers compete for jobs, but rather a place where "supplies of trainable labor are matched with training opportunities" (Thurow, 1975:79). Individuals compete with each other for jobs, not in terms of the wages they are willing to accept, but in terms of their relative trainability for particular jobs. Here, the competition for jobs should be more correctly seen as competition for a lifetime sequence of jobs which, if an individual is perceived as highly trainable, will begin at the entry port in an internal labor market with a steep job promotion ladder; but if the individual is perceived as being less trainable, it will begin in the secondary labor market or in an internal labor market with fewer and less rapid opportunities for promotion.

In Thurow's model, the number and type of job slots are technologically determined, as in SLM theory. Wages are rigid and jobs are allocated through a labor queue in which the first workers picked for the jobs with upward mobility will be those who appear to have the greatest promise of trainability and adaptability. In such a market, the distribution of skills in the market is a function of the demand for those skills, and wages are determined exogenously through wage bargains, but follow a systematic upward progression according to seniority within structured job ladders.

In Thurow's model of job competition, employers use race and sex as well as factors such as aptitude and education as "background characteristics" by which to rank workers in the job queue. This makes the theory of statistical discrimination crucial in the explanation of wage and unemployment differentials. Real differences in training costs and returns between men and women are assumed to exist, thus permitting employers to use race and sex as measures of trainability. This is assumed because Thurow does not believe that men desire either physical or social distance from women, as whites do from blacks. However, such as assertion makes sense only if social distance is very narrowly defined in terms of social class. The division of labor and specialization of function by sex creates substantial social distance between the sexes, within social classes and even within individual households. There is no question that many employers and fellow employees have no difficulty in relating to black janitors, or female typists, but find it difficult to relate to either group in positions of authority. Social distance is a crucial factor in sex as well as race discrimination.

The job competition model conveys the crucial elements which must exist for wage and unemployment differentials, initially based on supply differences and direct discrimination, to perpetuate themselves over time. In such a market, there would be no turning back once a stable signaling equilibrium à la Spence had been established, because men and women would be slotted into different training opportunities which would lead their actual productivity (as opposed to their innate ability) to diverge rapidly over time. While this outcome is similar to that obtained from a signaling model in a multimarket setting, it is considerably more difficult to break down, as it is not exclusively, or even primarily, informationally based. It has been shown in chapter 3 that employer investment in specific training is negatively related to turnover rates. In the job competition model, this would mean that women would be less likely to be hired than men for jobs containing a significant training component, because of their higher average turnover rates. This will negatively affect women's incentive to invest in training themselves, and increase the likelihood that they will find nonmarket opportunities relatively attractive at certain phases of their life cycle as well as at business cycle troughs. Therefore, high turnover rates are both the cause of less on-the-job training and the result. Occupational crowding will lower relative wages by restricting the opportunities for employment and advancement.

This same self-perpetuating cycle affects unemployment rates as well as wage rates. With access to training opportunities limited by higher perceived costs and lower perceived returns to training, many women are restricted to jobs where specific training is less important. If the labor market is divided into two sectors—primary and secondary—women are seen as being barred from "good" jobs in the primary sector, which are characterized by high wages, employment stability, good working conditions and opportunities for advancement, and confined to "bad" jobs in the secondary sector, which tend to be low-paying and unstable, and offer poor working conditions and little chance of advancement. Because discrimination perpetuates itself through the interaction of supply and demand, adaptive forces, such as lack of opportunities for advancement, will increase the likelihood that women's turnover rates will exceed those of men. The process of occupational crowding is seen as an important factor in raising women's unemployment rates relative to men's, both because women on the average have less to lose if they quit a job than men do, and because more women are forced to compete for fewer jobs.

It has been shown that job quit rates are greater for women than for men (Barnes and Jones 1974; Landes 1977). Although men are more likely to quit a job to move elsewhere in the job market, women are more likely to quit to exit from the labor force. The net effect of these two forces is that, on the average, women's turnover rates exceed men's. However, the more narrowly defined the occupational group, the smaller the sex differential in quit rates. Isabel Sawhill (1973) found that 50 percent of the differences in quit rates could be eliminated by adjusting for the occupational or industrial clustering of females. Barnes and Jones (1974) found that a 1 percent increase in earnings reduced job quitting three times more for women than men, indicating that, when given a chance, women become significantly more committed to their jobs. However, in order to be given a chance, women would have to present other unusually strong background characteristics (such as education) to counter the effect of their sex.

Given that women have historically participated in the labor force at lower levels and less continuously than men and have had substantial nonmarket responsibilities, and given that men and women are readily distinguishable by employers, a self-perpetuating long-run equilibrium situation is established in which women on the average have lower occupational status and earnings, and higher turnover and unemployment rates, than men. It is true that the group averages on which employers' perceptions and behavior are based are "correct," but it is also the case that these averages are themselves created by differential opportunities which employers offer to men and women. Furthermore, an individual woman cannot break out of this trap by acquiring the necessary training and experience or establishing a continuous work history, as she will still be judged on the basis of the group average rather than her individual behavior. Presumably, however, such behavior on the part of individual women does affect the group average slightly, and thus improves the image of, and opportunities open to, all women workers. Conversely, individual women who behave in "traditional" sterotyped fashion, leaving their jobs when they have children or when their husbands move, lower not only their own future opportunities but, to some extent, those of all women.

Although the roles of tastes, expectations, occupational segregation, and monopsony power in creating the observed sex differential in earnings (and, for that matter, in unemployment rates as well) are frequently presented as alternative or substitute theories of discrimination, one can equally well or better view them as coexisting or complementary. Tastes for discrimination or prejudices against women in certain roles constitute the starting point for labor market discrimination, but the interaction of these tastes with institutions and behavior creates ramifications much more extensive than the prejudices themselves. Actually, the concept of discrimination in economics should include both direct market discrimination, which results from any nonobjective behavior on the part of men in the evaluation of women's economic contribution, and indirect discrimination, which occurs in the socialization and educational process and affects the kinds of market choices women and men make. All economic literature on discrimination has concentrated on the former aspect. Indirect discrimination is mentioned, more or less as an afterthought, as an alternative explanation of differentials seemingly explained by objective economic factors.

Indirect discrimination is dealt with explicitly by Janice Madden (1975), who uses the term "cumulative discrimination," and defines this as occurring if a worker's productivity is lower than it would otherwise be in the absence of past discrimination. For example, this type of discrimination occurs when young women's choices about education, marriage, children, and career are affected by the experience of older women who have been victims of direct market discrimination.

Prejudices embodied in social mores create not only lower wages for women directly, but more importantly, occupational segregation (which in turn can give employers monopsony power vis-à-vis their female workers), historically self-perpetuating inferior status via statistical discrimination, and indirect discrimination in the form of limited opportunities, which reinforces and perpetuates all of the above difficulties in the path of women workers.

It is our belief that sex discrimination occurs in all these forms, and that they are closely interwoven. However, as we have emphasized, direct testing of any discrimination theory has been minimal, and testing the relative quantitative importance of different types of discrimination is still nonexistent. The empirical work embodying an indirect approach to discrimination can at best provide only an estimate of the total impact of discrimination, but contains no information as to the importance of the various discriminatory mechanisms.

Up to this point, we have devoted all our attention to the individual and the employer in analyzing the determinants of market outcomes. The individual and the employer, however, are not the only actors in this story. Even in a predominantly market economy such as ours, the government has the potential to play an important role in determining these outcomes through laws, taxes and subsidies, and employment policies. We have chosen to discuss these issues last, not because they are necessarily less important, but because it is easier to understand their full implications once all the market forces have been described and analyzed. The government, in the pursuit of conflicting goals, may have inadvertently or deliberately designed policies which in many cases compound the dynamic reinforcement of discriminatory outcomes in the labor market. Recent equal employment opportunity legislation seeks to combat these trends, but must fight practices and attitudes which in many cases have hardened into custom and even law.

NOTES

1. A production function embodying constant returns to scale throughout.

2. There are many statistical studies estimating the major determinants of either male or female earnings, but we are presenting only the results from those which attempted to do a symmetric analysis of men and women, so that earnings ratios and their determinants can be compared.

3. See U.S. President, *Economic Report of the President*, January 1973, p. 103. On the other hand, recent research, using time budget data, indicates that when total break time is subtracted from time at work, married women show the greatest effort per hour at work and therefore, a differential in hourly wage rates would underestimate the size of the differential return to effort. So these two factors (i.e., greater effort per hour and the shorter average work week for women) should roughly cancel each other out, leaving the differential in full-time year-round earnings a reasonably accurate estimate of the actual differential (Duncan and Stafford, 1977).

4. Another approach, which is econometrically equivalent, is to introduce interaction terms between sex and each of the other characteristics into the single earnings

equation. However, the two-equation approach discussed in the text is easier to conceptualize and more widely used.

5.   For example, in Landes' study (1977), the percentage of the gap explained by assigning women men's average characteristics was 67 percent, whereas if men were assigned average female characteristics, 101 percent of the gap was explained. The first approach seems more plausible, however, given that discrimination is most likely to take the form of reducing women's payoff for certain characteristics.

6.   Blinder defines a seven-equation structural model, in which the hourly wage rate, educational attainment, occupation, vocational training, union membership, service in the armed forces, and present job tenure are all endogenous and simultaneously determined. However, estimating this entire system simultaneously by means of either two-stage least squares or some similar econometric technique is impossible because of the underindentification of the wage equation (Blinder 1973).

7.   See Zellner (1975) for detailed discussion of this hypothesis.

8.   Bloch and Smith's study (1977) contains a result which appears to contradict these findings on the effect of the occupational distribution. They found that if women were given the male occupational distribution but their own occupation-specific employment probabilities, the gap between men's and women's employment probabilities would decrease by between 25 and 32 percent. This difference appears to be partly the result of including all labor force participants, rather than only the *experienced* labor force in the sample. The inclusion of inexperienced workers in effect creates another "occupation" for which the unemployment rate is 100 percent. Since a greater proportion of unemployed women than unemployed men have no previous work experience, what is described as the effect of occupation on unemployment in this case would be more accurately described as the effect of a high labor force entry rate. This interpretation is also consistent with the findings of Barrett and Morgenstern (1974:462).

9.   It has been suggested that the widening unemployment gap can be completely explained by the 1967 change in the definition of unemployment (Barnes and Jones 1975). However, this seems unlikely, because of the appearance of this trend as far back as 1961–1962, and the close correlation between the unemployment gap and female labor force participation over an extended period.

10.   Obviously, for the model to work the credential must be set at such a level that it does not pay for everyone to acquire it; otherwise it would not serve to distinguish between groups. With large subsidies to public education in the 1960s, more people found that education paid off. This has led employers to escalate job credentials as a way of maintaining a mechanism for differentiating groups with different levels of productivity.

11.   Spence's emphasis on the informational aspects of labor markets is such that changes in productivity after the individual is on the job (i.e., via training) are not of primary interest. Although his discussion of discriminatory mechanisms in a multi-market setting does imply the acquisition of skills on the job, he explicitly mentions training at only one point. One of the reasons why hiring is an investment decision and the employer has an incentive to determine potential employees' productivities in advance to the extent possible is that "[t]here may be a specific training required before the individual can handle certain kinds of jobs" (Spence 1974:14).

Appendix Table A5.1

Summary of Empirical Work on Sex Differentials in Earnings

Author and Source Number	Data Source and Population Group	Observed Earnings Ratio F/M	Adjusted Earnings Ratio (F/M)[a]	Controls Used	% of Gap "Explained"
A. General					
Sanborn (1)	1950 Census; BLS Wage Structure Series and Occupational Wage Surveys, 1945–49: employed civilian wage and salary workers	.58 (1949 median wage and salary income)	.76	age, education, hours of work, urbanness, race, detailed occupation	43%
			.82	above, plus more narrowly defined occupational classifications from BLS	57%
			.88	above, plus turnover, absenteeism, work experience	71%
Fuchs (2)	1:1000 sample of the 1960 Census: nonfarm employed persons	.60 (1959 average hourly earnings)	.61	color, schooling, age, city size	2.5%
			.66	above, plus marital status, class of worker,[a] length of trip to work	15%
Fuchs (3)	1:1000 sample of the 1970 Census: white nonfarm employed persons	.605 (1969 average hourly earnings)	.64	age, schooling	9%
Gwartney and Stroup (4)	U.S. Dept. of Commerce, *Current Population Reports*, P-60 series; 1950 and 1960 Census: employed persons	.60 (1959 mean hourly earnings)	.60	age, education	0

Study	Sample	Wage/Income measure		Control variables	Percent
	full-time year-round workers	.56 (1969 mean annual income)	.56	age, education	0
	single (never married) persons	.98 (1959 median annual income)	.93	age, education, annual hours worked	—
	married (spouse present) persons	.33 (1959 median annual income)	.51	age, education, annual hours worked	27%
Cohen (5)	Michigan Survey Research Center, 1969; persons aged 22–64, not self-employed, with a steady job and working 35+ hours per week.	.55 (December 1969 median annual income)	.73	hours of work, professional status, fringe benefits, absenteeism, seniority, education, unionization	50%
Oaxaca (6)	1967 Survey of Economic Opportunity: urban white and negro persons, aged 16 and over, who report an hourly wage for the week preceding the survey	.65 (1967 average hourly earnings of whites)	.72	children, city size, education, experience, health, hours of work, marital status, migration region, union membership	20%
		.67 (1967 average hourly earnings of blacks)	.69		6%
			.78 (whites)	above, plus industry, occupation, class of worker	37%
			.80 (blacks)		39%
Sawhill (7)	1967 Current Population Survey: employed wage and salary workers in the civilian labor force	.46 (1966 average annual earnings)	.56	race, region, age, education, weeks worked per year, hours worked per week	19%

Appendix Table A5.1 (continued)

Author and Source Number	Data Source and Population Group	Observed Earnings Ratio F/M	Adjusted Earnings Ratio (F/M)[a]	Controls Used	% of Gap "Explained"
Blinder (8)	Michigan Survey Research Center's "Panel Study of Income Dynamics": white persons, except household heads younger than age 25 or who did not work for money in 1967	.54 (1967 average hourly wage)	.54	age, region, parents' income, father's education, place of birth, number of siblings, health, local labor market conditions, geographic mobility, seasonal employment	0
			.69	age, region, education, vocational training, occupation, union membership, veteran status, health, local labor market conditions, geographic mobility, seasonal employment, time on job	33%
Mincer and Polachek (9)	1967 National Longitudinal Survey of Work Experience: white married and single women aged 30–44; 1967 Survey of Economic Opportunity: white married men aged 30–44	married women: .66 single women: .86 (1966 average hourly wage rates)	.81	education, actual labor market experience, tenure in current job, home time following first child, other home time (2-stage least squares)	45%
			.87		7%

Author	Data				
Sandell and Shapiro (10)	1967 Longitudinal Survey (corrected data): white married women aged 30–44; 1967 Survey of Economic Opportunity: white married men aged 30–44	married women: .66	.74	education, actual labor market experience, tenure in current job, estimated total home time (2-stage least squares)	23%
Mincer and Polachek (11)	1967 Longitudinal Survey (corrected data): white married women aged 30–44; 1967 Survey of Economic Opportunity: white married men aged 30–44	married women: .66	.83	education, estimated experience, estimated tenure, estimated home time following 1st child, estimated other home time via instrumental variables (2-stage least squares)	49%
Suter and Miller (12)	1967 Longitudinal Survey: women aged 30–44 unpublished data from the March 1967 Current Population Survey: men aged 30–44	.39 (1966 median wage or salary income)	.62	education, occupational status, work experience, hours of work	38%

Appendix Table A5.1 (continued)

Author and Source Number	Data Source and Population Group	Observed Earnings Ratio F/M	Adjusted Earnings Ratio (F/M)[a]	Controls Used[a]	% of Gap "Explained"
Kohen and Roderick (13)	Longitudinal Surveys: nonstudent men and women aged 18–25, employed full-time	white: .76 black: .82 (1968–1969 average hourly earnings)	.79 .81	family background, education, race, mental ability, quality of education, potential labor market experience, health, region of residence.	12% —
Chiswick, O'Neill, Fackler and Polachek (14)	1:100 sample of the 1970 Census: white and black persons aged 25–54 who worked in 1969 and in the survey week in 1970	white: .65 black: .78 (1969 hourly earnings)	.75 .83	detailed occupation	white: 28% black: 22%
Landes (15)	1967 SEO: whites, 14–65, employed in civilian labor force (aggregate in 96 occupations)	.71 (hourly wage)	.90	percent working full-time, percent who reported current job different from longest job in 1966, variance in weeks worked, growth in male earnings in occupation.	67%
Corcoran (16)	1976 Michigan Panel Survey of Income Dynamics: white men and women, 18–64	.62	.76	years out of labor force since completing school, proportion of years worked full-time, years of work experience before present employment, years of job tenure, plans to stop work	36%

B. Specific Occupations

Study	Description			Explanatory variables	%
Bayer and Astin (17)	NSF National Register of Scientific and Technical Personnel, 1964: natural and social science Ph.D.'s in full-time academic jobs, with 2–6 years of experience	.92 (1964 annual academic year (9–10 month) salary)	.97	experience, field of specialization, type of employer, rank	62%
Johnson and Stafford (18)	NSF Register: 1970 Ph.D.'s in 6 disciplines (anthropology, biology, economics, mathematics, physics, sociology)	by years since doctorate 0 .93 5 .88 10 .84 15 .82 20 .80 25 .79 30 .79	by years since doctorate .93 .93 .93 .93 .93 .93 .93	experience, field of specialization	0 42% 55% 62% 65% 67% 67%
Gordon, Morton and Braden (19)	full-time academic employees of a large urban university	.73	.90	age, race, years at the university, education, rank, department	63%
Hoffman (20)	Instructional faculty at U. of Mass./Amherst	.77	.84	education, experience	30%
			.85	above, plus minority group, school or division	35%
			.90	above, plus productivity in teaching, scholarship, and service	57%

Appendix Table A5.1 (continued)

Author and Source Number	Data Source and Population Group	Observed Earnings Ratio F/M	Adjusted Earnings Ratio (F/M)[a]	Controls Used	% of Gap "Explained"
Malkiel and Malkiel (21)	272 professional employees of a private corporation	.65 (1971 annual salary)	.84	education, experience, tenure in present job	55%
			.87	above, plus Ph.D. received, publications, marital status, critical area of study, absence rate	65%
			.99	above, plus job level	98%

[a] "Class of worker" refers to whether the individual is self-employed, a private wage and salary worker, or a government employee.

SOURCES:

(1) Henry Sanborn, "Pay Differences Between Men and Women," pp. 534–50.

(2) Victor R. Fuchs, "Differences in Hourly Earnings Between Men and Women," pp. 9–15.

(3) Victor R. Fuchs, "Recent Trends and Long-Run Prospects for Female Earnings," pp. 236–42.

(4) James Gwartney and Richard Stroup, "Measurement of Employment Discrimination According to Sex," pp. 575–87.

(5) Malcolm S. Cohen, "Sex Differences in Compensation," pp. 434–47.

(6) Ronald Oaxaca, "Male-Female Wage Differentials in Urban Labor Markets," pp. 693–709.

(7) Isabel V. Sawhill, "The Economics of Discrimination Against Women," pp. 383–96.

(8) Alan S. Blinder, "Wage Discrimination," pp. 436–55.

(9) Jacob Mincer and Solomon Polachek, "Family Investments in Human Capital," pp. S76–S108.

(10) Stephen H. Sandell and David Shapiro, "A Reexamination of the Evidence," pp. 103–17.

(11) Jacob Mincer and Solomon Polachek, "Women's Earnings Reexamined," pp. 118–34.

(12) Larry E. Suter and Herman P. Miller, "Income Differences Between Men and Career Women," pp. 962–74.

(13) Andrew I. Kohen and Roger D. Roderick, "The Effects of Race and Sex Discrimination on Early-Career Earnings."

(14) Barry R. Chiswick et al., "The Effects of Occupation on Race and Sex Differences in Hourly Earnings," pp. 219–28.

(15) Elisabeth M. Landes, "Sex Differences in Wages and Employment," pp. 523–38.

(16) Mary Corcoran, "Work Experience, Labor Force Withdrawals, and Women's Earnings," pp. 216–45.

(17) Alan E. Bayer and Helen S. Astin, "Sex Differences in Academic Rank and Salary among Science Doctorates in Teaching," pp. 191–200.

(18) G. E. Johnson and F. P. Stafford, "The Earnings and Promotion of Women Faculty," pp. 888–903.

(19) Nancy M. Gordon, Thomas E. Morton, and Ina C. Braden, "Faculty Salaries: Is There Discrimination by Sex, Race, and Discipline?" pp. 419–27.

(20) Emily P. Hoffman, "An Econometric Study of University of Massachusets/Amherst Faculty Salary Differentials."

(21) Burton G. Malkiel and Judith A. Malkiel, "Male-Female Pay Differentials in Professional Employment," pp. 693–705.

The following two review studies were also used in preparing this table: Andrew I. Kohen (1975), "Women and the Economy;" Harriet S. Zellner (1976), "A Report on the Extent and Nature of Employment Discrimination Against Women."

Chapter 6

The Effect of Law and Policy on Sex Differentials

A review of all government laws and policies affecting income support and labor market opportunity reveals a fundamental conflict between the notions of equality in a family context and in an individual context. On the one hand, society's concern for social stability and the proper rearing of the young has placed the emphasis on the family as the proper unit of income support. On the other hand, a philosophical commitment to equal opportunity has placed the emphasis on the protection of the rights of the individual. This inherent ambiguity in the design of government policy has important implications for sex differentials in the labor market.

Although recent legislation has given increased support and protection to women's rights in the labor market, many tax and transfer programs continue to reduce the relative advantage of market work for married women and/or mothers. Rapid growth in the number and proportion of women in the labor force has clearly contributed to the pressure for the antidiscrimination legislation passed in the last ten years. However, because sufficient numbers of dependent wives and mothers remain, other government programs continue to discriminate against the working woman in favor of the "wife and mother." The *working* wife and mother finds herself caught in the middle of a conflicting set of economic signals. The women's movement also symbolizes this confusion by pressing for equality in the labor market on the one hand, and, on the other hand, suggesting further income maintenance for the housewife, which would transfer her dependency from her husband to society. With female labor force participation rates hovering around 50 percent, countervailing interest groups confound any single movement toward the elimination of existing inconsistencies in the law.

Our previous analysis of the determinants of sex differentials abstracted from the potential implications of law and policy. In this chapter, we focus on policy implications, placing equal emphasis on the direct effects of policies specifically designed to affect sex differentials in the labor market, and on the indirect labor market effects of policies designed to achieve other goals, such as the general maintenance and redistribution of income or the increase of earnings. Although the primary rationale for such policies may be unrelated to sex differentials, their effects on the relative position of the sexes in the labor market may not be entirely unintended. We will begin by examining the assumptions built into income and payroll taxes and government transfers, which maintain income in the face of earnings loss, and as a result redistribute income across individuals in a way related to family status. Next, we will explore the indirect effects of policies explicitly designed to increase individuals' earnings, such as minimum wages, training programs, and public employment. Finally, we will trace the direct effect of policies concerned with sex differentials *per se*, such as protective labor legislation and affirmative action, on women's labor market position. In each case, we will analyze the differential effect of a particular policy on men's and women's labor supply decisions and/or firms' employment decisions, and its resulting implications for real wage and unemployment differentials.

Income Redistribution and Maintenance

The present payroll and income tax structures as well as the social security, unemployment insurance, and welfare systems, are the main mechanisms in the US for the maintenance and redistribution of income. Each of these individual institutions has its own unique historical roots and development, but each shares certain assumptions about the typical division of labor between the sexes which may have important implications for both men and women. The tax and social security systems are all-encompassing in their effects, whereas unemployment insurance and welfare are targeted to deal with particular contingencies and, therefore, affect most specifically certain subgroups of the population. However, everyone is potentially affected by each of these institutions.

PROGRESSIVE INCOME TAXES

The progressive tax system in this country was designed on the principle of the "ability to pay." Ability to pay was assumed to be dependent primarily on level of income and family size. Within any given marital category, the tax rate rises with the level of income. However, for the same level of income, a married couple pays the smallest percentage of income in taxes, then a single head of household, and a single person pays the highest percentage of income in taxes (see table 6.1). Since 1948, married couples have been permitted to aggregate their income for tax purposes (Blumberg 1971). Until recently, the tax on married couples was calculated by splitting their taxable income in half and taxing each half at the rate applicable to

Table 6.1

Taxes Paid by Different Family Units,[a] 1978

Adjusted Gross Income	Married-Joint[b]	Unmarried Head of Household[b]	Single Individual[c]	Married-Separate[c]
$ 2,000	0	0	0	2
$ 4,000	0	0	122	220
$ 6,000	119	289	453	593
$ 8,000	435	635	814	1024
$10,000	765	985	1227	1514
$15,000	1712	2091	2472	3038

SOURCE: Internal Revenue Service, *1978 Federal Income Tax Forms*, pp. 31–40.

[a] Standard deduction assumed.
[b] 2 Exemptions assumed.
[c] 1 Exemption assumed.

single individuals. With a progressive tax structure, this conferred a clear advantage on married couples. Single household heads are subject to a different tax structure. This arrangement implicitly assumes that each family unit contains only one earner. This, of course, implies that the burden of dependency is greatest in the case of husband-wife families, assumed to consist of a working man and a dependent wife and children. Single household heads are assumed to have responsibility for one adult plus any children, and single individuals to have no responsibilities other than for themselves.

However, the accuracy and equity of these assumptions is questionable at best. Only married couples can reap the substantial benefits of income splitting, although taxpayers who are not married may have similar responsibilities. Repeated charges of unfair treatment have led to several reductions in the tax burden of single relative to married people, the most recent and important of these being the 1969 Tax Reform Act. This served to narrow the differential between types of families in the fraction of any given taxable income that must be paid in taxes, but did not change the ranking. Single persons are now allowed to use a rate schedule with rates that do not exceed the rates for married couples filing jointly by more than 20 percent. Because the rates for single people were lowered, they now differ from those for married persons filing separately, as can be seen in table 6.1, whereas these two rate schedules had been identical prior to 1969.

An unintended side effect of the 1969 attempt to give the single taxpayer a fairer break was the so-called marriage tax, an interesting distortion in the treatment of working people by marital status that has received considerable publicity. While it is still true that a working man reduces his tax bill when he marries a nonworking wife, it is also true that when two working people marry, the tax on their joint income will exceed the total tax bill they would pay if they were not legally married. This is the case because the single tax rate is now slightly less than the tax rate applied to married couples with twice the income. As can be seen in table 6.2, the marriage tax has a larger dollar impact the higher the two incomes, and the smaller the difference between them.

Thus the (tax) tables have turned. The perennial (and justified) complaint of singles that the IRS made them pay dearly for their solitude

Table 6.2

1972 Tax Cost of Marriage for Couple Using the Standard Deduction

Total adjusted gross income	Spouse No. 1 earns 25% AGI				Spouse No. 1 earns 37.5% AGI				Spouse No. 1 earns 50% AGI			
	No dependents		1 dependent child		No dependents		1 dependent child		No dependents		1 dependent child	
	cost	%	cost	%	cost	%	cost	%	cost	%	cost	%
$ 8,000	$ 168	24.7	$ 190	36.8	$ 220	25.0	$ 474	48.9	$ 246	40.9	$ 473	49.3
$12,000	70	4.9	159	13.1	144	10.4	181	15.2	174	12.8	174	14.5
$16,000	132	5.8	263	14.4	175	7.9	265	14.5	185	8.4	217	11.6
$20,000	208	6.5	393	12.3	347	11.4	465	17.0	340	11.1	406	14.5
$24,000	262	6.1	510	13.4	512	12.7	669	18.4	636	16.3	717	20.0
$28,000	350	6.3	685	14.0	764	15.0	966	21.0	984	20.3	1087	24.2
$32,000	490	7.2	935	15.4	1043	16.7	1363	24.1	1311	22.0	1443	25.9
$36,000	654	8.0	1196	16.2	1438	19.3	1790	26.4	1674	23.0	1844	27.4
$40,000	1003	10.5	1520	17.4	1773	20.2	2208	27.5	2055	24.1	2285	28.7

SOURCE: Prepared statement by Grace G. Blumberg, *Economic Problems of Women*, hearings before the Joint Economic Committee, 93d Congress, 1st session, part 2, p. 236.

has given way to enraged outcries from two-earner families. While no one would argue that domestic arrangements are determined solely on the basis of tax minimization, a cost that, as table 6.2 illustrates, can be as much as $2,000 a year, cannot be dismissed as insignificant. There have been some well-publicized "tax divorces," including the extreme case of a couple who divorce each December and remarry in January. They intend to continue this annual ritual indefinitely, or until the tax law is changed. Since they are in fact divorced for part of each tax year, they can file as single taxpayers for the entire year with complete legality. Surely, this tax-induced behavior was not foreseen when the Tax Reform Act was passed.

Of more serious and general concern, of course, are the disincentives to labor force participation on the part of married women created not only by the marriage tax, but by several other aspects of our tax system as well, and the incentive to defer or refrain entirely from legal marriage. The cumulative effect of these provisions has clearly been in the direction of reinforcing a stereotypical division of labor by sex and perpetuating the secondary economic status of women. Questions relating to the deductibility of child care expenditures and the failure of the tax code to distinguish the relative ability to pay of two-earner and one-earner families at the same level of income are of particular importance in this context.

The deductibility of child care expenses, which was first introduced in 1954 and significantly expanded in the Revenue Act of 1971, added another variable to the determination of ability to pay. Prior to 1971, working wives in low-income families could take a small deduction if joint family income did not exceed $6,000, and single parent earners could take the same deduction regardless of income (Blumberg 1973). Apparently the underlying assumption here was that low-income wives and single mothers "have to" work and, therefore, child care is a necessary deduction from income; whereas wives in families with higher income do not need to work and, therefore, child care expenses are not a necessary criterion in the determination of the ability to pay.

The Revenue Act passed by Congress in 1971 allowed a deduction for "employment-related expenses" of up to $400 a month for household services. These services, with the exception of day care for a dependent under 15, had to be performed in the home. Day care expenses outside the home were limited to $200 a month for one child, $300 a month for two, and $400 a month for three or more. To take advantage of this provision, taxpayers had to itemize deductions and to file a joint return if married. The full deduction was allowed up to an adjusted gross income level of $18,000, and then tapered off up to an income level of $27,000, beyond which no further deduction was allowed. In 1975, the income limits for this deduction were raised by Congress. The adjusted gross income limit was raised from $18,000 to $35,000 and the sliding scale adjustments reached up to $44,000 before the deduction was eliminated. However, "substantially" full-time employment of both spouses was required for married couples to qualify (Blumberg 1973). Here the assumption seemed to be that parents working full time "have to" work, whereas parents working part time do not contribute essential income to the family even though they incur the same kinds of working expenses. In addition, because many low-income families could not take advantage of the itemization of deductions, it was only the middle-income families who benefited in terms of tax reduction. In 1976, the system was changed again. It has been converted into a tax credit of up to $400 for one child or $800 for two or more children, which is available to all individuals and families who pay tax and to spouses working part-time or studying full time. However, even this recent change in no way compensates working parents for the full child care costs associated with working, although the tax credit system is at least more equitable in that many more low-income parents are now eligible to receive some credit.

From the point of view of equity, it is not at all clear that the present system has succeeded in distributing the tax burden according to the ability to pay principle. The income-splitting provision of the Tax Code implies that a two-earner family has the same ability to pay as a one-earner family with the same income. This is not true. Not only does the second earner incur additional expenses, such as clothes, commutation and child care, but his or her absence from the home means the loss of untaxed nonmarket production. The tax laws were given their present form at a time when it was considered normal for the husband to work and the wife to remain at home. Today, this situation has changed drastically. The majority of couples have two earners, and it is no longer appropriate to treat the one-earner couple as the norm.[1] Nonetheless, the tax system still implicitly favors the traditional marriage and puts a disproportionate burden on the income of the second earner, who is taxed at the highest marginal rate applicable to the income of the primary earner. Therefore, the measured average wage differential between men and women should be recalculated to adjust for the differential effect of the tax. In the case of married men and women, the posttax gap in terms of take-home pay is wider than the pretax gap.

The tax structure as just described results in the anomalous situation that even a highly trained and skilled woman, who has what would appear to be excellent employment opportunities, finds that there is a real question as to whether it "pays" to leave unpaid household production for paid employment. Work-related expenses, the costs of substitute household services (especially child care), and/or the loss of some of these services, and especially the fact that her first dollar of earnings is taxed at her husband's relatively high marginal tax rate, all contribute to this situation. This can also produce a negative effect on her self-image in the face of her apparent inability to make any meaningful contribution to family income, and these doubts may well be explicitly or implicitly reinforced by her family, who have some vested interest in her remaining in the non-market sector.

When we examine the tax system in this light, the strong and continuing growth in the labor force participation of married women appears amazing in view of the substantial institutional barriers they face. However, we cannot infer from the observed trend in participation that these barriers are of little or no actual significance. We do not know what participation rates would be, or whether female labor force participation would be much more continuous and characterized by higher levels of investment in job skills, in the absence of existing tax disincentives to such behavior.

Until very recently, there had been no studies that attempted to measure directly the effect of the tax system on labor supply and, to our knowledge, there still are none measuring its impact on human capital investment. However, much has been inferred about these effects from existing knowledge about individual labor supply behavior. The effects inferred depend on certain assumptions about the net impact of the tax on individual and family income. If it is assumed that the tax revenues are respent to finance expenditures that leave real income unchanged and that there is no tax illusion,[2] then the effect of a tax on labor supply can be analyzed in terms of the pure substitution effect. However, if the imposition of or increase in taxes reduces or increases real income because of the redistributive nature of government expenditures, then an analysis of the effect of taxes on labor supply must weigh the effect of the change in real income against the reduction in the market wage.

Kosters (1969) estimated the hypothetical labor supply effect of a proportional income tax on older men (aged 50–64), using the one in a thousand sample from the 1960 Census, and on married women, using cross-sectional estimates of income and wage effects from Bowen and Finegan's study. For older men, the results indicated a compensated wage elasticity close to zero for hours of work. This would suggest that an income tax which left real income unchanged would have no effect on the hours of work of either older men, or, by assumption, prime-age men, because they typically display less variability in hours of work than older men. Using regression results from Bowen and Finegan, Kosters estimated that a tax would lead to a small reduction in labor force participation rates for older men. Using Bowen and Finegan regressions for married women, he found a signficantly larger negative compensated wage effect on labor force participation rates and thus a greater deterrent effect of a given tax on the labor supply of women. If income taxes redistribute income as well, one would expect that those gaining income would have the work-disincentive effect of taxes reinforced, while those losing income might not be affected as much or, in the case of men, might even be encouraged to work more.

The hypothetical tax that Kosters examined did not have any of the important features characteristic of the U.S. tax system—in particular, progressivity and the principle of income aggregation were lacking. Therefore, he did not explore the labor supply consequences of different marginal rates of tax for wives and husbands either at a point in time or over the life cycle.

Quester (1976) used data from the 1970 Census to estimate the labor-supply-disincentive effect on wives of the present system, which taxes second earners (who are usually wives) at the first earner's marginal tax rate. She argues that the strong negative relationship between husbands' income and wives' labor force participation usually observed is actually a tax effect, because the marginal tax applied to the wife's earnings rises with husband's income, leading to a reduction in her net wage. When the wife's wage is adjusted by the marginal tax rate applicable to the husband's income, and the husband's income is reduced by the amount of his tax, the positive effect of the wife's wage on the probability of her being in the labor force becomes considerably stronger. The effect of husband's income becomes insignificant. Since no adjustment is made for any redistributive effects on real income, the implicit assumption is that the tax always reduces real income as well as net take-home pay. She found the effect of taxes on hours of work to be similar to those on labor force participation. Although Quester clearly documents the additional disincentive effect of a progressive tax system for wives, she does not estimate its differential consequences for men, or its effects for both men and women over the life cycle. Leuthold (1978), using the NLS data, confirms Quester's finding that taxes have a significant negative effect on wives' hours of work, and also documents (1976) that for working couples the tax system reinforces the traditional division of labor by sex by increasing husband's working hours as well.

Boskin (1974) has speculated about some of the possible consequences of progressive income taxes for labor supply and human capital investment over the life cycle. The high marginal rates applied to wives' earnings reduce the discounted dollar gain from any human capital investment for either present or prospective wives for two reasons: (1) the investment yielding a higher income will be taxed at a higher rate, thus narrowing the absolute gain from the investment; and (2) the labor-supply-disincentive effect of such high marginal taxes reduces the number of years over which any returns will be realized. The progressive tax structure takes a larger and larger share of wives' earnings as their husbands' incomes rise over the life cycle and produces a strong deterrent to reentry among married women over 35. Thus the available evidence inevitably leads to the conclusion that the existing tax structure reinforces behavioral differences between the sexes, and thus creates larger sex differentials in labor supply and human capital investment than would exist under a tax system that treated each person as an individual regardless of marital status. However, even under such a system, sex differentials would be widened because of the greater responsiveness of women to any given wage rate change. The progressive tax system also causes a widening of sex differentials in labor supply with age, because of the increasing marginal tax imposed on the second earner in a two-earner family as income rises. Therefore, the larger sex differentials in labor supply, human capital, and wages among older men and women may be partially explained by the tax structure. Both the existence of the various sex differentials that we have observed and their tendency to worsen over the course of the life cycle are clearly related to institutional arrangements imposed on individual choices by society. Furthermore, our progressive tax system is only one of several such institutions which, being designed on the assumption of fairly narrowly perceived notions of proper sex roles, help perpetuate the very stereotypes on which they are based. This, of course, serves to reinforce and justify the original assumptions, and helps to retard any effective pressure for change.

SOCIAL SECURITY

Social security was first introduced in 1935 as an old-age insurance scheme for wage and salary workers in industry and commerce. It was originally financed according to the "benefit" principle of government finance, which relates an individual's benefit from the system to the same individual's contribution. However, by 1939, general concern for family protection had given rise to dependents' and survivors' benefits for insured workers. In order to avoid detailed investigations in individual cases, it was presumed that a man's wife and his children were his dependents and therefore automatically eligible for benefits in the event of his death or retirement. This change modified the basic benefit principle of taxation by providing benefits to some who had never contributed to the system, and thus redistributing income toward families with dependent wives. With the growth in the number of two-earner families, the resulting inconsistencies have increased over time, and, in effect, households with dependent adults are being subsidized by single people and two-earner families.

In 1978, the social security payroll tax for employees was 6.05 percent of the first $17,700 of earnings. There is no payroll tax on income above that level. Employers also contribute 6.05 percent, making the total effective tax rate 12.10 percent.[3] Over the next few years, the maximum amount of yearly income which will count toward social security is scheduled to rise sharply, and so is the tax rate. This is necessary in order to finance rapidly growing old age benefits as well as hospital benefits, which are now included under Social Security.

To be eligible for retirement benefits, an individual must have worked one-fourth of the time between age 21 or 1950 (whichever comes later) and retirement. If eligible, and, therefore, fully insured, his or her monthly benefits are determined according to post-1950 earnings minus the lowest five years. Quarters with no earnings are averaged in at zero. Although both benefits and contributions are related to earnings, they are related differently. The replacement rate declines as the level of earnings rises, so benefits are at a higher percentage of previous earnings for low-income individuals than for high-income individuals. This is an advantage to those with low wages as well as to those with intermittent labor force participation. However, up to the maximum benefit amount, the absolute size of the benefits is higher, the higher previous earnings. Dependents' benefits are determined as a percentage of the benefits received by fully insured participants.

Work requirements for disability payments are more stringent. If disabled, an individual can only be eligible for benefits if fully insured and if covered under the program for five out of the ten years *preceding* the disability. For survivors' benefits, it is required only that an individual have six quarters of coverage in the previous thirteen quarters.[4]

If fully insured, both men and women are eligible to retire and collect benefits at the age of 65, or at age 62 with reduced monthly payments. If fully insured workers continue to work after they reach the age of 65, they lose $1 of benefits for every $2 earned over the maximum allowable earnings of $4,000 a year in 1978. That means that continuation of a full-time job, which will inevitably pay more than $4,000 a year, will result in an incremental tax rate of 50 percent. This is incremental because payroll taxes, and federal and state taxes, will be paid as well. After the age of 72, individuals can earn any amount without jeopardizing their full benefits.

The automatic availability of wives' dependent benefits to fully insured male workers[5] creates two types of inequities in the present social security system. First, if inequity is measured in terms of benefits relative to contributions, working women married to working men gain less from their contributions than men or single working women with comparable earnings. In addition, two-earner families in many cases pay more taxes and receive lower benefits than one-earner families with comparable earnings. Because married women are guaranteed 50 percent of their husband's retirement benefits regardless of their own work experience, the payroll tax they pay on their earnings will at best increase their benefits only marginally. Because most women earn lower wages than men and also work less continuously, it is unlikely that their own work experience will entitle them to substantially more in benefits than they would be entitled to in any case. Therefore, the marginal contribution of their payroll taxes to benefits is in many cases very low or zero.

Despite the fact that low earnings have high replacement rates in the calculation of social security benefits, many two-earner families pay more taxes per dollar of benefits than one-earner families with the same income. The reason is that income earned above the maximum is not taxed, and the maximum is determined on an individual basis, not on a family basis. It has been estimated that the ratio of social security benefits received to taxes paid (appropriately discounted) is about twice as high for a family in which the wife does not work as in one where she does (O'Neill 1976). As in the case of the progressive income tax, the real wage of married women is reduced relative to single women and men because of the dependency assumption built into the Social Security system.

Consider the following illustrative example of the difference in retirement benefits between two families: a two-earner family where the wife earns 40 percent and the husband 60 percent of annual family income, and a one-earner family where the wife does not work.

Assume that each year the annual earnings of both families have been equal to the maximum base level used to compute contributions and benefits. If all four individuals were aged 65 and retired in 1975, the one-earner family would receive substantially larger monthly benefits than the two-earner family. The husband in the two-earner family would receive $266.50 monthly, while the wife, whose earnings had been less, would receive $179.60, for a total family retirement benefit of $406.10 monthly. On the other hand, the husband in the one-earner family would receive a primary benefit of $316.30 monthly, and his dependent wife would receive a secondary benefit of $158.20 monthly, for a total of $474.50, based on the husband's past earnings alone. Every year, the one-earner family receives $820.80 more than the two-earner family (before automatic adjustments for cost-of-living increases), although both families paid the same amount of payroll tax before retirement.[6]

A second type of inequity relates to the problem of untaxed household work. Housewives are not eligible for benefits as individuals but only as their husband's dependents. If a housewife is divorced, she is not eligible for any benefit unless the marriage has survived at least twenty years.[7] With rising divorce rates, many nonworking women are finding themselves unprotected against old age and therefore strongly motivated toward labor force participation as a means of achieving both short-run and long-run financial security. The assumption of dependency is a two-edged sword. Married women are damned if they work and damned if they don't. The rising probability of divorce will tend to reduce the deterrent effect of social security on labor force participation.

There are no studies to date which have attempted to estimate empirically the differential impact of the Social Security system on the labor supply of men and women. However, some passing reference is given to this question in the labor supply literature, and some of its possible differential impacts can be inferred. A consideration of the labor supply effects of the Social Security system requires an analysis of its effect on the trade-off between market and nonmarket work, both in the short run and over the life cycle. If the individual does not perceive the payroll tax as being in any way related to future benefits that may accrue,[8] the payroll tax may be seen as having income and substitution effects. Up to the taxable maximum, the payroll tax reduces the real wage, and above the taxable maximum, it reduces income by a fixed amount (MacRae and MacRae 1976). Thus it will act as a deterrent to labor force participation for those with earnings under the maximum, and as an inducement to labor force participation for those with earnings over the maximum. Because women on the average have lower earnings and are also more sensitive to any given wage change than men, the payroll tax will be more likely to have a negative impact on their aggregate labor supply. In addition, employers, who also must make contributions to the system, will favor more highly trained employees over less highly trained ones, and full-time workers over part-time ones, because of the lower tax costs. These tendencies could reduce employment opportunities for women relative to men.

Over the life cycle, the social security system taxes market work more heavily after the age of 65 than before (J. P. Smith 1975). If individuals see their present payroll contribution being translated into future benefits, they will be induced to work relatively more at younger ages and relatively less at older ages than would otherwise be the case. This intertemporal substitution of market work would affect men and women alike. However, married women would also experience an intertemporal income effect because of the dependent's benefits that they will be entitled to upon their husband's retirement, regardless of work experience. This expected increase in future unearned income will reduce work effort at all stages of the life cycle. Therefore, on balance, the present social security system tends to cause a reallocation of a given work effort to the younger ages. For married women, it is also likely to reduce the extent of the work effort, over the life cycle, both because of the reduction in the reward from market work at any point in time, and because of the expected increase in income. However, this effect will probably weaken over time with higher divorce rates.

In the United States, as in other industrialized countries, the role of the Social Security system in social policy had been a passive and reactive, rather than an active one, with programs adapting after a lag to changes in attitudes and behavior patterns. The majority of social security schemes have been implicitly based on the concept of a stable family unit containing a lifelong paid worker and a lifelong unpaid homemaker. Whether or not assumptions such as these ever really reflected social realities, there is growing consensus that they can no longer provide the basis for fair and adequate social security protection.[9]

Despite the time lags that have existed, however, substantial reform of our Social Security system is now under serious consideration, and there have been a variety of creative proposals concerning possible changes. A memo from President Carter to the heads of executive departments and agencies on August 26, 1977 included the following statement: "I am now requesting the heads of all Federal agencies and departments to initiate a comprehensive review of all programs which they administer in order to identify any regulations, guidelines, programs or policies which result in unequal treatment based on sex." (Report of the HEW Task Force on the Treatment of Women under Social Security, 1978, p. 2). More specifically, in the Social Security Amendments of 1977 (PL 95-216), Congress required the Secretary of HEW to study and prepare a report on proposals to eliminate dependency as a factor in entitlement to spouse's benefits and to eliminate sex discrimination (U.S. Dept. of Health, Education and Welfare 1979: 161).

In the wake of increasing female labor force participation, the rising divorce rate, and the growing perception of the family as an interdependent economic unit, three types of issues with respect to the treatment of women and families have to be confronted. These relate to (1) equity for single workers and two-earner couples relative to one-earner couples; (2) gaps and inconsistencies in the protection of full-time or part-time homemakers; and (3) provisions of the social security law that explicitly treat women and men differently. Although it might appear at first glance that this last set of issues would be the most serious, the reverse turns out to be the case, because relatively few people are actually affected by these provisions, which in any case are likely to be changed soon. In general, such provisions have treated women workers' dependents less generously than those of men, and have thus ended up by providing benefits to women (dependent on men) under more liberal conditions than to men (dependent on women).[10] The first two issues, which affect the entire population, are of immediate and crucial concern. In response to the 1977 congressional mandate, HEW has come forward with two successive documents proposing major new options, which present a very encouraging picture of the possibilities for reform.

The eight proposals reviewed in the preliminary February 1978 HEW *Task Force Report* involve variations on two major themes, both of which attempt to put claims to social security benefits on an individual basis and eliminate derived claims. These are: (1) the sharing of social security credits equally between spouses during their years of marriage; and (2) the awarding of credits for nonmarket work to individuals who remain at home. The plan that best addressed all the issues and did more than any other proposal to clear away basic assumptions about dependency was the earnings sharing plan developed by the Department of Justice, which would divide social security credits of married couples equally between spouses on a year-by-year basis. This plan was chosen as one of the two basic options presented in the final February 1979 HEW Report. Earnings sharing is one of the most effective ways of reducing the differential treatment of one-earner couples relative to two-earner couples and single individuals, and provides increased protection for divorced homemakers in their own right. The major alternative option which also deals with these issues is a two-tiered system with Tier I financed out of general revenues and available to everyone, regardless of past work history or current income, and Tier II providing supplementary benefits to those with past work history. With Tier I providing a floor under income, then an earnings-related contributory social security program need only relate individual entitlement to individual contributions, and the relationship between benefits and earnings need not vary with family circumstances as it does at present.

Now that HEW has completed their congressionally mandated study, it no longer seems unrealistic to expect some major reform in the near future. Either option presented would eliminate most of the inequities present in the current system. Thus recent developments serve to generate more optimism concerning the future effects of social security on sex differentials than would have been justified only a short time ago.

WELFARE AND PROPOSED ALTERNATIVES

Although present welfare schemes vary to some extent from state to state, the same assumption of female dependency pervades the design of present income transfer programs for low-income families. Until 1961, the program of Aid to Families with Dependent Children (AFDC) was available only to female-headed households, the presumption being that a family with a healthy male would not and should not be in need of income support. In fact, when it was designed originally in the 1930s, the primary intent was to permit mothers to stay at home (Honig 1974).

The continued absence of publicly available day care for all except a tiny fraction of the welfare population makes it appear that this continues to be the policy's intent. Although changes introduced in 1961 now make it possible for intact families with unemployed male heads to receive aid, in many states the aid available under these circumstances is much more limited. The welfare standards are the same for intact and female-headed families if neither has any income, but significant differences arise if either type of family has some earnings, because of varying allowances for work expenses and varying income "disregards" (Bernstein 1973). For example, in the more generous states, a two-parent family of four whose head is working full time could be earning $4,500 per year and be eligible only for $900 in food stamp subsidy, whereas an AFDC family of the same size could have a small amount of earnings and receive benefits in cash, food stamps, Medicaid, and housing assistance worth as much as $8,000 annually (Palmer and Minarik 1976).

Several studies of the present system have estimated that welfare as it is presently designed, with its presumption of female dependency and its emphasis on the financial support of women in their role as mothers, has created strong incentives for marital instability and non-market work, which in the long run worsen the cycle of poverty, by limiting the accumulation of human capital and increasing the probability of unemployment. The strongest evidence of the work disincentive effect of present programs can be found in Durbin's (1973) study of welfare in New York City. She brings out the important point that when a mother has been deserted and accepted on welfare, the government takes on the role of the "primary earner." With high marginal tax rates on supplemental earnings, steady labor force participation is discouraged and the secondary earnings role of the mother is reinforced. In addition, men, whether actually or only "statistically" separated from their families, also take on a secondary earner role, because their earnings are no longer essential to family support. It was found that for every ten women coming on to AFDC, four women and two men dropped out of the labor force. Among low-income groups, this may cause a narrowing of sex differentials in labor force participation and wage rates, as both men and women become secondary members of society. Work disincentive effects and marital instability effects have been confirmed in other studies, using very different data sets (e.g., Honig 1974; Shea 1973). However, in the most recent study by the Urban Institute, findings indicate that welfare is more likely to inhibit remarriage than encourage divorce and separations (Sawhill et al. 1975).

The debate about alternatives to the present system has been concerned primarily with definitions of the poverty population and work disincentive efforts. If the "working poor," (including intact husband-wife families) are included in the potentially eligible population, then incentives for separation and divorce are effectively eliminated, and interactions within the family become the important factor underlying the likely effects on labor supply. Killingsworth (1976) points out the possibility that, within a two-earner, low-income family, the result of a negative income tax (NIT) might be a rise in labor supply rather than a fall. If a NIT reduces earnings for both men and women by an equal percentage, then it is possible that the "added" worker effect resulting from the decline in husband's wage might dominate the decline in labor supply due to the reduction in *own* wage, and thus increase labor supply among women who have displayed such labor supply flexibility. However, in all cases, it is expected that a NIT will reduce the labor supply of husbands, because their labor supply decision is relatively unaffected by changes in their wives' wages. Greenberg and Hosek (1976) used 1970 Census data to test these hypothetical effects for husband-wife families and found that labor supply disincentive effects for wives over the life cycle would be small, because few wives in NIT-eligible households where both spouses are present currently work an appreciable number of hours, and also because in some regions the encouragement to work because of a reduction in the husband's marginal earnings may outweigh the discouragement resulting from the decline in the wife's own wage. If NIT replaced existing welfare schemes, they estimated less than a 1 percent reduction in hours worked, with little or no change in sex differentials between husbands and wives.

These results are not entirely consistent with the results of the New Jersey-Pennsylvania NIT experiment. There, husbands showed little response and wives a significant negative response in labor supply (Pechman and Timpane 1975). However, people would not reasonably be expected to make long-term adjustments to temporary changes. Therefore, to the extent that families eligible for the experiment conformed to traditional sex roles, it would be expected that such a temporary experiment would only serve to reinforce these roles. On the other hand, long-run permanent income support, unprejudiced by preconceptions concerning dependency, might well serve to break down stereotypical sex roles within low-income families. However, it appears to be quite unlikely that such an evenhanded and neutral system of general income maintenance will actually be instituted in the near future.

UNEMPLOYMENT INSURANCE

Unemployment insurance (UI) is another "event-conditioned transfer"[11] which is related to previous work experience. It was designed in the 1930s to provide partial replacement of earnings for those involuntarily unemployed. Although the program is federally initiated and regulated, the individual states have considerable latitude in setting various parameters. Because of the complexity of different state programs, it is possible to make only certain broad generalizations. Most workers are now covered by individual state systems and those who are not usually covered (like state and local government employees, farm workers and private household workers) were included temporarily during the recent recession under the Special Unemployment

Assistance Program enacted in 1974. Usually, an individual's weekly benefit level is computed as half of his or her usual average weekly earnings, up to some maximum level of earnings. However, because unemployment insurance payments are not taxable, the effective rate at which earnings are replaced is higher. On the average, Feldstein (1974) found average replacement rates for all states to be between 60 and 80 percent of previous earnings. This is probably, if not an overestimate, at least an upper limit. The U.S. Unemployment Insurance Service puts benefit rates in the range of 50 to 70 percent of net wages, while Munts and Garfinkle (1974) have estimated that, in Ohio, unemployment insurance replaces 40 to 50 percent of total remuneration after taxes. Unlike Feldstein, they took into account the effects of fringe benefits and average wage increases, as well as taxes. The average replacement rate nationwide appears to be between half and two-thirds, indicating that unemployment insurance does not eliminate the cost of unemployment to the individual, although it does significantly reduce it (Marston 1975; Hamermesh 1977a). In addition, the replacement rate for married women may be higher than for single women or for married men because of higher marginal tax rates.

Given that an unemployed worker is covered by the state UI system, actual eligibility for benefits is defined in terms of prior work attachment and the reason for separation. The standards for prior work attachment vary from state to state, but they all involve some minimum amount of earnings and/or number of weeks worked in a recent base period (usually the first four of the five preceding quarters or simply the preceding year). The general purpose of all these provisions is to determine that the individual has more than a casual attachment to the labor force. In most states, workers who quit their jobs voluntarily or were fired for cause are either automatically ineligible or, less frequently, eligible for benefits after a waiting period of six weeks or more. In many states, the allowed duration of benefits, as well as their amount, varies with base period earnings.

Because of its temporary nature,[12] any inequities or possible disincentives built into the system do not have as far-reaching ramifications as the other programs discussed. However, it is interesting to note some of the same biases concerning women's work which are apparent in the other programs. Although many states have provisions denying benefits to pregnant women during stated time intervals before and after delivery, this was declared unconstitutional by the Supreme Court on November 17, 1975. However, it is still unclear whether states can deny benefits to women who have lost their jobs specifically because of pregnancy. In eleven states, claimants are eligible for dependents' benefits as well as their own benefits if they provide more than 50 percent of the dependents' support. Even though a woman's earnings may be crucial to family well-being, if she earns less than her husband, it is presumed that her husband provides the children's support and, therefore, her unemployment will not permit her to collect dependents' benefits. In many states, individuals leaving work involuntarily for family-related reasons are denied benefits, even if they are available to take another job in another location (if a husband's job has caused family relocation) or with different hours (if there has been an illness in the family). It should be noted that the trend has generally been in the direction of greater restrictiveness, with more states in 1970 than in 1960 having special disqualification provisions concerning unemployment due to pregnancy or marital obligations.[13] A final inequity which is particularly felt by women, who are more likely to work part time than men, is that part-time workers who lose jobs involuntarily may be declared ineligible for benefits if they are not available to take full-time work, despite the fact that the wages of part-time workers are subject to unemployment taxes.

Above and beyond the fact that the characteristics of state unemployment insurance laws described above clearly do embody preconceptions about the role of women and make it more difficult for unemployed women to collect benefits, one can often observe what can only be described as a strong strain of bias against women in discussions of the unemployment insurance system, especially by those who feel it is too liberal.[14] This parallels and is closely related to the widespread attitude that unemployed women "don't count" in the way that unemployed men do, and that high female unemployment rates, as observed in chapter 4, need not be considered a serious problem. Obviously, this philosophy will have implications for macroeconomic policy as well as unemployment insurance coverage.

Given the different sources of unemployment for men and women, as seen in table 4.3, it should come as no surprise that women represent a smaller fraction of the insured than of the total unemployed. In March 1973, a time of relatively low aggregate unemployment, 43.9 percent of the unemployed, but only 38 percent of those collecting unemployment benefits, were women. The corresponding percentages two years later, in the depths of the recession, were 41.5 percent and 33.8 percent (Hamermesh 1977a:22, table 3). On the other hand, women are more than proportionately represented among exhaustees (those who use up all the weeks of benefits to which they are entitled), since they are more likely than men to have base-period employment and earnings below those of the average claimant and thus a below-average potential duration of benefits.

The question of whether the existence of unemployment insurance raises the unemployment rate has been the subject of both heated debate and many empirical studies. Since several aspects of unemployment insurance interact to affect behavior, the total effect of the system on labor supply, and on the unemployment rate, is complex. Given the definition of the unemployment rate, as discussed in chapter 4, unemployment insurance could increase it by increasing labor force participation and/or the average duration of a spell of unemployment via workers' supply decisions, or by increasing the number of spells per worker, largely via employer decisions with respect to layoffs. Many empirical studies on the effect of unemployment insurance and the size of benefits on either weeks of unemployment per spell, or, less ideally, benefit weeks per spell, have found some lengthening effect. The best rough estimate appears to be that an additional half week of unemployment results from each 10-percentage-point increase in the earnings replacement ratio.[15]

It is difficult to ascertain whether this increased duration of unemployment represents productive search or leisure. If the former is the case, we would predict an improvement in postunemployment wages because of the longer search effort. Ehrenberg and Oaxaca (1976) found that, for the groups studied (men 45–59, women 30–44, and men and women 14–24), there was a significant increase in wages for both older men and middle-aged women, indicating little difference between the sexes in job search commitment. Among younger women, there was some slight evidence of substituting unemployment for out-of-labor-force status, thus possibly increasing the labor force participation rate and unemployment rate for that group.

Extensions of the duration of benefits in recessions have no doubt induced some exhaustees of regular benefits to remain in the labor force rather than dropping out. Hamermesh (1977a) cites the absence of a drop in the labor force participation rate in 1973–1975 as possible evidence of this effect. However, studies covering 1958, 1961, and 1974–1975 reveal that most exhaustees showed strong labor force attachment, and only a small fraction dropped out after exhausting all benefits. It appears that most claimants who eventually exhaust their benefits are not merely those who would have left the labor force in the absence of unemployment insurance. Labor force participation, in contrast to the amount of time spent in the labor force by those who participate, is not signficantly related to the characteristics of unemployment insurance programs. By increasing hours supplied, unemployment insurance results in a higher level of employment as well as longer spells of unemployment. Hamermesh (1977b) found that prime-age women who are already in the labor force are induced to substitute market for nonmarket work, and to work more weeks than they would otherwise. However, these effects are small in magnitude. The unemployment insurance system has at most a marginal effect on sex differentials in wages and unemployment duration, and cannot be seen as an important explanation of women's higher unemployment rates.

It is clear that the increased pressure for equal rights has forced some changes in entitlement to social security and unemployment insurance. However, the changes made so far involve minor variations on a basic structure rather than a reevaluation of the structure itself. All the policies discussed here continue to be based on two major assumptions about the structure of households: (1) the importance of the nuclear family as a social and economic unit of support; and (2) women's dependent position within the family because of their secondary commitment to the labor force. Because of the rising divorce rate and the growth of two-earner families, increasing numbers of men and women have no experience with the traditional family structure described above, and many others experience it as only a transitional phase in their life cycles. Other economic changes discussed in previous chapters have induced a breakdown in traditional sex roles, despite any deterrents to that process built into the policies discussed here. Thus, policies which once reinforced the division of labor by sex are now responsible for growing inequities between men and women. And policies which were once supportive of women within the institution of marriage are now creating disincentives to marriage rather than only disincentives to work. However, the very design of institutions and programs such as progressive income taxes and social security reinforces certain myths of female dependency, which slow the underlying process of social and economic change which is taking place.

On the other hand, there are signs that this outdated institutional framework is at last beginning to respond to the pressures of underlying social change, and that overall restructuring may well take place in the foreseeable future. A major revision of the social security system, along either of the lines suggested in the recent HEW Report, would almost inevitably lead to reconsideration of and eventual changes in other income redistribution programs as well. The elimination of outmoded assumptions concerning female dependency in any one area should make it easier to challenge analogous assumptions elsewhere.

We will now turn our attention to a set of policies and programs designed to develop individual earnings potential, either by increasing productivity and thus hourly wages, or by decreasing unemployment and the accompanying loss of earnings, or both.

Policies and Programs Designed to Increase Earnings

The redistribution of existing earnings is only one part of a two-pronged attack on poverty and inequality. A complementary approach is to increase earnings directly in the labor market by increasing the wages of the working poor and by increasing employment opportunities for those on the margin of the labor force. The maintenance of economic growth and the smoothing of cyclical fluctuations through fiscal and monetary policy is the most general approach to earnings improvement through an economy-wide increase in job opportunities. An approach that can be both an alternative and a complement to aggregate demand manipulation is the development of employment and training programs targeted to meet the needs of specific groups, both in terms of improved access to market opportunities and/or the acquisition of new skills. The minimum wage laws are another example of a very specific approach to earnings improvement which may, in fact, benefit one group of workers at the expense of another. Each of these very different approaches to earnings improvement has an impact on the individual regardless of family attachment, which differentiates these from the policies previously discussed. However, because of differences between men and women in their occupational distributions as well as their responsiveness to market opportunities, the impact of these policies may not in fact be entirely symmetrical. Nevertheless, because none of these policies target sex differences in market opportunities and rewards as a particular area of conern, we are treating them separately. Their differential effects, if any, are generally unintended. In the section that follows, we will examine macroeconomic policy, employment and training programs, and minimum wages in turn as they impact on sex differentials in earnings and unemployment rates, both through their direct effects on wages and job opportunities and through their indirect effects on labor supply and skill acquisition.

MACROECONOMIC POLICY

Increases in aggregate demand generated through monetary and fiscal policy are linked to earnings improvement through a resulting increase in job opportunities. Such a stimulus in aggregate demand would presumably leave the structure of demand for labor unchanged. Therefore, the major question to raise here concerns the differential impact of macroeconomic policy on the unemployment and labor force participation rates of men and women.

Since the passage of the Employment Act of 1946, there has been a government commitment to the goals of "maximum employment, production, and purchasing power." These general goals are completely sex-neutral; the Employment Act nowhere refers to "maximum male employment" or "maximum employment of primary earners."

However, as women have become a more important component of both the labor force and unemployment, there has been some tendency to minimize the seriousness of an unsatisfactorily high level of unemployment by drawing attention to their increasing numbers. This occurred in both the 1970–71 and 1974–76 recessions.[16] In other words, it has been repeatedly suggested that macroeconomic policy to reduce unemployment is a less important priority than in the past because so many of the unemployed today are women. Fortunately, such attitudes have not become a major force in the formulation of macroeconomic policy.

Two aspects of differential unemployment discussed in chapter 4 are of particularly direct relevance to questions of short-run and long-run macroeconomic goals respectively: these are the lesser amplitude of cyclical fluctuation of the female relative to the male unemployment rate, and the widening over time of the unemployment gap. This would appear to indicate at first glance that women would have relatively less to gain than men from the smoothing of short-run fluctuations in aggregate demand, but might have more to gain from a long-run pattern of sustained economic growth. This is in fact partially correct, but the situation is actually more complex, particularly with respect to the effects of short-run fluctuations.

The less pronounced relative impact of recessions on the female unemployment rate is the net result of several opposing factors: (1) the concentration of women workers in industries and occupations that are less affected by cyclical fluctuations; (2) the fact that women have been especially likely to react to a reduction in job opportunities by leaving the labor force or, even more importantly, by postponing entry; and (3) the fact that women's relative lack of specific training makes them more vulnerable to layoff within industries in recession, which works in the opposite direction. With respect to the 1973–1975 period, R. E. Smith (1977) demonstrates convincingly that this recession was "an equal opportunity disemployer," largely because of the industrial and occupational distribution of the female labor force. For example, the construction and automobile industries, which experienced sharp declines, employ relatively few women. If the decline in total employment had affected all industries proportionately, female employment losses would have been considerably greater. Although such detailed analyses have not been performed for previous recessions, it appears that similar patterns have prevailed. No recession ever affects all industries and occupations proportionately, and many "women's jobs" do tend to be in less cyclically volatile sectors.

As we saw in chapter 2, labor supply varies procyclically, and these variations have been more pronounced for women, whose average participation rates are lower, than for men.[17] Thus a comparison of the unemployment rates of men and women over the business cycle may well be misleading as an indicator of the relative effects of short-run fluctuations in demand. As we saw in chapter 5, one way to deal with this problem is to look at cyclical changes in *employment*, rather than unemployment, for men and women. Data on cycles in total employment by sex during the period 1947–1968, adjusted for the trend of secular growth, show clearly that female employment exhibited greater variability over the business cycle than male employment,[18] although in the most recent recession, male employment was especially hard hit. Another closely related approach, developed at the Urban Institute, is to compute the jobless rate, a measure that combines both unemployment and labor force variation. Joblessness is measured as the difference between the number of people who would be available for work if the economy were at full employment and the number actually employed. Thus the jobless rate estimates the percentage of the *potential* labor force without jobs, while the conventional unemployment rate estimates the percentage of the *current* labor force without jobs (R. E. Smith 1977:6). The gap between female and male jobless rates shows considerably less cyclical variation than the gap between the corresponding unemployment rates, and provides a better indication of the relative effects of recession and recovery.

While it appears on balance that the short-run gains and losses from the ups and downs of the business cycle impinge with approximate equality on men and women workers, women clearly stand to gain relatively more than men from a rapid and sustained recovery and growth path in the long run. Women will account for roughly six-tenths of net employment growth for the remainder of the decade.[19] A simulation model of the American labor market broken down by demographic groups predicts that, by 1980, half of the job gains would go to women if GNP growth were 6 percent instead of 5 percent annually, although women would make up less than 50 percent of the potential labor force (R. E. Smith 1977). Women's gains in employment will come more from their increased labor force participation than from reductions in unemployment. Because women's labor force participation rates are more responsive to employment conditions than men's, increased growth rates will reduce their unemployment rates relatively less than men's.

The occupations that are predicted to grow relatively more rapidly than average employment growth under several alternative scenarios are service workers (excluding private household), clerical workers, and professional and technical workers.[20] These are all female-dominated sectors; however, in the case of the professional and technical category, growth is expected to be fastest in traditionally male-dominated subsectors. On balance, the present occupational distribution should allow a continued growth in women's employment. To the extent that women enter occupations where training and experience pay off, a faster growth option will permit women to build up seniority and experience which will improve their wages relative to men. However, in many of the areas where growth is expected, there are no well-established seniority systems.

If instead the economy limps on in semi-recession with excess capacity and high unemployment rates, it is likely that the mythology of women's secondary status will be revitalized in an attempt to justify the persistence of high unemployment rates. In the extreme scenario of zero economic growth (ZEG, which is proposed by various environmental groups) there would be no way to increase the employment of women without disemploying men, given the present institutional structure. There is a delicate balance between too little and too much stimulus. The tighter the market, the greater the percentage of newly created jobs which will remain unfilled, given the structure of the labor market and the skill distribution.

However, given the sex composition of the labor force growth and the expected growth patterns by occupation, women's employment stake in achieving a higher growth rate is larger than men's. In fact, every measurable market differential will improve in relative terms for women under an assumption of greater growth. The gap in labor force participation rates will narrow further because of the relative responsiveness of women's labor supply to improved employment conditions. The occupational distributions will become less segregated, because of the increase in career and training opportunities for women. To the extent that crowding has contributed to higher unemployment rates for women, this should narrow the gap between men and women in unemployment rates. The wage gap should also narrow because of increased job experience for women.

All these rosy predictions make general macropolicy appear to be a simple panacea for all existing inequality between the sexes. Although the direction of change seems good, the policy is unfocused. A benefit-cost analysis of such policies may weigh heavily against them if sex differentials are defined as their only target, particularly given inflationary fears. Training programs and affirmative action, because they are more directed at particular goals, are more likely to have a positive yield in terms of benefits relative to costs. In fact, given recent high rates of inflation, general macropolicy is viewed as tackling the employment problem much more effectively on the downswing of the business cycle than during periods of relative prosperity. As an example, the Humphrey-Hawkins bill focused on public service jobs rather than fiscal and monetary policy to achieve "full employment."

EMPLOYMENT AND TRAINING PROGRAMS

While macroeconomic policy seeks to raise earnings and lower employment by increasing the aggregate demand for labor sufficiently to absorb a given supply, employment and training programs approach these same goals more selectively, by facilitating the acquisition of marketable skills and job training for certain target population groups. Training programs provide schooling and job training in an institutional setting, whereas employment programs provide direct access to jobs in which on-the-job training can be acquired through the subsidization of private employers or the financing of public service employment. Originally, training programs were seen as a panacea for structural unemployment which was resistant to general macroeconomic policy. However, in more recent years, the focus has shifted toward employment programs with the recognition that training does not guarantee employment, but employment provides not only a job but usually some training as well. Employment programs provide a middle road between general macroeconomic policy and institutional training by increasing the demand for labor and at the same time channeling it toward certain targeted disadvantaged groups.

The theory of investment in human capital presented in chapter 3 underlies the development of training programs as a policy approach to employment and earnings inadequacy. Workers who cannot compete successfully in the labor market are provided with the requisite skills via public investment. These programs may be an important factor in raising the economic status of minorities and women *if* their disadvantaged position is largely the result of supply considerations, such as skill acquisition and labor force commitment. However, an adequate demand for labor must be present, both in the sense of sufficient aggregate demand on the macrolevel and an absence of discriminatory barriers on the microlevel. Training programs cannot operate in a vacuum, and vigorous application of both macroeconomic policy and antidiscrimination legislation is necessary if the gains from such training programs are to be maximized. However, in a real sense, these programs can only be as successful as their theoretical underpinnings are correct. If, for example, Thurow's job competition model is descriptive of reality and most relevant training is acquired on the job, then employment programs which provide disadvantaged groups with direct access to jobs which would otherwise be offered to groups with more favored background characteristics are more likely to be successful.

In the early 1960s, the focus of manpower programs was on structural unemployment, which developed even during periods of general prosperity in certain industries, occupations, or geographic areas, as a result of technological change. Thus the aim was to retrain skilled workers in response to shifts in demand, a policy expressed in the Manpower Development and Training Act of 1962 (MDTA). During the War on Poverty in the mid-1960s, the emphasis shifted to minority groups and the disadvantaged, who lacked skills because they were not properly educated or trained to meet the productivity requirements of the available jobs. An additional legislative mandate was provided through the Economic Opportunity Act of 1964.[21]

When unemployment rose again in the early 1970s, there was increasing pressure for the federal government to become the employer of last resort. The Public Employment Program (PEP) was created in 1971 through the passage of the Emergency Employment Act and was the first major job creation effort since the 1930s. PEP provided funds to state and local governments to hire the unemployed and subsidize their wages in "temporary" public service jobs. However, it is unclear whether these funds have really created new jobs, or just helped to alleviate the fiscal crisis in state and local governments through the simple internal substitution of funds. Titles II and VI of the Comprehensive Employment and Training Act of 1973 (CETA) continues the funding for public service employment geared to local needs, which are evaluated on the basis of previous allocations and the local unemployment rate. The emphasis through CETA is now on decentralization, with programs under local control. Some previous programs will be phased out, others will be continued under local control, and others, such as the Work Incentive (WIN) program and the Job Corps, will remain national programs.

Many manpower program evaluation studies have been conducted, but few have used a methodology which is sufficiently sophisticated to provide meaningful results. In analyzing the effect of a particular program on participants' earnings, it is crucial that there be a control group with which the participants' experience can be compared. Without this, all programs would appear quite successful, because enrollees are most often individuals who have suffered some recent adversity in the labor market or are entering the labor market. Without a control group, any subsequent improvement in their employment or earnings status would appear to be due to participation in the program, whereas some gains might have occurred in any case. Few studies have used the necessary controls, and only a handful have attempted to draw any conclusions about the differential impact on men and women.[22]

The enrollment pattern revealed in table 6.3 shows that, although they were numerically significant in most employment and training programs, female trainees were heavily concentrated in programs hav-

Table 6.3

Number and Percent of Enrollees in Major Manpower Programs by Sex, Fiscal Years 1965–1972

(1000's)

Program	Enrollment		Percentage Distribution Among Programs	
	Women	Men	Women	Men
1. Skill training programs	720	1090	18.5	21.8
MDTA—Institutional	530	654	13.6	13.1
MDTA—OJT	190	436	4.9	8.7
Women as percent of total	40%			
2. Job development programs	256	496	6.5	9.9
JOBS	99	214	2.5	4.3
PSC	72	40	1.8	0.8
AOP		22		0.4
PEP	85	220	2.2	4.4
Women as percent of total	34%			
3. Employment development programs	632	639	16.1	12.8
OIC	114	49	2.9	1.0
CEP	199	270	5.1	5.4
WIN	256	150	6.5	3.0
JOBS CORPS	63	170	1.6	3.4
Women as percent of total	50%			
4. Work experience programs	2300	2777	58.8	55.5
NYC	2277	2710	58.2	54.2
OM	23	67	0.6	1.3
Women as percent of total	44.8%			
Total	3908	5002	100.0	100.0

SOURCE: Calculated from table I-2 in Perry, Charles R., Bernard E. Anderson, Richard L. Rowan, Northrup, et al., *The Impact of Government Manpower Programs.*

NOTE: MDTA-OJT = MDTA—on-the-job training.
 JOBS = Job Opportunities in the Business Sector.
 PSC = Public Service Careers.
 AOP = Apprenticeship Outreach Program.
 PEP = Public Employment Program.
 OIC = Opportunities Industrialization Centers.
 CEP = Concentrated Employment Program.
 WIN = Work Incentive Program.
 NYC = Neighborhood Youth Corps.
 OM = Operation Mainstream.

ing a limited emphasis on the acquisition and development of marketable skills. Male enrollees had a roughly similar enrollment pattern, although a slightly larger percentage of them were found in programs categorized by Perry et al. (1975) as skill training or job development. Within programs, however, there was significant variation in the role of women. In the Opportunities Industrialization Centers program, which focused on entry-level jobs geared to local employment opportunities, 70 percent of the participants were women. In the WIN program, 63 percent of the enrollees were women. This is not surprising, considering that the eligible population is restricted to those on welfare, the overwhelming majority of whom are women. Since the expansion of the WIN program, through subsidies to employers and the requirement of participation for all except exempt groups, the share of women in total enrollment has increased still further (U.S. Dept. of Labor 1974:367). In 1975, 45.6 percent of those enrolled in institutional training programs under CETA were women (Kiefer 1979). On the other hand, the representation of women in PEP and the Job Corps has been quite low (28 percent and 27 percent respectively).

Within the skill development programs such as MDTA institutional training and JOBS, studies using control groups consistently show that women's earnings improvement has been better than men's.[23] In order to enhance participants' chances of finding a job opening, certain high turnover areas such as the clerical and health fields were emphasized in MDTA particularly. Because these areas were traditionally female-dominated and growing sectors, it is not surprising that women, who were trained primarily as clerical and service workers, did better as measured by relative earnings gains than men, who were trained primarily as craftsmen and operatives (see table 6.4). It is interesting to note that, contrary to the above generalization, a large percentage of black women were trained as operatives in the JOBS program. However, Kiefer (1976) indicates that, although black women's earnings increased substantially relative to their comparison group after participation in the JOBS program, white women's relative earnings improvement was twice as great. This suggests, but certainly does not prove, that training along traditional sex lines for women may be more successful in the short run than preparing them to enter male-dominated fields, given barriers to entry, such as union control, in

Table 6.4

Occupation of Training by Program, Race, and Sex

Percent of Trainees Trained as:

	Professional & technical workers & managers	Clerical workers	Sales workers	Craftsmen	Operatives	Service workers	Laborers
Males							
Black							
MDTA	4.3	4.8	1.3	44	40	4.8	0.4
JOBS	1.2	8.8	1.8	11	56	7.0	15
JC	1.8	1.8	0	67	16	5.3	8.8
NYC	1.9	20	0	22	15	37	3.7
Nonblack							
MDTA	10	2.6	0.0	55	29	2.6	.5
JOBS	3.9	12	2.6	18	43	9.1	12
JC	3.7	1.9	0	72	5.7	9.4	7.5
NYC	2.1	17	0	25	10	31	15
Females							
Black							
MDTA	1.3	64	0	2.6	8.6	23	0
JOBS	1.3	39	1.3	1.9	53	1.9	1.9
JC	2.1	44	2.1	8.3	0	44	0
NYC	1.8	66	0	0	1.8	30	0
Nonblack							
MDTA	1.8	63	1.2	.6	2.4	31	0
JOBS	0	67	2.1	0	29	2.1	0
JC	10	50	0	5.0	0	35	0
NYC	0	63	1.6	0	3.2	32	0

SOURCE: OEO/DOL sample (1969/70), computed by N. Kiefer, "The Economic Benefits from Manpower Training Programs," p. 70.

traditionally male occupations. For example, Kiefer (1979) found that MDTA institutional training had a positive effect on both the probability of employment and the level of earnings for a sample of black women, but that there were no significant effects for those trained in occupations other than clerical or service. The strongest gains accrued to those trained in service occupations. Training which channels men and women into traditional lines of work may enhance women's employability in the short run, because of the relative availability of jobs and the lack of resistance, but will reinforce the traditional segmentation of the labor market by sex and limit women's long-run upward mobility. Without coordination of training programs with affirmative action policy and without overall manpower policy planning, it is unlikely that these programs alone can or will affect the occupational distribution by sex.

Another reason why the measured gains for women in these adult training programs may have been greater than men's is that these programs attract new female labor force participants by facilitating labor force entry. Because women have traditionally been particularly responsive to employment conditions, the availability of programs teaching marketable skills may have been a strong inducement to labor force entry. Therefore, some gains in earnings may be deceptive because a higher percentage of women in the control group than in the program will probably remain outside the labor force. Because women's opportunity costs are not estimated, the higher labor force participation of program participants will create the impression of greater earnings gains than in fact took place. If training programs were just facilitating the entry of women who would have entered the labor force in any case, their impact would be significantly overestimated.

One important exception to the general patterns described above was the early phase of the WIN program (1967–71), when it was primarily a skill-training program. During this period, women had lower placement rates than men and, at the completion of the program, lower labor force participation rates as well. This is not surprising, given the welfare population to which the program is directed. There is less motivation for women to follow through because their support on Aid to Dependent Children is not contingent on WIN participation.

Employment and training programs directed at youth have shown a different pattern of effects. In the Job Corps and Neighborhood Youth Corps, the relative gains have been divided along racial lines, with black males gaining the most and white women experiencing actual losses. This may be explained by the high unemployment rates of black teenage males in urban areas, where these programs are concentrated. In relative terms, they should be expected to show more improvement. It is not entirely clear why women appear to have benefited so little and in some cases suffered losses. This may be partially explained by decreases in labor force participation upon entering the program (Kiefer, 1976, p. 65). In the case of the NYC, which really functions as a "combination income maintenance device and an aging device to help youths (stay) out of trouble until they are old enough to get a sustaining job or to become involved in a training program" (Woltman and Walton 1968:80), women may be participating in the program as a transition between school and childbearing.

There is no data yet with which to evaluate systematically the relative effect of public employment programs on men and women. The enrollment of women in 1971 and 1972 (see table 6.3) was low, and there was some evidence to indicate that women were less successful in being promoted and transferred to "permanent" positions (Perry et al. 1975:63). In 1973, the fraction who were women (26 percent) was well below their proportion of all unemployed persons (47 percent) (U.S. Dept. of Labor 1974:154). This was probably primarily due to the emphasis placed on finding jobs for Vietnam veterans, although the types of jobs available may also have had some effect. Education, public works, and transportation absorbed by far the greatest proportion of PEP funds, and public works and transportation are traditionally male-dominated. Typical job titles included engineering aide, clerk-typist, traffic engineer, street and highway repairman, housing and fire inspector, classroom aide, police dispatcher, apprentice fireman, park laborer, and maintenance helper—almost all traditionally associated with the male sex. Although some public employment proposals were seen by Berkeley City Manager John L. Taylor as "a good opportunity to integrate, both by race and sex, the traditionally white, male-dominated jobs,"[24] there is no evidence that this has occurred to any significant extent.

Although alleviating labor market inequality between the sexes was not one of the explicit goals of the Emergency Employment Act of 1971, it is certainly not inconsistent with the general objective of promoting equal employment opportunity. Public employment programs have a definite potential for reducing sex differentials in earnings and unemployment, but this potential has not been fully exploited. Nor does it appear likely that it will be in the near future: young people, veterans, and male heads of low income families seem to have a higher priority than women, even those who head low-income households, when it comes to using public employment as a tool for lowering employment rates. In fact, recent data show that, within each Title of CETA, women make up a larger proportion of those eligible for services than those being served, and this is most dramatically the case in the public employment program (Underwood 1979). In view of the fact that inflationary pressure, both actual and potential, may well make such programs a more viable countercyclical measure in the future than general fiscal and monetary policy, there is cause for concern. The greater enrollment of women in public employment programs, and especially in nontraditional jobs within those programs, is essential to the improvement of women's economic status.

The available evidence that government has provided a partial escape from wage discrimination for women workers (Corazzini 1972; Long 1976; S. P. Smith 1976, 1977) lends credence to the importance of equal opportunity in public employment. The greater wage advantage for women relative to men in government employment at every level does indicate there may be less sex discrimination in the public sector. However, it is far from nonexistent, despite the requirement that "federal agencies take affirmative action to assure equal employment opportunity" (Office of Management and Budget 1976:231). S. P. Smith (1976) finds that, for otherwise equally qualified women workers, employment by federal, state or local government resulted in a wage advantage relative to private employment of 31 percent, 12 percent, and 3.6 percent, respectively. On the other hand, while men employed by the federal government enjoyed a 19-percent wage advantage, male employees of state and local government earned no more than comparable workers in private employment. In fact, private employment yielded a 5-percent wage differential over local government employment for male workers (pp. 195–97). Nonetheless, there are sizeable gross earnings differentials and apparently substantial discrimination in every sector. Table 6.5 presents results, analogous to those in table A5.1, on the size and decomposition of the earnings gap by sector. S. P. Smith (1977) argues that these wage patterns are probably passed on from the private to the public sector through wage policies based on comparability, but may also reflect tastes on the part of public sector employers and fellow employees.

The one available study of the effect of PEP on sex differentials is

Table 6.5

Gross Female/Male Wage Ratios and Proportion of Gap Explained
by Sector, 1973 and 1975

	Observed Earnings Ratio = F/M	Earnings Gap = 1 − F/M	% of Gap "Explained" by Characteristics[a]	% of Gap due to Discrimination[b]
1973				
Federal	.662	.338	48%	52%
State	.699	.301	44%	56%
Local	.787	.213	29%	71%
Private	.588	.412	42%	58%
1975				
Federal	.675	.325	26%	74%
State	.725	.275	47%	53%
Local	.813	.187	29%	71%
Private	.645	.355	43%	57%

SOURCE: Computed from S. P. Smith, *Equal Pay in the Public Sector: Fact or Fantasy*, p. 109, table 6.1.
NOTE: See chapter 5 for a full discussion of these measurement concepts.

[a] $\dfrac{(F/M)^* - F/M}{(1 - F/M)}$

[b] $\dfrac{1 - (F/M)^*}{(1 - F/M)}$

consistent with the above evidence on public sector employment in general. Simeral (1978) found that, for 1278 men and 566 women who participated in PEP in 1971, the wage differential by sex was smaller during participation than in the jobs they held either before or subsequently, apparently because PEP wages were more standardized with respect to individual characteristics. However, the relative importance of discrimination (once again measured indirectly via the residual method) remained roughly constant over all three periods. The beneficial effect of public employment on relative wages does not appear to carry over to employment opportunities and occupational structure. Long (1976) found that relative employment opportunities for women in federal service were only slightly more favorable than in private industry. Simeral (1978) reports that the evaluation of requirements for specific jobs under PEP resulted in occupational segregation by sex; if anything, the jobs held by the PEP participants were even more sex-stereotyped than the jobs they had held previously. With the decline in unemployment in 1972 and 1973, the need for a counter-cyclical tool diminished. Funding for PEP continued at a low level in fiscal 1974 and 1975. In its place, Title II of CETA authorized a public employment program targeted to those regions where unemployment rates remained high despite falling national unemployment rates. By 1975, with unemployment rates rising again, the allocations to public employment through CETA funding rose rapidly to more than $1 billion during fiscal 1975 (U.S. Dept. of Labor, Manpower Administration 1975:49). Although unemployment rates have declined gradually since 1975, funding for public service employment under Titles II and VI of CETA has remained at high levels. Supplementary appropriations for fiscal years 1977 and 1978 authorized a further rapid build-up in the number of such jobs. Despite a 1976 provision targeting 50 percent of new vacancies in Title VI to low-income persons, which actually increased the proportion female among those eligible from 54 to 65 percent, the percentage of women enrolled under the new rules actually decreased between 1976 and 1977. (Underwood 1979:22)

Given the continuing tendency to stereotype women as secondary workers and to treat their unemployment as less important than that of men, the concern remains that the rationing of training slots and public service jobs may be biased against women, particularly in times of high unemployment. Bell (1976) first voiced this fear in connection with the then-pending Humphrey-Hawkins bill (the Full Employment and Balanced Growth Act of 1976), which was never passed. Goals for veterans have been a major deterrent to increased female participation in public service employment, as has the increasing tendency to ration jobs by means of a "one per family" limitation. (Underwood 1979:24).

In conclusion, it is unlikely that employment and training programs have had a dramatic effect on trends in sex differentials. Whether this is because of the inadequacy of the human capital approach per se in this context or because of the fairly conservative approach to sex roles taken by the individual programs is difficult to say. Adherents of the dual labor market theory would argue that training and skills alone will not lift women or other disadvantaged groups out of their secondary economic status, if they still remain sequestered in secondary labor markets, characterized by inferior jobs with little or no opportunity for advancement. In this view, the essential problem is not lack of necessary skills at all, but rather artificial barriers to entry into the primary labor market, created not only by employers but also by training program staff personnel, and therefore the present training approach is seen as largely irrelevant and inappropriate. The demand side of the market must be attacked directly through the enactment and enforcement of legislation guaranteeing equal opportunities and prohibiting discrimination, and employment programs must focus on opening up job access in the primary sector. This type of direct attack on demand is the subject of the final section of this chapter.

On the other hand, one could well argue that, while providing investment in and access to training is a perfectly valid and effective way to decrease sex differentials in earnings and unemployment rates, the manpower programs have had much less effect in this area than they could potentially have, because of the traditional and uncreative approach that has been taken. Certainly, none of these programs has attempted in any dramatic way to seek out female participants or to break loose from prevalent sex stereotyping of occupations. Women, to the extent they have been enrolled in training programs, have been trained in traditionally female occupations and men have been trained in traditionally male occupations. Probably it has been easier for these programs to place their trainees successfully by not rocking the boat, and the number of placements is the usual criterion by which the success of a program is measured. Although the traditional occupational distribution has been reinforced through these programs, their existence is likely to have provided some inducement to female labor force participation and some relative improvement in female wages, at least in the short term, thus slightly narrowing the gap in wages and labor force participation rates. Unfortunately, however, these beneficial effects have fallen far short of their potential.

MINIMUM WAGES

Another approach to earnings improvement for low-wage workers is through minimum wages. However, this can only benefit those who can get and keep a job. Therefore, it is a superficial approach to an underlying problem that is primarily related to the distribution and level of demand on the one side, and the distribution and availability of skills on the other.

Given the downward sloping demand curve for labor discussed in chapter 4, raising the wage rate will result in fewer workers being employed, other things being equal. Only under conditions of monopsony is it possible for legislation to raise wages with no negative effect on employment; in this case, the minimum wage serves as a countervailing force, balancing the employers' power to control the level of wages. However, if the demand curve is shifting to the right over time as the economy grows, we will observe not an actual decrease in employment, but a slower rate of employment growth than would have occurred in the absence of minimum wage legislation.

While macroeconomic and manpower policies (and also the anti-discrimination legislation to be discussed shortly) seek to increase earnings by affecting both wage rates and hours of employment, minimum wage legislation is concerned only with the former component of earnings. Therefore, the actual effect on total earnings is unclear: the higher hourly wage rate may be outweighed by shorter hours and/or more unemployment, resulting in an actual fall in earnings. Those at the bottom of the earnings distribution, including many young people, women and minorities, will be most likely to suffer from these unintended side effects of minimum wage legislation. A minimum wage is clearly inferior to the other policies considered as a technique for increasing earnings. Such legislation can only be truly effective in achieving this goal where labor markets are riddled with monopsonistic imperfections, and workers would be consistently paid less than their marginal product in the absence of a legal floor under wage rates.

Minimum wage legislation was first passed by individual states and was primarily designed to protect women and minors from wage exploitation through discrimination in trade, service, and manufacturing industries.[25] Since the passage of the Fair Labor Standards Act in 1938, which set up minimum wages at the federal level for men and women, most states have passed legislation to cover men as well. In most cases, state legislation usually extends only to those areas not covered by federal legislation. As federal minimum wage levels rise and coverage expands, state legislation becomes less important, except in a few states (Alaska, Connecticut, and New York) where state minimums exceed federal levels (Welch 1976a). Today, minimum wage legislation is not seen as being in any way related to the issue of sex discrimination. However, because of differential coverage and different behavior patterns between the sexes, it is possible that the minimum wage has had dissimilar effects.

When the Fair Labor Standards Act was first passed in 1938, the coverage of the law varied considerably across industries, with the most "machine-intensive" and, therefore, the most "male-intensive" industries being the most thoroughly covered. Coverage was increased in 1961, and again in 1966 and 1974. As can be seen in table 6.6, the extension of coverage in retail trade and services has been most notable, and coverage rose further to 63 percent in retail trade and to 83 percent in services under the 1974 legislation (Welch 1976a). It is interesting to note that until the 1974 changes, the most extensively covered industries were the male-dominated industries. Table 6.7 shows women as a percentage of total employment by industry. It appears that the smaller the percentage of women in the industry, the

Table 6.6

Percentage of Employed Persons in Firms Covered by Minimum-Wage Legislation by Industry and for the Aggregate, Selected Years

Industry	1947	1962	1968
Mining	99	99	99
Construction	44	80	99
Manufacturing	95	95	97
Transportation and communication	88	95	98
Wholesale trade	67	69	76
Retail trade	3	33	58
Finance, insurance, and real estate	74	74	74
Services	19	22	67
Aggregate	56	61	79

SOURCE: Unpublished data obtained from the U.S. Dept. of Labor, Bureau of Labor Statistics. Taken from: Finis Welch, "Minimum-Wage Legislation in the United States," p. 2.

Table 6.7

Women as a Percentage of Total Employment in Selected
Nonagricultural Industries, 1950, 1960, 1970, and 1977

Industry	1950	1960	1970	1977
Mining	2	5	8	9
Construction	3	4	6	6
Manufacturing	26	25	29	30
Transportation and communications	16	18	22	23
Wholesale trade	21	22	24	24
Retail trade	41	44	47	50
Finance, insurance, real estate	44	49	52	56
Services	58	62	63	63
Aggregate	32	36	40	43

SOURCES: 1950, 1960, 1970: E. Waldman, B. J. McEaddy, "Where Women
Work," p. 4, table 1.
1977: Computed from unpublished BLS data.

more extensive the minimum wage coverage. In more recent years,
extensions of the law have had a larger impact on women than on
men, because the industries where they are concentrated have been
experiencing the largest percentage of changes. In fact, in 1970, 60
percent of all women in nonagricultural industries were concentrated
in service and retail trade (Waldman and McEaddy 1974).

When coverage is incomplete, minimum wage legislation affects the
industrial distribution of low-productivity workers by reducing their
employment in the covered sector (where legislated wages now exceed
their productive value) and increasing their employment in the
uncovered sectors. It also exacerbates the cyclical employment
instability of these workers, because as demand falls in recession, they
will be the first to be fired, particularly if the firm is unable to adjust
wages downward. Some of the loss in employment may show up as a
rise in unemployment and some may show up as a decline in labor
force participation.

As indicated above, women, along with younger workers and
members of minority groups, are most susceptible to these effects, as
the legal minimum wage is raised relative to average hourly earnings
for the economy as a whole. It has been observed that the ratios of the

unemployment rates of teenagers relative to adult workers, and women relative to men, tend to be greatest in periods immediately following an increase in the minimum wage (Burns 1966). The worsening of the sex differential in unemployment rates described in chapter 4 does appear to have some relation to minimum wage coverage. Female-male differences in unemployment rates since 1962 have tended to be significantly larger than was the case in earlier years, and young and nonwhite women actually began to have higher rates of unemployment than their male counterparts for the first time in 1962. This phenomenon is related to the 1961 extension of the coverage of the Fair Labor Standards Act. In September 1961, in addition to raising the minimum wage from $1.00 to $1.15 an hour, the 1961 amendment to the act extended coverage of 4.3 million more workers, including 2.9 million in retail trade and services.[26]

Several recent studies have calculated disemployment effects of minimum wages, but none has focused specifically on the differential impact on men and women. For the 1954–1969 period, Mincer (1976) found small disemployment and discouragement effects for women 20 and over, but he does not provide an exactly comparable figure for men. Teenagers and men aged 20–24 showed sizeable effects, but men 25 and over showed no significant effect. It is possible that with incomplete coverage in services and retail trade, the major effect of women so far has been on the distribution of employed between the covered and uncovered sector. In 1950, 54 percent of all nonagricultural women workers were employed in retail trade and services, whereas in 1970 this had risen to 60 percent (Waldman and McEaddy 1974). This may partially be explained by their lower coverage in those sectors. Therefore, at least until recent extensions of the minimum wage to cover more retail trade and service workers (including domestic employees), low-wage men may have suffered more disemployment than low-wage women, because of the low-wage opportunities for women in sectors uncovered by the law. Recent extensions may have a larger disemployment effect on low-wage women.

The major earnings-augmenting policies discussed here have been shown to have only minor effects on sex differentials. Because these policies are designed to deal with the individual and not the family, they do not have the problems inherent in the whole array of programs related to income redistribution and maintenance, which were previously discussed. However, because both levels and the rates of change of labor force participation, earnings, and unemployment differ significantly between women and men, these policies may still have different implications. Clearly, rapid growth rates and employment and training programs should facilitate women's rapid entry into the labor force, both by creating more jobs and by training women for the kinds of jobs that are available. Changes of this sort should eventually work toward narrowing the sex differentials that exist in earnings and unemployment rates. On the other hand, recent extensions and increases in the minimum wage will probably have the opposite effect. Because none of these policies question in any basic way women's present status in the labor market or their occupational distribution, they all may well have a tendency to reinforce existing patterns in sex differentials, rather than creating any impetus for change.

Policies and institutions, like the basic sex differentials that we have observed, clearly interact with and reinforce one another. Thus it is to some extent misleading to discuss the general policy effects with which we have been so far concerned in the absence of any reference to the legal framework concerning discrimination and equal opportunity. The distribution of the benefits of prosperity and growth and of employment and training programs, in particular, will depend in large part on whether past discriminatory patterns are allowed to perpetuate themselves. On the other hand, the opening up of new opportunities to women will be much more feasible in a context of sustained economic growth than under conditions of continuing economic stagnation. Thus, as we turn our attention to those policies that impinge directly on sex differentials, it is important to keep in mind their relationship to both the availability of training opportunities and the general health of the economy as a whole. In fact, improvements in the functioning of labor markets, from both the supply side in terms of providing opportunities for training and mobility, and from the demand side in terms of eliminating various types of discrimination and providing access to jobs with upward mobility, can be of great importance in the achievement of the general economic goal of prosperity and noninflationary full employment.

Direct Policies Designed to Affect Sex Differentials

Recent government legislation has focused on equal employment opportunities for minorities and women. The purpose of the legislation has been to tackle directly inequality in the labor market, by making certain kinds of typical employment behavior illegal, and, in some circumstances, requiring affirmative action on the part of employers to assure open access to jobs on a nondiscriminatory basis. This is not the first time in American history that government policy makers have been concerned about sex differentials in the job market. In the early 1900s, much labor legislation was passed at the state level to "protect" women (and children) from exploitation through long hours, low wages, and unduly strenuous work. These laws, by treating women as a group, reinforced certain stereotypes about women's frailty and their secondary attachment to the labor force. Recent legislation has emphasized the importance of the individual, regardless of sex, and is attempting to tackle the sources, as well as the consequences, of discriminatory behavior.

This section will begin with a review of the major legislation at the state and federal levels and some of the most important judicial decisions. This will be followed by a discussion and analysis of the likely consequences for various sex differentials, and a summary of recent empirical evidence of actual effects.

REVIEW OF LEGISLATION

Until the early 1960s, all legislation affecting sex differentials was passed on the state level. Many states not only passed various labor laws protecting women in the early 1900s, but twenty-two of them had passed laws requiring equal pay in most kinds of private employment by the time the federal Equal Pay Act was passed in 1963. In addition, two states (Hawaii and Wisconsin) had fair employment practice laws prohibiting discrimination by sex before passage of Title VII of the Civil Rights Act, while twenty-five states had already passed laws prohibiting racial discrimination in employment at that time (U.S. Dept. of Labor, Women's Bureau 1975:322–24).

The laws protecting women in the labor market can be broken down into three broad categories: (1) laws providing supposed benefits; (2) laws restricting women's employment under certain circumstances; and (3) laws excluding women from certain jobs (Task Force on Working Women 1975). Examples of laws providing benefits include minimum wages for women only, and requirements specifying that employers provide a meal or a rest period. By 1923, sixteen states had minimum wage laws for women. In that year, these laws were declared unconstitutional in *Adkins v. Children's Hospital*, in which the judge declared that "we cannot accept the doctrine that women of mature age require or may be subjected to restrictions upon their liberty of contract which could not be imposed in the case of men under similar circumstances" (Munts and Rise 1970:4). This was reversed in a one-vote shift in the Supreme Court in 1936, when Chief Justice Hughes was quoted as saying, "What can be closer to the public interest than the health of women and their protection from unscrupulous and over-reaching employers?" (*ibid.*, p. 5).

Laws restricting women's employment include maximum hour regulations and regulations restricting night work. By 1931, twenty-seven states had created maximum weekly or daily hours to protect the "health and morals" of women. There were also state laws excluding women from certain kinds of jobs, such as mining, bartending, or jobs requiring weight-lifting, or from any employment before or after childbirth. For a time, these laws coexisted with a ruling declaring minimum wages for women illegal, reflecting an ambiguity in policy that still exists today, although in less extreme form.

The 1960s and the 1970s have seen the passage of many equal employment opportunity laws at the federal level, each having different coverage, different enforcement mechanisms and different agencies of administration. However, because of certain conflicts with previous state "protective" laws, actual action against sex discrimination did not become significant until the 1970s. Amendments have broadened laws and strengthened enforcement, and regulations have been changed to meet unanticipated problems. Interpretive rulings by the courts have set important precedents in the application of the law. Because of the enormous cost of individual suits, the emphasis over this period shifted to class actions dealing with systematic patterns of discrimination. More recently, the "pattern and practice" approach, which results in plant- or company-wide agreements giving women and/or minorities back pay and access to better jobs, has again been weakened. The current trend appears to be toward dealing with sex discrimination complaints on an individual, case by case basis, or in the framework of "small" class action suits, where each individual member of the affected class is specifically named. However, the Equal Employment Opportunity Commission (EEOC) has not abandoned the pattern and practice approach, and is currently developing new standards and guidelines for systematic proceedings.

The Equal Pay Act of 1963 is the oldest federal legislation dealing with sex discrimination. It prohibits differential rates of pay to women and men in the same establishment who "do equal work on jobs, the performance of which requires equal skill, effort and responsibility, and which are performed under similar working conditions, except where such payment is made pursuant to (i) a seniority system, (ii) a merit system, (iii) a system which measures earnings by quantity or quality of production; or (iv) a differential based on any other factor than sex" (Task Force on Working Women, p. 87). Until July 1972, only employees covered by the federal minimum wage law were covered. At that time, the Education Amendments of 1972 significantly expanded coverage to include employees of small firms, and executive, administrative, and professional employees, including teachers and other professional personnel in educational institutions at all levels. Although coverage has been expanded, there are still discriminatory practices that this law does not address. If jobs are sex-segregated by firm and pay differentials by sex result, this does not constitute a violation of the Equal Pay Act, so long as each firm employs only members of one sex in each occupational category.

On July 1, 1979, the authority to enforce the act was transferred from the Wage and Hours Division of the Employment Standards Administration of the Department of Labor to the EEOC as part of a general reorganization of civil rights enforcement. In the first eight years, the Wage and Hours Division found $47 million in back pay owing to 113,000 employees, almost all of whom were women. However, by the end of 1972, only about one-third of this amount had actually been paid. Some small percentage of the total has also been recovered through costly court action (Task Force on Working Women 1975:90).

Title VII of the Civil Rights Act of 1964 is the most far-reaching federal legislation dealing with discriminatory practices, both in terms of coverage and in terms of the type of behavior outlawed. With extensions of coverage in 1972 and 1973, the law now affects all employers and labor unions with more than fifteen employees or members, as well as those employed by educational institutions and state and local governments and federal agencies. It is an unlawful employment practice "for an employer covered by the law (1) to fail or refuse to hire or to discharge any individual or otherwise to discriminate against any individual with respect to his compensation terms, conditions or privileges of employment . . . or (2) to limit, segregate or classify his employees in any way which would deprive or tend to deprive any individual of employment opportunity or otherwise adversely affect his status as an employee. . . . " (Kanowitz 1969:108). Labor unions and unemployment agencies are also covered by the law. Exceptions are permitted only when sex is a *bona fide* occupational qualification (BFOQ) reasonably necessary to the normal operation of business. Differentials in compensation are also permitted if they result from a seniority or merit system.

In revised guidelines laid out by the EEOC in 1972, the conflict between state protective laws and Title VII was resolved. In the case of state laws restricting or prohibiting women's employment in certain circumstances, Title VII is said to supersede these laws because of the inherent conflict between them. In no case does the existence of state laws justify the use of BFOQ exceptions. In the case of state laws providing benefits to women only, in the form of minimum wages or premium overtime, the EEOC deemed it unlawful for an employer either to refuse to hire women in order to avoid the provision of mandated benefits, or not to provide them to men (U.S. Dept. of Labor, Women's Bureau 1975:292–93.)

Until 1972, the primary responsibility for enforcing Title VII was with the injured individual through the court system, or with the attorney general in the government's name in a case where a pattern or practice of discrimination had occurred. Until that time, the Equal Employment Opportunity Commission had no power to go into the court on behalf of the government or the aggrieved individual, but could only act as a friend of the court. In 1972 the Equal Employment Opportunity Act, which extended coverage of Title VII to employees of educational institutions and to state and local government employees, also gave the EEOC court enforcement powers. In 1974, the enforcement power of the attorney general was also transferred to the commission in pattern cases (Task Force on Working Women 1975:93).

Because of the enormous number of charges received, the EEOC has not been able to keep up with the current level of cases. Since 1966, the inventory of unresolved cases has grown from 2,300 to 106,700 in 1975, despite a significant increase in appropriations, from $3250 million in 1966 to $55081 million in 1975 (U.S. Equal Opportunity Commission, *Tenth Annual Report* 1975).

Executive Order 11375, effective October 13, 1968, amended a previous executive order (11246, issued in 1965) to prohibit discrimination based on sex by federal contractors, subcontractors and employers on federally assisted construction. These two orders establish the practices and policies required of all contractors who have more than $10,000 in federal money, and apply to the entire institution within which the contract is held. The key section reads:

The contractor will not discriminate against any employee or applicant for employment because of race, color, religion or national origin. The contractor will take *affirmative action* to ensure that applicants are employed, and that employees are treated during employment, without regard to their race, color, religion, sex or national origin. Such action shall include, but not be limited to the following: employment, upgrading, demotion, or transfer; recruitment or recruitment advertising; layoff or termination; rates of pay or other forms of compensation; and selection for training, including apprenticeship.

Private contractors with contracts totaling $50,000 or more, as well as educational institutions and medical facilities, must develop written affirmative action plans within 120 days of commencement of a contract. Revised Order No. 4, effective December 4, 1971, strengthened guidelines relating to sex and specifically required the contractor to analyze his work force to "determine if women and minorities are underemployed and set numerical *goals* and timetables by job classification and organization unit to correct any deficiencies" (Task Force on Working Women, 1975:105).

The overall compliance program for Executive Order 11246 is administered by the Office of Federal Contract Compliance Programs (OFCCP) of the Department of Labor. Local and state governments have their own contract compliance programs as well. Eleven individual government agencies were originally delegated the responsibility to achieve compliance among contractors to which they award contracts. In the case of educational institutions, the Office of Civil Rights of the Department of Health, Education and Welfare was designated the agency responsible. In October 1978, all enforcement was consolidated under OFCCP.

The potential impact of these executive orders is large because roughly one-third of the total labor force works in companies holding government contracts. However, during the three-year period from 1970 to 1972, only 18 percent of federal contractors were subject to compliance review, and, although 700 notices to "show cause" why sanctions should not be imposed were issued, only two contracts were suspended during that time (Goldstein and Smith 1976). The punishment specified is suspension or cancellation of all or part of existing contracts and/or the disbarment from any future contracts.

The most recent legislation of significant importance to women has been Title IX of the Education Amendments of 1972, which states: "No person in the United States shall, on the basis of sex, be excluded from participation in, be denied the benefits of, or be subjected to discrimination under any educational program or activity receiving Federal financial assistance." (U.S. Dept. of Labor, Women's Bureau 1975:300). This is particularly important for women because one important source of inequality between the sexes in the labor market has been differential access to certain education and training opportunities.

Although the precise ways in which this law will be applied in the future remain to be seen and will be determined in part by judicial rulings, it appears reasonable to assume that a variety of widespread "role-differentiating" practices are no longer legal. These include: requiring all male or female students to take specific classes, unless students of both sexes are required to take these classes; denial of admission to either sex in classes traditionally reserved for the opposite sex; guidance practices that tend to establish one-sex classes, or counseling, including testing, that pushes students toward sex-linked career areas; employment placement systems that classify jobs by sex, or differentiate by sex in terms of the occupational level of placement for students with similar educational background (Hallam 1973:804). The provision that admissions policies may not discriminate on the basis of sex may well have a significant impact on the representation of women in graduate and professional schools and, eventually, on the occupational distribution of women workers.

JUDICIAL INTERPRETATION AND PRECEDENT

A significant body of case law has now developed on issues of employment, equal compensation and other terms and conditions of employment. Until very recently, the courts have been fairly consistent in interpreting the scope of the laws broadly. On January 13, 1970, in a precedent-setting case under the Equal Pay Act, *Schultz* v. *Wheaton Glass Company* (421 F. 2d 259, 61 LC ¶32,284 [CA-3 1970]), the Third Circuit Court of Appeals explained:

Congress in prescribing "equal" work did not require that the jobs be identical, but only that they be *substantially equal.* Any other interpretation would destroy the remedial purpose of the Act. (Task Force on Working Women, p. 88)

Therefore the concept of equal pay for equal work was seen to go well beyond comparisons within narrow job classifications.

Two other major decisions under the Equal Pay Act involved the Daisy Manufacturing Company (*Hodgson* v. *Daisy Manufacturing Company*, 317 F. Supp. 538 63 LC ¶32,392 [DC Ark. 1970]) and the Midwest Manufacturing Corporation (*Wirtz* v. *Midwest Manufacturing Corporation*, 58 LC ¶32,070 [DC Ill. 1968]). The former case reaffirmed the principle, set forth in *Wheaton*, that jobs need not be absolutely identical to require equal pay. More specifically, the *Daisy Manufacturing* case set the important precedent that greater physical effort, in the form of occasional heavy lifting required of male workers, does not make jobs unequal or provide any basis for a wage differential. This is of considerable significance, inasmuch as claims of this sort have been commonly used by companies attempting to justify paying higher wages to men, and have been consistently disallowed by the courts (Burns and Burns 1973:97).

The significance of the *Midwest Manufacturing* case lies in the fact that it addresses the crucial issue of "statistical discrimination," and finds such behavior to be in violation of the Equal Pay Act. The corporation in question had been paying male employees higher wages, on the grounds that hiring women involved higher employment costs. The court's decision specifically made it illegal to judge individuals on the basis of (supposed) group averages, and to pay lower wages on the grounds of (alleged) differences in group costs, such as turnover or absenteeism rates, based on sex (*ibid.*).

Judicial interpretation of Title VII focused broadly on effects rather than intentions in the early 1970s, and thus challenged a wide variety of common employment practices that excluded minorities and women from many positions. This approach is best exemplified in the Supreme Court's opinion in *Griggs* v. *Duke Power Co.* (401 U.S. 424, 3 EPD ¶8137 [1971]), a crucial case under Title VII which defined the potential scope of illegal discriminatory acts. Although this case related to hiring criteria for blacks, it has broad implications for all types of discrimination. In this case, tests, the results of which were not necessarily correlated with performance on the job, were used as a prerequisite for hiring. The result was that fewer blacks were hired, because fewer blacks had the requisite educational background. The Court ruled that, even if the intent had not been discriminatory, the result was discriminatory, and, therefore, not permissible. The Supreme Court held that

Under . . . (Title VII), practices, procedures, or tests neutral on their face, and even neutral in terms of intent, cannot be maintained if they operate to "freeze" the status quo of prior discriminatory employment practices . . . The Act proscribes not only overt discrimination but also practices that are fair in form, but discriminatory in operation. . . . Congress directed the thrust of the Act to the *consequences* of employment practices, not simply the motivation. (Edwards 1973:413).

Decisions in general sex discrimination cases under Title VII have tended to conform to this principle until very recently. Two important examples of cases in which "neutral" practices were found to be discriminatory *in effect*, and therefore ruled illegal, are *Danner* v.

Phillips Petroleum Co. (447 F. 2d, 3 EPD 8319 [CA- 5 1971]) and *Meadows* v. *Ford Motor Co.* (5 EPD 8468 [W.D. Ky. 1973]). The former case involved a system in which only employees in certain job titles had seniority rights, and there were no women in those particular jobs. The latter case concerned a policy requiring production workers to weigh at least 150 pounds. This restriction eliminated 80 percent of all women aged 18–24 from eligibility for these jobs, although there was no evidence that weight was directly correlated with the ability to do the work required (Edwards 1973:414).

This "pattern and practice" approach was seized on by EEOC, and became the major weapon in class action cases involving sex or race discrimination. The most dramatic and widely publicized of these cases involved the American Telephone and Telegraph Company (AT&T). On January 18, 1973, a consent decree between AT&T, the Equal Employment Opportunity Commission (EEOC), the United States Department of Labor and Department of Justice was approved in the District Court. The Bell system is the largest employer in the country and the remedial wage adjustment, which will amount to at least $38 million, or roughly $1,000 in back pay and $640 annual increment per worker, was the largest and most comprehensive civil rights settlement ever agreed to (Wallace, 1976:1 and 272). This and some other similar settlements indicated that the heat was on the large employers. The following statement made by Judge Constance Motley concerning this case makes it clear that intent is not seen to be the relevant issue in determining whether or not particular employment practices are discriminatory:

The wide statistical disparities . . . in the company's employment of women in various job categories in training programs *places a burden on the defendant* to show that the disparities are not the product of discrimination against women on the basis of their sex. . . . (Edwards 1973:414; italics ours)

In the same vein, faced with the threat of continuing suits, the United Steelworkers and nine steel companies agreed, in a 1974 consent decree, to $30.9 million in back pay and a restructuring of seniority systems to allow freer movement from one job to another (*Business Week*, June 20, 1977:28). Although Title VII originally permitted exceptions to equal compensation in the case of a seniority system, the *Griggs* case had made clear that it was a policy's consequences, not its intent, that was important to the proof of discrimination. The case dealt with practices which perpetuated the effects of past direct discrimination, but the broad language of the decision has been interpreted by the EEOC and the courts to cover any practice which has a disparate impact on any group protected by Title VII, even in the absence of any prior discrimination (Lopatka 1977). Certainly, Chief Justice Burger's words in the Court's unanimous opinion lend themselves to such an interpretation:

Congress directed the thrust of the Act to the *consequences* of employment practices, not simply the motivation. More than that, Congress has placed on the employer the burden of showing that any given requirement must have a manifest relationship to the employment in question. (Quoted in Lopatka 1977:32)

The lower courts have built up an immense body of Title VII law on the *Griggs* principle that outcome, rather than intent, is the key determinant of a Title VII violation, and that the burden of justifying a practice with disparate impact (be it an intelligence test, a minimum height requirement, a seniority system, or any such rule) falls on the accused employer (the so-called "business necessity" doctrine). Nevertheless, almost exclusive emphasis on effects has been qualified somewhat by recent Supreme Court decisions that again raise the issue of discriminatory purpose.

In *Washington* v. *Davis* (426 U.S. 229 [1976]), the Supreme Court appears to have introduced a distinction between Title VII violations and constitutional violations, with discriminatory intent as the key distinguishing factor. Although this case did not actually involve Title VII, its Title VII implications are very important and more than a little confusing. The basic finding was that a positive correlation between a literacy test for District of Columbia policemen and performance in a training program was sufficient to validate the test, without requiring further proof of correlation with later performance on the job (Lopatka 1977:48). This can be interpreted to mean that Title VII is not completely analogous to equal protection under the Constitution. Disparate impact alone may constitute a *prima facie* violation of Title VII, but does not establish the denial of equal protection under the Fourteenth Amendment, in the case of state and local government employees, or of Fifth Amendment due process, in the case of federal government employees (Lopatka 1977:36). A constitutional violation requires discriminatory purpose, but a Title VII violation does not. However, there has also been a retreat recently from the former position that a disparate outcome by race or sex, in and of itself, is evidence that Title VII has been violated.

This trend is apparent in the recent treatment of seniority systems. In a Supreme Court case in 1976 (*Franks v. Bowman Transportation Co.*, 44 U.S.L.W. 4356), the Supreme Court ruled that individuals denied jobs in violation of the act can be awarded retroactive seniority after being hired. On May 31, 1977, the Supreme Court in *Teamsters v. U.S.* (97 S. Ct. 1843 [1977]) issued a complicated ruling that reaffirmed their previous ruling on the award of retroactive seniority, but also held that Title VII does not prohibit the use of *bona fide* seniority systems even when they perpetuate acts of discrimination which occurred prior to the date Title VII took effect (July 2, 1965).[27] "As long as there is no *intent* to discrimination, employers and unions may continue to use the seniority systems" (Oelsner 1977a:1). Although there is the clear implication that acts of discrimination subsequent to the date of Title VII's implementation might not be similarly protected by seniority systems, this could be difficult to enforce, given the problem of proving intent and the necessity of timely filing of complaints. While the emphasis on intent as a legitimate criterion for determining the illegality of a discriminatory act was a definite break with past precedent, this does not necessarily appear to have drastically altered the application and interpretation of Title VII. The Supreme Court let stand a lower court ruling which rejected a challenge by three unions, charging that the promotion plan required by the AT&T affirmative action program violated seniority rules in union contracts (*Miller v. AT&T*, 77-1524 Cert. denied June 19, 1978). However, it is premature to read much meaning into this unexplained decision.

At the same time as the courts appear to be retreating from a broad to a much more narrowly defined interpretation of sex (and race) discrimination, there remain important unresolved issues relating to particular applications of Title VII; these include the BFOQ exception, fringe benefit plans and the controversial question of whether a quota is constitutional in the absence of a judicial finding of discrimination.

Title VII allowed exemptions to its ban against discrimination in hiring in the case of sex as a BFOQ. (Race or color, on the other hand, can never be a BFOQ.) The courts have interpreted the BFOQ requirement very narrowly, making it permissible only in the case of actors and actresses to specify sex as a requirement of the job. *Dias* v. *Pan American World Airways* (442 F. 2d 385, 3 EPD ¶8166 [1971]) was one of the strongest cases interpreting the BFOQ. In this case, Pan American refused to hire Dias (a man) as a flight attendant because they claimed that strong consumer preference for women constituted a BFOQ. The Circuit Court reversed the District Court decision, stating that "discrimination based on sex is valid only when the *essence* of the business operation would be undermined by not hiring members of one sex exclusively" (Task Force on Working Women, p. 96). In another case, *Phillips* v. *Martin-Marietta Corp.* (400 U.S. 542, 3 EPD ¶8088 [1971]), the Supreme Court upheld the principle that motherhood by itself was not a reasonable basis for exclusion from a job. In this case, the company rejected applications for a job from mothers with preschool children. The Court ruled:

The existence of such conflicting family obligations, if demonstrably more relevant to job performance for women than a man, could arguably be a basis for distinction. . . . But that is a matter of evidence tending to show that the condition in question "is a *bona fide* occupational qualification reasonably necessary to the normal operation of that particular business or enterprise." (Hawkins 1974:28)

The general view that the BFOQ exception should be interpreted very narrowly is probably best expressed in the Fifth Circuit Court of Appeals opinion in *Weeks* v. *Southern Bell Telephone and Telegraph Co.* (408 F. 2d 228, 59 LC ¶9213 [CA-5 1969]), which states:

In order to rely on the *bona fide* occupational qualification exception an employer has the burden of proving that he had reasonable cause to believe, that is, a factual basis for believing, that all, or substantially all, women would be unable to perform safely and efficiently the duties of the job involved. (Edwards 1973:416)

Another significant case in this area was *Rosenfeld* v. *Southern Pacific Company* (444 F. 2d 1219), where the court specifically ruled that state protective laws do not make sex a BFOQ, but that each applicant must be considered on the basis of his or her own individual qualifications.

A very recent ruling, in early 1977, has mixed implications with regard to the future interpretation of the BFOQ exception. In a decision involving restrictions on the employment of women as prison personnel in Alabama (*Dothard* v. *Rawlinson*, 97 S. Ct. 2720 [1977]), the Supreme Court invalidated height and weight restrictions, which would have automatically excluded many women without regard to capabilities, but permitted a ban against women guards in "contact" positions, as falling within the BFOQ exception. It is possible that this latter ruling may encourage employers who have previously had BFOQ claims disallowed to appeal in the hope of convincing the Supreme Court that their restrictions on the employment of women are in fact valid under this provision (Oelsner 1977b:A8).

The legality of fringe benefit plans which treat men and women differently remains in question. Different compulsory retirement ages for women and men have been found to violate Title VII in *Bartmess* v. *Drewrys* (444 F. 2d 1168, 3 EPD ¶8271 [1971]). The Supreme Court has also ruled that employer pension plans which require larger contributions of women (which are most common among public employees) are in violation of Title VII (*Los Angeles* v. *Manhart*). However, many pension plans defer discrimination by paying larger monthly benefits to men than to women upon retirement on the actuarial grounds that women as a group will outlive men as a group. The question of whether or not such systems are in fact discriminatory remains unresolved, although a recent decision appears to reject actuarial figures as a legitimate basis for creating differences by sex in retirement benefits (*Rosen* v. *Public Service Electric Co.*, 5 EPD ¶8499 [CA-3 1973]).

Certainly one of the most difficult issues in the area of fringe benefit plans is the whole question of maternity leaves and maternity benefits. The 1972 EEOC guidelines stated that an employment policy that automatically excludes pregnant women from employment or from certain jobs would be considered a case of sex discrimination under Title VII, and, furthermore, that employment policies having to do with maternity leaves and health insurance benefits must "be applied

to disability due to pregnancy or childbirth on the same terms and
conditions, as they are applied to other temporary disabilities"
(Edwards 1973:421). Until 1976, every federal court of appeals that
had considered this matter had held the exclusion of pregnancy from
temporary disability coverage to be illegal sex discrimination under
Title VII (Oelsner 1977b:A8). However, in December 1976, the
Supreme Court ruled that private employers who have programs temporarily compensating employees for a wide range of disabilities may
refuse to compensate women for absences due to pregnancy (*General
Electric* v. *Gilbert*, 97 S. Ct. 401 [1976]). More recently, in December
1977, the Supreme Court ruled that, although employers can deny
pregnant employees sick pay for maternity leave, they cannot take
away accumulated seniority when they return to work. Fortunately,
these setbacks proved to be only temporary. On October 31, 1978,
President Carter signed into law the much-debated pregnancy
disability bill which amends Title VII to prohibit all discrimination on
the basis of pregnancy.

Although quotas to remedy past discriminatory practices have been
generally accepted as both constitutional and in accord with Title VII,
it can be argued that, in the absence of such past illegal discrimination, preference for one individual over another on the basis of race or
sex (so-called reverse discrimination) very probably violates Title VII
(Lopatka, 1977:54). This issue, in the context of "benign" racial
discrimination, was raised in the *DeFunis* case (*DeFunis* v. *Odegaard*,
416 U.S. 312 [1974], vacating for mootness, 82 Wash. 2d 11, 507 P.
2d 1160 [1973]), but was not resolved. The California Supreme Court
held, in *Bakke* v. *Regents of the University of California* (18 Cal. 3d
34, 132 Cal. Rptr. 680, 553 P. 2d 1152 *cert. granted* 97 S. Ct. 1098
[1977]), that granting such preference is unconstitutional, but the
court's opinion in upholding this decision appears to circumscribe its
relevance so narrowly that it has no implications for affirmative action
programs with respect to such areas as hiring, promotion, and occupational segregation by sex.

However, as this book goes to press, *Weber* v. *Kaiser*, which
appears to be the case that will either eliminate or exonerate voluntary
affirmative action, is being heard by the Supreme Court. The Kaiser
Aluminum & Chemical Corporation is being sued for reverse discrimi-

nation under Title VII by a white male employee, who was denied admission to a crafts retraining program, because of a requirement that half the trainees be black or female. The Kaiser program was held to be illegal by both the Federal District Court in New Orleans and the Fifth Circuit Court of Appeals. The Supreme Court's decision in this case is expected to decisively define the future course of affirmative action. As things stand now, a company with no proven record of past bias could conceivably be sued for discrimination under Title VII for either establishing or failing to establish an affirmative action plan. A decision in Kaiser's favor would legitimize strong voluntary efforts to upgrade female and minority workers, but there is little hope that equal employment policies can spearhead a rapid elimination of occupational segregation and earnings differentials, if the Kaiser plan is found to violate Title VII.

PREDICTED IMPACTS ON SEX DIFFERENTIALS

In analyzing the impact of state and federal employment laws on sex differentials in the market, we will assume that discrimination is widely practiced. Given our discussion in the previous chapter, this seems to be a totally reasonable assumption. We will analyze each of the major pieces of legislation reviewed above in terms of its predicted impact on sex differentials in wages, employment, and occupational distribution. We have seen that this legislation falls into two broad classes: (1) "protective" labor laws; and (2) "equal employment opportunity" (EEO) laws. The crucial distinction between them is that EEO laws attempt to make discrimination itself illegal, whereas protective laws allow discrimination to persist but, instead, attempt to compensate for some of its consequences. In practice, the actual effect of many so-called protective laws has been not to protect women workers, but to restrict the opportunities open to them and to help perpetuate discrimination.

Early state laws requiring minimum wages and overtime pay for women but not for men reflected a concern for one consequence of discrimination: namely, women's low wages relative to men's. However, because no restrictions were placed on the number of women employed, the result was a shrinking of job opportunities for women in the sectors covered by the law, with the unemployed finding jobs in sectors not covered by the law or dropping out of the labor force. The resulting implications for relative wages are unclear, and depend primarily on (1) the proportion of total employment covered by the law; (2) the discrepancy between minimum wages and prior wages for women; and (3) the elasticity of demand for women in the covered and uncovered sectors. The wages of women who retain their jobs in the covered sector will be higher than before, and the wages of women in the uncovered sector will be lower than before because of the increase in supply. The demand for men would also increase in the covered sector as they become *relatively* cheaper. The net result could be an increase or a decrease in relative wages because the mean wage for women and men would be a weighted average of their wages in the two sectors.

Other protective laws restrict or prohibit women's employment in certain specific occupations (i.e., those requiring long hours, night work, weight lifting, and other specific occupations like mining), again forcing women to seek employment elsewhere. This has clearly contributed to occupational segregation by sex. It also reduced women's relative wages by crowding them into fewer occupations. Early state legislation tended to reinforce all the sex differentials that have come to seem traditional, particularly occupational segregation. By limiting job opportunities, they inhibited the growth in women's labor force participation and human capital accumulation as well. These negative effects have been recognized, at least implicitly, in decisions that have invalidated such state laws where they are seen as being in conflict with Title VII.

Recent federal legislation is attempting to reverse these trends by making discrimination itself illegal. However, when behavior which is typical and pervasive is declared illegal, we cannot assume that it will necessarily be eliminated or even substantially reduced. The impact of the legislation will be a function of (1) the completeness of the law in specifying every manifestation of discrimination as illegal behavior; (2) the percentage of employment covered by the law; (3) the enforcement of the law; and (4) the extent of the penalties imposed. If the law makes certain forms of discrimination illegal but leaves others unmentioned, then employers are free to adjust their behavior so that discrimination persists and is reflected in new and unanticipated forms of disadvantage. But even illegal forms of discrimination will persist if the benefits of continued discrimination are seen to exceed the costs, in terms of the chances of being caught and the penalty if and when that occurs.

The first major piece of federal legislation which attempted to legislate equal employment opportunity was the Equal Pay Act. Although we have seen that equal pay for equal work was interpreted broadly to mean equal pay for similar work, it did not require the employment of women in any particular proportion and, therefore, a firm with an all-male labor force would be in compliance with the law. Even a firm employing both men and women would be in compliance with the law if all men were in management positions and women were in unskilled positions, or if all men and women were sorted so that in no case were members of both sexes doing similar work. With no specific employment provisions and incomplete coverage, the result would be a movement of women out of the covered sector (which initially was the same male-dominated sector covered by the minimum wage law discussed above), and the effect on relative wages is unclear. However, because Title VII was passed within a year of the Equal Pay Act and was more all-encompassing in its prohibitions, it does not seem necessary to predict the effect of the Equal Pay Act independently.

Title VII of the Civil Rights Act included both pay and employment provisions, and therefore goes beyond the Equal Pay Act in tackling various prevalent discriminatory patterns, including occupational segregation. By requiring equal treatment in hiring, promotion, firing, and compensation (including fringe benefits) employers were left little room to maneuver in complying with the law and, therefore, the costs of compliance were increased. Under these circumstances, unless the costs of noncompliance are also increased through extensive enforcement and expensive penalties, it is likely that a large percentage of covered employers will defy the law. Those firms who find the cost of compliance less than the cost of defiance will experience increases in operating costs, and this may force some smaller and less profitable firms out of business. To the extent that output and employment decline, any increases in female employment in the covered sector will be dampened. It is even possible that the result could be a net decline in employment for women if the overall decline in production were severe enough. This seems unlikely, however, particularly if employers with the most to lose are the ones most likely to defy the law, and, therefore, suffer no increase in operating costs unless they get caught.

Increased wages in the covered sector may attract new labor force entrants, some of whom may remain unemployed or may ultimately be forced to seek employment outside the covered sector. The result should be at least some improvement in relative wages and occupational distribution overall as all male occupations begin to include some women. However, in the long run relative wages may not improve if employers, no longer allowed to discriminate in money wages, discriminate instead in nonwage components of compensation, such as access to on-the-job training (Lazear 1979). It is also possible that relative wages could even decline if the reduction in employment in the covered sector were so severe as to cause further crowding in the uncovered sector and a decline in wages there.[28] However, this also seems unlikely.

The significant extensions of coverage in 1972 for both Title VII and the Equal Pay Act increased the probability of some positive effect on wage differentials and the occupational distribution. However, if output and employment were significantly affected, there might well be some negative effect on unemployment differentials, if women's labor force participation rates continue to rise rapidly and the rate of increase of new job opportunities is slowed. In the long run, however, if most discrimination is based on erroneous notions of women's productive potential, EEO legislation should not cause permanent increases in operating costs, but merely temporary ones, as firms make the transition to new modes of behavior.

The executive orders affecting government contractors go one step beyond Title VII by mandating positive timetables and goals for future hiring. However, they cover less than one half of total employment. Although "quota" is a dirty word to some observers, the effects of affirmative action can be analyzed as if certain female-male quotas were required and widespread enforcement is assumed. If the goal or quota mandated exceeds the available proportion of requisitely skilled women in the labor force, then, in order to meet the quota, employers could reduce their total skilled employment. Alternatively, they could engage in "skill bumping," which offers an option for utilizing workers who would otherwise be unemployed, by simple reclassification of job titles (Welch 1976:S112). In the simplest scenario, by increasing the proportion of skilled job titles, some less skilled women could be promoted to fill the quota and nothing else need be disturbed. There would be a redistribution of income from men to women, with women's relative wages improving somewhat, even if their reallocation caused the wage differential between "skill" groups to narrow. One problem, however, would be the allocation of skilled jobs to less skilled women, with possible adverse effects on productivity.

On the other hand, if the quota were in line with the availability of male and female labor, skill bumping would not be necessary, and productivity and output would improve as skilled women previously underemployed in less skilled occupations find more appropriate opportunities in the covered sector. Women's relative wages would rise more substantially than in the first case as some additional skilled men are forced to compete for skilled jobs in the uncovered sector. This seems more realistic because, in actuality, affirmative action goals are being set in accord with the proportion of women in the relevant labor pool. Particularly at the entry level, quotas based on available labor pools should not require any major dislocations, because of the rapid increases in women currently in training for certain traditionally male occupations. In many cases, the proportion of women available at the entry level will even exceed mandated goals or quotas, which are based on the proportion of women of all ages available.

ESTIMATES OF ACTUAL EFFECTS

Empirical research measuring the effects of EEO laws on minority employment and earnings has been available only relatively recently and, in most cases, has focused only on black males. This may partially be explained by the ambiguity prevailing in the law as it related to women, with EEO laws and state protective laws coexisting until the early 1970s. Recent extensions of coverage and increased enforcement powers of the EEOC occurred roughly at the same time that new EEOC guidelines declared that state protective laws were superseded by Title VII. It was also not until April 1972 that affirmative action guidelines from the OFCC relating to sex were implemented (Goldstein and Smith 1976:566). Therefore, it is now possible to engage in a before-and-after-1972 comparison. However, it is difficult to separate the effects of various laws because they coexist and, qualitatively at least, are predicted to have similar effects.

There have been two common empirical approaches to analyzing the effect of EEO legislation on minority employment and earnings: (1) a time series approach in which the time trend in minority or female earnings is related to variables measuring economic conditions and EEO enforcement; and (2) a cross-section approach in which firms which are more susceptible to government enforcement efforts are differentiated from other firms, by means of contract status or geographic location (Flanagan 1976:494). The time series approach has not yet been used to examine changes in sex differentials, because enforcement of EEO legislation has been so recent. Most cross-section studies have focused on the contract compliance aspect of EEO legislation, because it is possible to separate firms into two categories: contractors and noncontractors, or firms reviewed and not reviewed. However, it is not clear whether a result indicating that contractors have higher percentages of minorities necessarily means that the law has had any effect. Heckman and Wolpin (1977) found that firms with high levels of minority employment are more likely to get contracts and, therefore, such cross-section studies would overestimate the effect of the contract compliance program on firms' employment patterns.

The two cross-section studies which have investigated contract compliance by sex show negative effects for white women and negligible effects for black women. Goldstein and Smith (1976) looked at the determinants of relative change in employment and wage status for four race-sex groups across 74,563 individual establishments between 1970 and 1972. Dummy variables measuring the presence of a government contract and the occurrence of a compliance review were included. Although blacks showed small employment gains relative to whites in contract firms, men seemed to have gained relative to women. This can be explained by the lack of emphasis on sex discrimination before 1972. Heckman and Wolpin (1977), using data for 1973, found similar results. If any group gained relatively in the early 1970s, it was black men, simply because they were the only group really protected.

The only study which has examined the effect of the expansion and strengthening of EEO legislation in 1972 on women's earnings on an economy-wide basis was conducted by Beller (1979). This study is based on a cross-section of individuals in both 1967 and 1974, with variables measuring the incidence of enforcement of Title VII (ratio of total investigations completed by the EEOC to the number of women) and the probability of a successful settlement of a case (ratio of successful to attempted settlements) assigned to individuals according to geographic region. Enforcement of the federal contract compliance program was measured by the federal share of industry production, and values were assigned to individuals by industry of employment. Her findings suggest that, after the law was amended, the mean incidence of enforcement for sex discrimination tripled but still remained lower than that for race discrimination. The mean probability of successful settlement also appears to have increased following the amendments. Her results suggest that increased enforcement in this period raised women's earnings in most cases and narrowed the male/female wage ratio or, more accurately, prevented the gap from widening more than it did. However, these results must be interpreted with extreme caution because of the assumption that the impact of the programs evaluated varies mainly by geographical region and sector rather than by industry type and size of firm. For example, the impact of the AT&T settlement was more likely to be felt among large firms in general or firms in the same industry than by firms located in the same region where the AT&T case was conducted (Killingsworth 1979b).

Thus we find that empirical research suggests that the effects of EEO on earnings and employment of women have been small or even negligible and raises questions about the possible interpretation of results. Nevertheless, the degree of enforcement may be an important determinant of the actual impact. However, qualitative data on the EEOC compliance process in an earlier period indicated that the recession which began in 1969 enlarged the cost of settlement for firms, and increased the probability that firms would risk the threat of civil suit and court-imposed settlement rather than agree to conciliate (Adams 1973:26). Therefore, it is not entirely clear what role the state of the economy played in Beller's seemingly positive results.

Although the theoretical effects of EEO legislation are clear, the data do not yet show that any dramatic change has taken place. The recession and recent reversals in the courts strongly suggest that research using 1975–1977 data will find previous small positive effects eroded for blacks and women. It is unlikely that the positive changes in the law in 1972 were translated into any significant long-term shift in the direction of narrowing sex differentials. However, this should not imply that EEO programs are not useful. It only suggests that present methods of administration and enforcement are unimpressive and attention should be directed to methods for making the programs work, through better coordination and enforcement. If nothing else, the programs have heightened women's consciousness about themselves and their employment opportunities, and encouraged the pursuit of careers in nontraditional fields. However, as we have seen, the future of voluntary affirmative action is in doubt, and its elimination could easily destroy or reverse these incipient trends. Even if voluntary affirmative action is legitimized, these programs cannot be fully successful without the full support of the administration and cooperation between various branches of the enforcement machinery.

Conclusion

An assessment of the entire array of government policies and programs to date suggests that, if anything, the government has reinforced traditional sex roles in the labor market rather than serving as an impetus for change. In fact, social and economic change has outpaced government legislation in most instances, creating serious inequities between working and nonworking women and between one- and two-earner families. Even manpower programs and EEO have done little or nothing to date to alter the sharply divergent occupational distributions of men and women. Any slight earnings and employment gains achieved by women through manpower programs and EEO have been counteracted by the effect of inflation on the progressive income tax structure and the payroll tax, particularly as it affects working wives, who find themselves in rapidly rising marginal tax brackets. Slight adjustments in eligibility for social security benefits do not yet reflect a fundamental change in attitudes about the fairness of using the family as the unit of income support, although we have seen that more dramatic change may well be on the way.

Although some policy ambiguities have been resolved, others remain in force. The conflict between EEO and state protective laws has been eliminated by the courts. However, the family and the individual continue to vie with each other for government support and protection. As the nature of the family and woman's role within it change, this conflict is intensified. At the same time, certain principles of fairness compete in the courts: one pressing current issue is the conflict between equal employment opportunity on the one hand and seniority on the other. The recent recession intensified these conflicts by pitting groups against each other, thus reducing the chance that the government could have any real positive impact on sex differentials in earnings, employment, or the occupational distribution. Despite this lack of success, women's labor force participation rates continue to rise, defying the forecasters and exacerbating labor market inequities, both between men and women and between different groups of women.

Even if the government is not going to be a leader in initiating social change, it should at least keep laws and policies consistent with the social and economic change that has already taken place. This will require that the individual become the unit of income and earnings support regardless of family status. Beyond that, it is only possible for the government to provide the impetus for further change if it commits substantial resources to the effort, both in terms of dollars and of talent, so that those who discriminate will find the cost of its continuation prohibitively expensive.

As things stand now, the effects of policies that tend to reinforce outdated stereotypes and perpetuate the status quo continue to have a stronger influence than the well-publicized, but relatively weak, pressures from laws requiring equality of treatment. This is not surprising in view of the self-perpetuating nature of women's secondary status, and its close relationship to past patterns of discrimination and outmoded institutions. Simply declaring discrimination illegal cannot break such well-established behavioral patterns; often it is unclear exactly how the discriminatory behavior to be eradicated manifests itself.

As economic growth and technological change continue, behavior is modified in response to changing incentives, although expressed values and institutions may lag behind and continue to reflect choices that are no longer optimal. At this point it remains an open question whether strengthened and effective antidiscrimination policies or the ongoing pressure of primary economic change will provide the decisive impetus toward a break in the vicious circle of existing sex differentials.

NOTES

1. The 33.5 million families with two or more earners in 1975 accounted for 59 percent of all families where the husband was in the labor force, an increase from 47 percent in 1965. See Hayghe (1975b, 1976).

2. A recent study of Rosen (1976) explicitly tests for the presence of tax illusion and finds none, thus confirming that the after-tax wage is the important variable in decision-making.

3. There has been some debate as to whether the full burden of the employer tax is shifted to the employee. However, it is clear that at least some of the burden is shifted. Cf. Feldstein (1972) and Brittain (1972).

4. This material was drawn primarily from Ball (1973), and Hoskins and Bixby (1973).

5. Upon retirement, a fully insured female worker can get a 50 percent benefit for her husband only if she can prove that he received at least 50 percent of his financial support from her. However, in the case of widowers with dependent children (March 1975) or over the age of 60 (March 1977), the Supreme Court has declared them eligible for the same benefits as a widow would be entitled to in similar circumstances. The recent case invalidates the requirement for men to prove dependency to receive old age benefits on the basis of their wives' contributions as well. However, it is unlikely that many men will take advantage of this option, because in most cases their own entitlement will exceed the dependent's entitlement.

6. This example was derived from "Reports of the Quadrennial Advisory Council on Social Security," 1975, p. 74.

7. Starting in 1979, the duration-of-marriage requirement will be reduced from twenty to ten years.

8. Although people may perceive the payroll taxes they pay as being translated into credits accumulating in their account, this is in fact not the case, because payroll taxes collected from the working population are immediately redistributed to social security recipients and are, therefore, part of the government mechanism for redistributing income.

9. See Gordon (1978) for a comparative analysis of problems relating to the treatment of women under social security in France, Germany, Sweden, and the United Kingdom, as well as the United States.

10. Many such provisions have been eliminated by actions of the Congress over the years and recent decisions of the courts. A list of the remaining gender-based distinctions (ten in number) can be found in Appendix A (pp. 75–76) of the 1978 HEW *Task Force Report*. Amendments to eliminate these remaining anomalies were recommended by the Carter Administration to the Congress in 1977. However, the Congress deferred action on these changes, but agreed that this question would be included in the six-month study, provided for by the Social Security Amendments of 1977, of proposals to eliminate dependency and sex discrimination under social security.

11. Terminology suggested by Feldstein (1976).

12. Even with extensions passed at the federal level during the recent recession, the maximum number of weeks was sixty-five (up from the usual twenty-six weeks) or one and one-quarter years (Skolnik 1975).

13. In 1960, benefits were denied by thirty-five states when unemployment was due to pregnancy and twenty-one states when unemployment was due to marital obligations. By 1970, these numbers had risen to thirty-eight and twenty-three states, respectively (Adams, 1971, table 4, p. 71).

14. A somewhat extreme, but unfortunately not atypical, article in the December 1975 *Reader's Digest* (Kenneth Y. Tomlinson, "Let's Stop the Unemployment Compensation Rip-Off," pp. 100–4) illustrates this point. Five of the eight examples given of "abuses" of unemployment benefits by "undeserving" recipients involved women, including the two that he appears to consider more reprehensible. The first of these is the case of seasonal fruit packers ("mostly wives of working husbands") who receive benefits during the off-season, "although few seriously look for jobs." The second is the case of a woman who quit her job because her husband had taken a new position in another area. When she was unable to find another job, she drew unemployment benefits after the disqualification period. Having seen the importance of such exogenous geographic mobility in putting women workers at a disadvantage with respect to both earnings and unemployment, one might think that providing unemployment compensation for covered women workers who cannot find employment in the new area would be the least we could do. However, this woman was actually not a typical case, as indicated above. Many women in her position receive no benefits at all, no matter how long they remain unemployed. And when women do qualify for unemployment compensation under these circumstances, it never fails to arouse someone's outrage.

15. See Hamermesh (1977a, ch. 3) for a summary of the major studies and the derivation of this estimate.

16. See Niemi (1975:61–62) 61–62 for some examples from 1970–71. Examples from the more recent and severe downturn include the statements of Alan Greenspan (then chairman of the Council of Economic Advisors) in the *New York Times*, September 4, 1976, and "Unemployment—A Story the Figures Don't Tell," *U.S. News and World Report*, November 18, 1974:43–45.

17. See Lloyd and Niemi (1978) for some interesting evidence that the cyclical labor supply patterns of men and women are changing, and have become more similar over time. R. E. Smith (1977) also confirms this behavioral change in the most recent recession: "The evidence that changes in women's behavior did occur is strong. Past cyclical patterns suggest that after a recession as long and severe as this one, the labor force participation rate of females should be below its current magnitude. The difference between the unemployment rates of women and men is much larger than expected; in previous recessions, the difference narrowed, reflecting, in part, women leaving the labor force. In this recession the difference narrowed but not by as much as in the past because women's participation rate continued to rise. This certainly resulted in a higher unemployment rate" (p. 15).

18. See Niemi, (1974:338–39 and p. 341, table 4).

19. This may be an underestimate because the growth rate of the female labor force has been consistently underestimated by the BLS. Although it is easy to predict the growth in the working age population, it is much more difficult to predict the probability of labor force participation (R. E. Smith 1977:20).

20. This is assuming a 3.8-percent rate of growth (Carey 1976:10–12).

21. For an excellent recent review of all employment and training programs until 1972, see Charles R. Perry et al. (1975).

22. Both Kiefer (1976) and Perry et al. (1975) review the studies to date. In addition, Kiefer does his own empirical analysis of four of the major programs.

23. Because MDTA has been in effect a longer time, more studies have been done of this program than any other. All except Kiefer's study are reviewed in Perry et al.

24. "Public-Service Jobs—A way to Put the Untrained to Work," *U.S. News and World Report*, August 5, 1974, p. 62.

25. *1975 Handbook on Women Workers*, U.S. Department of Labor, Employment Standards Administration, Women's Bureau, Bulletin 297, p. 317.

26. U.S. Senate, *Hearings before the Subcommittee on Labor and Public Welfare* (Washington, D.C.: Government Printing Office, 1961), p. 14.

27. "Prior discrimination" actually includes not only pre-1965 discrimination, but also post-Act discrimination that has not been made the subject of a timely charge (Lopatka 1977:68).

28. An extensive discussion of the likely employment and wage effects of EEO legislation on blacks can be found in Andrea Beller, "The Effect of Title VII of the Civil Rights Act of 1964 on the Economic Position of Minorities," Ph.D. dissertation, Columbia University, 1974.

Chapter 7

Breaking Out of the Vicious Circle

At this point it is all too clear that the separation of the various aspects of women's secondary economic status—labor force participation, education and training, occupational distribution, earnings, unemployment—is an artificial one. Each aspect is part of the same problem and stems from a common source, involving women in a vicious circle with respect to work experience, human capital accumulation, earnings, and unemployment. Attitudes based on an outdated perception of reality still prevail, and in fact permeate our laws and institutions. Thus the "normal" role for a woman is still seen to be that of a wife, sometimes out of the labor force entirely but, in recent years, more typically a secondary worker with substantial nonmarket responsibilities. Women are still conditioned to expect to spend at least some portion of their working lives outside the labor force, and are implicitly and explicitly discouraged from investing heavily in market-oriented skills and career preparation. Direct discrimination against women in the labor market as well as institutional arrangements that treat men and women differently reinforce these effects, and help to make the socially conditioned expectations of secondary economic status a self-fulfilling prophecy.

Not only is the perpetuation of women's secondary economic status a circular process, but it is impossible to say with certainty at which point and with which factor the entire process begins. One could start, and many analysts have in fact done so, in the home, with the division of labor between the sexes and its resulting implications for the pattern of men's and women's labor force participation. Since the allocation of time of each household member is determined by both personal opportunities and opportunities open to other members, marriage is a primary determinant of sex differences in labor supply. Differences by

312

sex in market and home productivity form the basis of the observed differences in labor force participation and hours of work. Since, as we have seen, labor supply is closely linked to all other components of economic status, lower and less continuous market labor supply on the part of women results in less investment in training, both by themselves and by their employers, a different occupational distribution, higher unemployment, and lower wages.

At this point, however, uncertainty as to the direction of causation becomes painfully evident. Wages and job opportunities are affected both by individual and employer expectations of lifetime labor supply and by actual work experience, but the division of labor by sex, and the resulting differences in labor supply and occupational distribution, were initially described as the consequence of different opportunities facing men and women in the market and nonmarket sectors. Even if men and women were equally productive in the nonmarket sector, higher male market earnings would provide a strong incentive for the observed asymmetrical division of labor by sex, which turns out to be not a simple starting point or primary cause after all, but to be determined by, as well as determining, the other dimensions of women's economic status.

We could just as well start at any other point in the circle—with wage levels, occupational selection, investments in training, or, indeed, with government policies. In each case, we could trace out a chain of causation leading from the starting point to all the other components of economic status, but we would eventually find that the factor originally taken as primary is also itself partially determined by everything else. Thus it is impossible to define where or how this vicious circle begins, although the process of its self-perpetuation is readily traced. Given that women's economic status has historically been a secondary one, it is not surprising that it continues to be so. A related and equally difficult question is the one of how this vicious circle can be broken.

Are some links in the process weaker than others and more likely to yield to pressures for change? Would a decisive breakthrough at any point change the entire pattern? Can such a breakthrough be achieved on an individual level by changes in behavior, or is it necessary for aggregate behavior patterns to change? Is change more likely to come through specific policies directed to that goal or through the more impersonal forces of technological change and economic growth?

What is rather striking is that apparently it is possible for significant changes to take place in some areas without destroying the basic circular pattern. Most obviously, the dramatic and continuing increases in female labor supply have not yet led to a restructuring of the relative economic status of men and women. As we have seen, changes in the direction of greater similarity in the occupational distribution have been minor, and the earnings and unemployment rates of women relative to men have actually worsened. Does this imply that changes in labor supply will not be the source of decisive and far-reaching economic change, or simply that such changes have not yet progressed to the point where they will result in the breakdown of established patterns?

In this concluding chapter we will suggest some tentative answers to these questions, which emerge from our analysis of patterns and trends in sex differentials and our review of the relevant literature. These answers must be tentative, not only because the future is uncertain, but also because many of the personal and market dynamics which determine the market outcomes we seek to predict are not yet fully understood. The major findings of this book will enable us to analyze such predictions concerning labor force participation, education, and occupation as are available, and to speculate about the future unraveling of the vicious circle.

Major Conclusions

All the evidence we have collected documents strongly the radical behavioral change taking place among American women in all dimensions of labor supply. Not only are a majority of working-age women now in the labor force in any given week, but each successive cohort of women is displaying higher levels and more continuous patterns of labor force attachment than the preceding one. In other countries, such as Sweden, this same upward trend in labor force participation among women has been accommodated by a large increase in part-time work but this has not been the case in the United States, where the average work week for women has declined less than for men in the past ten years. In fact, among the group of working women most likely to work part-time (ages 25–34), there has actually been an increase in average hours over the last ten years.

Historically, marriage has been the major institution which has sustained and reinforced the traditional division of labor between the sexes because of the complementary roles played by men and women in the rearing of children. However, this has not always been as true of the black minority of the U.S. population. Labor market discrimination has hindered black men in the fulfillment of the breadwinner role and has resulted in less stable marriage patterns, as well as in a longer tradition of work among married women. Interestingly enough, in recent years, it has been married white women, and most recently white women with young children, who have contributed the most to the dramatic changes in women's overall labor supply patterns. This is not only because they are entering the labor force in greater numbers than before, but also because marriage and children are no longer causing them to withdraw from the labor force to as great an extent as was the case among their predecessors. Thus it is the sex differentials in labor supply that were originally the largest that are narrowing most rapidly.

Men's behavior has been changing as well, but by no means as rapidly or as radically as women's. This lack of complementary change has created strains and stresses both at home and on the job. Traditional functions must still be performed, but they are by no means equally shared. As a result, most working women are in fact moonlighting, holding down one job during the day and another in the evening, in order to sustain the physical, financial, and emotional health of the household.

Economic research shows clearly and consistently the importance of both the level of the family's financial resources and a woman's labor market opportunities as determinants of her work choices. Research on men's labor supply behavior, on the other hand, has shown them to be remarkably unaffected, except possibly at the beginning and end of their working lives, by the economic opportunities and work choices of their wives. There is some evidence, however, that their allocation of time within the home is affected. Unfortunately, the lack of time series analysis of labor force trends in the United States leaves us with only piecemeal explanations, derived from cross-sectional analyses, of the changes that are taking place. We lack the full interactive framework which would be necessary for a complete understanding of the sustained coexistence of radical change among women on the one hand, and relatively little change among men on the other hand.

Although we do not yet completely understand the dynamics of labor supply decisions, the analysis of panel data confirms that women are a heterogeneous group whose individual differences are, if anything, being accentuated over time by their respective worklife experiences. Working women's propensity to remain in the work force from year to year is increased by the specific skills acquired on the job, whereas nonworking women's propensity to enter or reenter the labor force is reduced over time by the growing gap between their skills and those demanded in the market place. Thus the changes that are taking place do result in conflicts of interest, not only between men and women but also between groups of women, at least in the short run.

These rapid changes in women's labor supply patterns also show up to some extent in educational trends. Although the average educational attainment of men has been rising slightly more rapidly than that of women, recent changes in college enrollment patterns by sex, as well as changes in fields of study, suggest that average educational attainment among women will continue to rise and become increasingly job-oriented. Not only is education a particularly necessary credential for women who seek careers, but the very process of education itself increases women's propensity to see a market-oriented career as more productive and personally rewarding than homemaking. Women as a group are a notable anomaly in the human capital framework, because they have relatively high levels of educational attainment and relatively low levels of earnings. Education has nonetheless proved to be a good investment for women, who also have lower opportunity costs than men.

Over the same period that labor supply has been undergoing dramatic change, there has been no overall change in the degree of occupational dissimilarity by sex and, if anything, a deterioration in wage and unemployment differentials. Not only is the duration of women's unemployment spells on average longer than men's, but the incidence of unemployment among women has been rising more rapidly than it has among men. Differences between men and women in lifetime labor supply are often used as an explanation for their sharply dissimilar occupational distributions. The same explanation has also been applied to the wage gap, and even to the unemployment gap, because of the differential importance of inter-labor force turnover for men and women. Although the gap between men and women in labor supply still remains large, its substantial narrowing has not been reflected in the trends for any of these indicators of market outcomes. Even the segmented labor market approach, which emphasizes the structure of the labor market and the importance of differential estimates of training costs in the job allocation process, would be at a loss to explain this lack of change without resort to the independent importance of discrimination, not only in creating differentials but in sustaining them.

Despite significant changes in the occupational distributions of men and women, there has been no resulting decrease in the degree of occupational dissimilarity between the sexes. Growth in demand has been primarily concentrated among just those occupations which have been strongly male- or female-dominated, thus washing out the effect of any shifts that have occurred in women's and men's occupational choices. Barriers against women to job and occupational mobility have limited their ability to translate gains in job experience into gains in earnings, job rank, or occupational standing. Recent evidence from panel data shows clearly that the quality of working experience acquired by men and women, in terms of the amount of actual training received, differs substantially. This suggests that as more women work, discrimination is becoming a more rather than less effective factor than in the past in constraining women from exercising their full range of work choices.

No study of wage differentials has been able to explain more than 50 percent of the wage gap between the sexes without resorting to factors, such as job rank and occupation, which are themselves at least partially the consequences of discrimination. At the same time that the wage gap has been widening, the sex differentials in average experience and job tenure have probably been narrowing, although average educational attainment rose faster for men than for women. Recent trends and research findings confirm the independent importance of discrimination as a factor creating and sustaining sex differences in market rewards. Individual work histories from panel data show that one year of job experience is not necessarily equivalent to another in terms of either its specific training content or its potential for wage growth and upward mobility. Women's experience in general is not concentrated in the types of jobs which require much training. Therefore, although training is crucial to wage growth, it is not synonymous with job experience, as the human capital approach has sometimes led us to believe. It is entirely possible for women's average years of work experience to increase without any narrowing of the wage gap. However, it would seem rational for women increasingly to seek out careers with training and wage growth potential because of their expectations of growing labor market attachment.

Rapidly rising unemployment rates among women have paralleled declines in their turnover rates. Given occupational segregation, it seems that demand has not grown rapidly enough to absorb the unprecedented number of women moving into and staying in the labor market.

The government has also been shown to have an unmeasured but nonetheless important impact on the evolution of sex differentials over time. While the government's programs and policies are often designed to sustain and reinforce the underlying social reality, they sometimes can act as a catalyst for change. Although most policies and programs are still based on traditional notions of male and female roles, recent enforcement of Title VII of the Civil Rights Act, as well as recent proposals for reform of the social security system, suggest that at least the government signals are no longer unidirectional. However, at this point in time, most income redistribution schemes still differentially penalize married women who work, thus reinforcing traditional work roles in the home and creating serious inequities both between working and nonworking women and between one- and two-earner families. In addition, employment and training programs have not admitted women in proportion to their eligibility, and have also taken the easy way out by training women for women's jobs and men for men's jobs, thus reinforcing the traditional division of labor between the sexes in the job market. Unresolved conflicts in the enforcement of equal opportunity laws and affirmative action create little incentive for employers to comply voluntarily with the law. In the meantime, social and economic change continues apace.

We are at a critical moment in this social revolution, as working women move into the majority. Although 50 percent is only one point on a continuum, it is an important one in a society committed to majority rule. To date there is little to suggest that men in general, or employers and policy makers in particular, have substantially changed their assumptions or patterns of behavior in response to this underlying social change. However, not only is the working wife and mother now becoming the rule rather than the exception, but soon the typical male employer or policy maker will have a working wife. Further projections of demand and supply patterns should suggest some answers to questions raised at the beginning of the chapter. Are we in the throes of some natural historical process, like the demographic transition, which has not yet run its course, or are there critical intervening variables which can halt or distort this transformation of sex roles which is taking place?

Projections and Future Sex Differentials

The continued growth in the labor force participation of women does not show any signs of leveling off in the near future. The assumption that a slowdown in the rate of increase was imminent has resulted in repeated underestimates of the projected female labor force by the Bureau of Labor Statistics. In fact, BLS projections worsened through time as the rate of growth of the female labor force accelerated. Because a long time period is used for linear projections and it is assumed that no further increases will take place after a terminal year, the lower rates of increase of the female labor force in past years are reduced still further as projected growth is tapered toward the terminal year. BLS projections revised as recently as 1976 (Fullerton and Flaim 1976) predicted that female labor force participation rates would rise from 46.3 percent in 1975 to 51.4 percent in 1990. As the aggregate female labor force participation rate passed the 50-percent mark only two and a half years later, it rapidly became apparent that female labor force growth had again been significantly underestimated, and that a reexamination of the assumptions underlying the BLS projections was called for. New forecasts, which differed from earlier ones in projecting three different possible paths based on high, intermediate and low rates of growth, were issued in August 1978. The high growth forecast shows the female labor force participation rate rising to 60.4 percent by 1990, a rate of increase that is more in line with recent experience (Flaim and Fullerton 1978).

BLS projections have been subjected to increasingly severe criticism in recent years because of their arbitrary assumptions. The most recent projections, although based on more complicated assumptions than have been used in the past, are by no means immune to this charge. Empirical research on labor supply has demonstrated that the size of the labor force is not mechanically determined by changes in population size and age distribution, although these factors are important, but is also dependent on the relative attractiveness of labor market opportunities and on real income levels. However, labor force projections derived from functional relationships are subject to the same criticism of arbitrariness leveled at the BLS, because their derivation requires projections of critical independent variables, such as future wage growth and family size, which are themselves dependent on, among other things, future labor force growth. There are also many alternative functional specifications from which to choose. R. E. Smith's (1979) projections based on this approach show the crucial importance of strong economic growth and improved relative wages for sustained increases in female labor force participation.[1] Future improvement in relative wages could have a particularly powerful impact on future labor force growth among women, because of reinforcing income and substitution effects.

Predictions concerning future birth rates were not incorporated into Smith's analysis, but this factor will obviously play a role as both a determinant and a consequence of future levels of labor force participation. The low-growth scenario in the most recent BLS projections involves the assumption that the total fertility rate (the number of children per woman) would rebound from the current low of 1.8 to 2.7, and that increases in participation among women aged 20 to 44 would be correspondingly slowed. Under this and other low-growth assumptions, the female labor force participation rate would be only 53.8 percent by 1990. However, the grounds for assuming such a rise in the birth rate are questionable, given the continuing strong upward trend in labor market attachment among young women.

One problem with the BLS projections is that they completely ignore any complementarity and interaction between male and female labor supply decisions. According to the high-growth scenario, participation rates are higher for all groups, and in the low-growth scenario, they are lower for all groups; the distinct possibility that male and female participation might change in opposite directions is not dealt with. The low-growth path, which incorporates increased birth rates, is assumed to result as well in a decline in male participation in the age groups between 20 and 54, but past experience might lead us to believe that this fertility increase and the accompanying slowdown of female labor force growth would be accompanied by constant or increasing participation on the part of prime-age males. On the other hand, the high female participation rates of the high-growth scenario could well be accompanied by lower, not higher, male participation, due to the greater flexibility they would thus acquire.

Educational projections for the labor force, because they are linear projections of past trends, reflect a continuation of the present shifts in college enrollment patterns for men and women (Johnston 1973). By 1990, not only will a larger percentage of female than of male labor force participants have high school diplomas, but, among those under 34, women will also be more likely to have college degrees. For example, in the age group 20–24, 19.8 percent of female labor force participants are forecast to have had four or more years of college, whereas the corresponding percentage for men will be only 17.0 percent.

Despite their arbitrary assumptions, the BLS projections of labor force participation and educational attainment raise the question of how the status quo of treating women as secondary workers and earners can possibly be maintained if these projected changes actually occur. Not only do they imply much greater participation in the labor market in the near future, but they also necessarily indicate that male-female differentials will narrow significantly. The predicted narrowing of the sex differential in labor supply is particularly striking among those aged 20–24. In 1975, the labor force participation rates for men and women in this age group were 84.4 percent and 64 percent, while these rates in 1990 are projected to be 89.1 percent and 85.2 percent respectively, under a high-growth scenario. In other words, the difference between male and female participation rates in this age group would be less than 5 percentage points! Furthermore, these estimates do not take into account the implications for female labor force growth of the increases in educational attainment predicted for women. Given this convergence at the crucial age when lifetime career decisions are being made, it is surely unlikely that this cohort will revert to a rigid and stereotyped division of labor by sex in the later years of their working lives. In fact, recent empirical work by Heckman (1979) suggests that the increased labor force experience of young women will strongly increase the probability that they will remain in the labor force in the future.

It is possible that the continuation of present trends in labor supply, as described above, can generate the momentum to carry sex differentials in market outcomes beyond their current stalemate. However, the likelihood that these trends alone will be sufficient to accomplish this breakthrough in the near future is very much dependent on the outlook for changes in the occupational structure. The future of the occupational structure is dependent, not only on the differing growth rates of industries, but on the occupational mix within industries, which changes in response to technological change. The two fastest growing occupational categories are predicted by the BLS to be clerical and service (other than private household), both of which have traditionally been female-dominated (Carey 1976). Therefore, job opportunities for women in the next ten years are more likely to arise from employment growth and replacement needs in fields in which women are already well represented than from large-scale penetration into new fields (Lecht 1976). Forty-four percent of total employment increases projected by the Conference Board (Lecht 1976) for women between 1970 and 1985 will be accounted for by growth in the clerical occupations alone. The greatest opportunities for breakthroughs in employment for women exist in relatively high-growth and traditionally male-dominated fields, such as professional, managerial and technical occupations, which require high levels of education. However, the opportunities here are unlikely to be sufficient to change the degree of occupational dissimilarity dramatically. Therefore, economic growth and technological change will not provide any independent impetus toward a further breakdown of typical patterns.

Prospects for women's wage growth and a narrowing of the wage and unemployment gaps are dependent on the characteristics of the occupations women will enter. To date, younger women have shown a tendency to follow older women into the same female-dominated occupations (Lecht 1976:39). It is not clear to what extent this represents socialized choice and to what extent it results from occupational barriers. No official wage growth projections have been made, but these would, like other projections, depend on the assumptions made. By focusing on the link between occupation and earnings, the Conference Board projections predict no change in the wage gap in the next ten years, because they predict essentially no change in occupational dissimilarity (Lecht 1976:31). On the other hand, Lazear (1979), who focuses instead on actual recent changes in wage growth between cohorts of young women, predicts a steady narrowing of the wage gap between the sexes as women enter jobs with greater potential for earnings growth and accumulate more job experience. These projections represent alternative future scenarios, and the difference between them depends on whether present occupational barriers remain in place or cease to be operational, as working women continue to accumulate job experience.

During this transition period, policies that reinforce women's secondary economic status continue to receive support, and to coexist with legislation that mandates equal opportunities in employment. Although these policies are mutually inconsistent and pull in opposite directions, each of them meets the needs of a substantial fraction of women today. Present ambiguities inherent in government programs, as well as unresolved conflicts in the enforcement of equal opportunity laws, make it difficult for the government to impact significantly at this time on the determination of sex differentials. Of particular concern are the unresolved issues in the employment area which are up for Supreme Court resolution in *Weber* v. *Kaiser* (Chase 1978). If lower court rulings are upheld, then employers will not be allowed to implement affirmative action plans unless previously found guilty of discrimination in the courts. If behavior is only allowed to change when the law is enforced in the courts, the elimination of discrimination will be an extremely long and expensive process. On the other hand, if voluntary affirmative action is given a clean bill of health by the Supreme Court, the government will have much more power to accelerate the process of social change.

With female labor force participation rates currently hovering in the range of 50 percent, heterogeneity within the female population is at its historical maximum. There is not a strong majority committed either to the nonmarket sector (as in the past) or to market work (as appears will be the case in the future). Given this current situation, one of the most important questions to be answered is whether an individual woman will be able to break out of her own personal "vicious circle" simply by behaving in a manner substantially different from the average pattern. Will a woman who chooses a nonstereotyped occupation, participates continuously in the labor force, and invests heavily in training achieve a level of earnings as high and an incidence of unemployment as low as comparable male workers? We know from personal experience and anecdotal evidence that it is very unlikely that she will, and the interactions between demand and supply that lead to pervasive statistical discrimination help to explain why this is the case. Rather than take the risk, employers will continue to judge all women workers largely on the basis of group averages, and new opportunities will tend to open up to women only as those averages change. In most cases, breaking out of the vicious circle of secondary economic status on an individual basis has been extremely difficult in the past, although it may become slightly easier as employers' perceptions adjust slowly to the underlying changes in statistical reality.

If and when the crucial breakthrough is made and the vicious circle begins to unravel, the wage and unemployment gaps will narrow and men's and women's occupational distributions will become more similar. These changes themselves will then have important feedback effects on labor supply and patterns of educational investment. Men will not be as likely as in the past to be the higher earner in the family, and women will see a greater payoff to a continuous career and to educational and training investment. The extent of subsequent shifts in the division of labor between the sexes within the home will depend to some extent on the adaptability of certain key institutions such as the firm, the school system, and the government to the pressures of social change. Firms will have to adjust to the fact that each employee is likely to function as a parent as well. Schools will have to set hours that are consistent with the working day. The government will have to shift fully away from the family to the individual, regardless of sex, as the basic unit of support.

The crucial question remaining becomes one of timing. How long will it take? Is discrimination largely statistical in nature and therefore likely to diminish as more women develop continuous work histories, or is discrimination more fundamentally engrained in attitudes about male and female roles? If the former is correct, the change will take place smoothly, and should not be long in coming now that women have crossed the critical 50-percent divide. With only a moderate time lag, the vicious circle which has perpetuated women's secondary economic status could then reverse itself, as a result of pressure generated solely by changes in women's labor supply behavior.

On the other hand, if the latter is correct, then discrimination will become the critical barrier to change. In that case, strong enforcement of equal employment opportunity laws, which we have seen to be problematical, will be the necessary catalyst for change if the break in the vicious circle is to come soon. Otherwise, we must wait for a change of attitudes which will come only slowly. Even if we are confident that these attitudes will eventually be altered in the face of changing economic reality, it is disturbing that this might well take several generations to accomplish under this alternative scenario. If concern for the opportunities and rewards of current generations of individual women is to overcome complacency about the eventual achievement of equity, then the future must be actively shaped by institutional changes rather than left to gradual evolution.

The next ten years will give a clear indication of which type of discrimination we are really dealing with. In the meanwhile, the employers and husbands of working women are already making some adjustments to a new reality. And children, particularly those of working parents, are growing up with some of the awareness of the diversity of roles available to men and women that is an essential prerequisite for basic attitudinal changes.

NOTES

1. R. E. Smith's (1979) hybrid wage and income coefficients are derived from the labor supply functions estimated by Ashenfelter and Heckman (1974) and Cain and Dooley (1976).

Bibliography

Adams, Avril V. 1973. "Evaluating the Success of the EEOC Compliance Process." *Monthly Labor Review* 96(5):26–29.

Adams, Leonard P. 1971. *Public Attitudes Toward Unemployment Insurance.* Kalamazoo: Upjohn Institute for Employment Research.

Aigner, Dennis J. and Glen G. Cain. 1977. "Statistical Theories of Discrimination in Labor Markets." *Industrial and Labor Relations Review* 30(2):175–87.

Arrow, Kenneth J. 1972. "Models of Job Discrimination." In Anthony Pascal, ed., *Racial Discrimination in Economic Life*, pp. 83–102. Lexington, Mass.: Lexington Books.

—— 1973. "The Theory of Discrimination." In Orley Ashenfelter and Albert Rees, eds., *Discrimination in Labor Markets*, pp. 3–33. Princeton, N.J.: Princeton University Press.

Ashenfelter, Orley and James Heckman. 1974. "The Estimation of Income and Substitution Effects in a Model of Family Labor Supply." *Econometrica* 42(1):73–85.

Ball, Robert M. 1973. "The Treatment of Women under Social Security." Statement prepared for Joint Economic Committee, U.S. Congress, 93rd Congress, 1st session, part 2, pp. 311–18.

Barnes, William F. and Ethel B. Jones. 1974. "Differences in Male and Female Quitting." *Journal of Human Resources* 9(4): 439–51.

—— 1975. "Women's Increasing Unemployment: A Cyclical Interpretation." *Quarterly Review of Economics and Business* 15(2):61–69.

Barrett, Nancy and Richard D. Morgenstern. 1974. "Why Do Blacks and Women Have High Unemployment Rates?" *Journal of Human Resources* 9(4):452–64.

Barth, Peter S. 1968. "Unemployment and Labor Force Participation." *Southern Economic Journal* 34(3):375–82.

Barzel, Yoram and Richard J. McDonald. 1973. "Assets, Subsistence, and the Supply of Labor." *American Economic Review* 63(4):621–33.

327

Bayer, Alan E. and Helen S. Astin. 1968. "Sex Differences in Academic Rank and Salary among Science Doctorates in Teaching." *Journal of Human Resources* 3(2):191–200.

Becker, Gary S. 1957. *The Economics of Discrimination.* Chicago: University of Chicago Press (2nd ed., 1971).

—— 1960. "Underinvestment in College Education?" *American Economic Review* 50(2):346–54.

—— 1964. *Human Capital.* NBER General Series, no. 80. New York: Columbia University Press.

—— 1965. "A Theory of the Allocation of Time." *The Economic Journal* 75(299):493–517.

—— 1967. *Human Capital and the Personal Distribution of Income: An Analytical Approach.* Ann Arbor: University of Michigan, Institute of Public Administration.

—— 1973. "A Theory of Marriage: Part 1." *Journal of Political Economy* 81(4):813–46.

Becker, Gary S. and Barry R. Chiswick. 1966. "The Economics of Education: Education and the Distribution of Earnings." *American Economic Review* 56(2):358–69.

Bell, Duran. 1974. "Why Participation Rates of Black and White Wives Differ." *Journal of Human Resources* 9(4):465–79.

Beller, Andrea. 1979. "The Impact of Equal Employment Opportunity Laws on the Male/Female Earnings Differential." In Cynthia B. Lloyd, Emily Andrews, and Curtis L. Gilroy, eds., *Women in the Labor Market.* New York: Columbia University Press.

Benham, Lee. 1974. "Benefits of Women's Education within Marriage," *Journal of Political Economy* 82(2/2):S57–S71.

—— 1975. "Non-Market Returns to Women's Investment in Education." In Cynthia B. Lloyd, ed., *Sex, Discrimination, and the Division of Labor*, pp. 292–312. New York: Columbia University Press.

Ben-Porath, Yoram. 1973. "Labor Force Participation Rates and the Supply of Labor." *Journal of Political Economy* 81(3):697–704.

Bergmann, Barbara. 1974. "Occupational Segregation, Wages and Profits When Employers Discriminate by Race or Sex." *Eastern Economic Journal* 1(2):103–10.

Bergmann, Barbara R. and Irma Adelman. 1973. "The Economic Role of Women: A Review." *American Economic Review* 63(4):509–14.

Bernstein, Blanche. 1973. "Discrimination and Inequity in Public Assistance and Related Programs." Statement prepared for Hearings before the Joint Economic Committee, U.S. Congress, 93d Congress, 1st session, part 2, pp. 396–401.

Blau, Francine D. 1976. "Longitudinal Patterns of Female Labor Force Participation." *Dual Careers* 4:27–55. Washington, D.C.: U.S. Department of Labor, R & D Monograph no. 21.

—— 1977. *Equal Pay in the Office.* Lexington, Mass.: Heath.

—— 1978. "The Impact of the Unemployment Rate on Labor Force Entries and Exits." Paper presented at the Secretary of Labor's Invitational Conference on the National Longitudinal Surveys of Mature Women, January 1978.

Blau, Francine and Wallace Hendricks. 1979. "Occupational Segregation by Sex: Trends and Prospects." *Journal of Human Resources* 14(2):197–210.

Blaug, Mark. 1976. "The Empirical Status of Human Capital Theory: A Slightly Jaundiced Survey." *Journal of Economic Literature* 14(3):827–55.

Blinder, Alan S. 1973. "Wage Discrimination: Reduced Form and Structural Estimates." *Journal of Human Resources* 8(4):436–55.

Bloch, Farrell E. 1975. "The Allocation of Time to Household Work." Working Paper no. 64, Industrial Relations Section, Princeton University.

Bloch, Farrell E. and Sharon P. Smith. 1977. "Human Capital and Labor Market Employment." *Journal of Human Resources* 12(4):550–60.

Block, M. K. and J. M. Heineke. 1973. "The Allocation of Effort under Uncertainty: The Case of Risk-Averse Behavior." *Journal of Political Economy* 81(2/1):376–85.

Blumberg, Grace G. 1971. "Sexism in the Code: A Comparative Study of Income Taxation of Working Wives and Mothers." *Buffalo Law Review* 21(1):49–98.

—— 1973. "Household and Dependent Care Services: Section 214." Statement prepared for Hearings before the Joint Economic Committee, U.S. Congress, 93d Congress, 1st Session, part 2. pp. 240–53.

Bonin, Joseph M. and William Y. Davis. 1971. "Labor Force Responsiveness to Short-Run Variations in Economic Opportunity." *Southern Economic Journal* 38(2):161–72.

Boskin, Michael J. 1973. "The Economics of Labor Supply." In
Harold W. Watts and Glen G. Cain, eds., *Income Maintenance
and Labor Supply*, pp. 163–81. Chicago: Markham.
—— 1974a. "A Conditional Logit Model of Occupational Choice."
Journal of Political Economy 82(2/1):389–413.
—— 1974b. "The Effects of Government Expenditures and Taxes on
Female Labor." *American Economic Review* 64(2):251–56.
Bowen, William and T. A. Finegan. 1969. *The Economics of Labor
Force Participation*. Princeton, N.J.: Princeton University Press.
Brittain, John A. 1972. "The Incidence of the Social Security Payroll
Tax—A Reply." *American Economic Review* 62(4):739–42.
Brown, Gary D. 1976. "How Type of Employment Affects Earnings
Differences by Sex." *Monthly Labor Review* 99(7):25–30.
Burns, Arthur F. 1966. *The Management of Prosperity*. Washington:
American Enterprise Institute for Public Policy Research.
Burns, John E. and Catherine G. Burns. 1973. "An Analysis of the
Equal Pay Act." *Labor Law Journal* 24(2):92–99.
Butler, Arthur D. and George D. Demopoulos. 1971. "Labor Force
Behavior in a Full Employment Economy." *Industrial and Labor
Relations Review* 24(3):375–85.
Cain, Glen G. 1966. *Married Women in the Labor Force*. Chicago:
University of Chicago Press.
—— 1976. "The Challenge of Segmented Labor Market Theories to
Orthodox Theory: A Survey." *Journal of Economic Literature*
14(4):1215–57.
Cain, Glen G. and Martin D. Dooley. 1976. "Estimation of a Model
of Labor Supply, Fertility, and Wages of Married Women.
Journal of Political Economy 84(4/2):S179–S199.
Cain, Glen G. and Harold W. Watts. 1973. "Towards a Summary and
Synthesis of the Evidence." In Glen G. Cain and Harold W.
Watts, eds., *Income Maintenance and Labor Supply*, pp. 328–67.
Chicago: Markham.
Cardwell, Lucy A. and Mark R. Rosenzweig. 1975. *Monopsonistic
Discrimination and Sex Differences in Wages*. Discussion Paper
No. 222, Economic Growth Center. New Haven: Yale Univer-
sity.
Carey, Max L. 1976. "Revised Occupational Projections to 1985."
Monthly Labor Review 99(11):10–12.
Carnoy, Martin and Dieter Marenbach. 1975. "The Return to School-
ing in the United States, 1939–1969." *Journal of Human
Resources* 10(3):312–31.

Chase, Marilyn. 1978. "Kaiser Aluminum Case May Help in Clarifying Reverse Job-Bias Issue." *The Wall Street Journal*, September 21, 1978.

Chiplin, Brian. 1979. "The Evaluation of Sex Discrimination: Some Problems and a Suggested Reorientation." In Cynthia B. Lloyd, Emily Andrews, and Curtis L. Gilroy, eds., *Women in the Labor Market*. New York: Columbia University Press.

Chiswick, Barry R. 1973. "Racial Discrimination in the Labor Market: A Test of Alternative Hypotheses." *Journal of Political Economy* 81(6):1330–52.

Chiswick, Barry R., June A. O'Neill, James Fackler, and Solomon W. Polachek. 1974. "The Effect of Occupation on Race and Sex Differences in Hourly Earnings." *Business and Economic Statistics Section Proceedings of the American Statistical Society*, pp. 219–28.

Cogan, John F. 1975. "Labor Supply and the Value of the Housewife's Time." RAND Publication, no. R-1461-OEO/EDA/RF.

Cohen, Malcolm S. 1971. "Sex Differences in Compensation." *Journal of Human Resources* 6(4):434–47.

Cohen, Malcolm S., Samuel A. Rea, and Robert I. Lerman. 1970. "A Micro Model of Labor Supply." U.S. Department of Labor, Bureau of Labor Statistics, Staff Paper no. 4.

Corazzini, Arthur J. 1972. "Equality of Employment Opportunity in the Federal White-Collar Civil Service." *Journal of Human Resources* 7(4):424–45.

Corcoran, Mary. 1978. "Work Experience, Work Interruption, and Wages." In Greg Duncan and James Morgan, eds., *Five Thousand American Families: Patterns of Economic Progress*, 6:47–103. Ann Arbor: University of Michigan, Institute for Social Research.

—— 1979. "Work Experience, Labor Force Withdrawals, and Women's Earnings: Empirical Results Using the 1976 Panel Study of Income Dynamics." In Cynthia B. Lloyd, Emily Andrews, and Curtis L. Gilroy, eds., *Women in the Labor Market*. New York: Columbia University Press.

Corcoran, Mary and Greg Duncan. 1978. "A Summary of Part I Findings." In Greg Duncan and James Morgan, eds., *Five Thousand American Families: Patterns of Economic Progress*, 6:3–46. Ann Arbor: University of Michigan, Institute for Social Research.

Denison, Edward F. 1962. *The Sources of Economic Growth in the United States and the Alternatives Before Us.* New York: Committee for Economic Development.

Dernberg, Thomas and Kenneth Strand. 1966. "Hidden Unemployment 1953–1962: A Quantitative Analysis by Age and Sex." *American Economic Review* 56(1):71–95.

Deutermann, William V., Jr. 1973. "Educational Attainment of Workers, March 1973." U.S. Department of Labor, Bureau of Labor Statistics, Special Labor Force Report No. 161.

Deutermann, William V., Jr. and Scott Campbell Brown. 1978. "Voluntary Part-Time Workers: A Growing Part of the Labor Force." *Monthly Labor Review* 101(6):3–10.

Doeringer, Peter B. and Michael J. Piore. 1971. *Internal Labor Markets and Manpower Analysis.* Lexington, Mass.: Heath.

Douglas, Paul H. 1934. *The Theory of Wages.* New York: Macmillan.

Duncan, Greg and Frank Stafford. 1977. "The Use of Time and Technology by Households in the United States." University of Michigan. Mimeo.

Duncan, Greg and Saul Hoffman. 1978. "Training and Earnings." In Greg Duncan and James Morgan, eds., *Five Thousand American Families: Patterns of Economic Progress*, 6:105–50. Ann Arbor: University of Michigan, Institute for Social Research.

Durbin, Elizabeth. 1973. "Work and Welfare: The Case of Aid to Families with Dependent Children." *Journal of Human Resources* 8(Supplement):103–25.

Edwards, Harry T. 1973. "Sex Discrimination Under Title VII: Some Unresolved Issues." *Labor Law Journal* 24(7):411–23.

"The EEOC Retreats after a Seniority Ruling." *Business Week*, June 10, 1977, p. 28.

Ehrenberg, Ronald G. and R. L. Oaxaca. 1976. "Unemployment Insurance, Duration of Unemployment and Subsequent Wage Gain." *American Economic Review* 66(5):754–66.

Fair, Ray C. 1971. "Labor Force Participation, Wage Rates and Money Illusion." *Review of Economics and Statistics* 53(2):164–68.

Feldstein, Martin S. 1968. "Estimating the Supply Curve of Working Hours." *Oxford Economic Papers* 20(1):74–80.

—— 1972. "The Incidence of the Social Security Tax—Comment." *American Economic Review* 62(4):735–38.

—— 1974. "Unemployment Compensation: Adverse Incentives and Distributional Anomalies." *National Tax Journal* 27(2):231–44.

—— 1976. "Seven Principles of Social Insurance." *Challenge* November/December:6–11.

Finegan, T. Aldrich. 1962. "Hours of Work in the United States—A Cross-Sectional Analysis." *Journal of Political Economy* 70(5):452–70.

Flaim, Paul O. and Howard N. Fullerton, Jr. 1978. "Labor Force Projections to 1990: Three Possible Paths." *Monthly Labor Review* 101(12):25–35.

Flanagan, Robert J. 1976. "Actual versus Potential Impact of Government Anti-Discrimination Programs." *Industrial and Labor Relations Review* 29(4):486–507.

Frank, Robert H. 1978. "Why Women Earn Less: The Theory and Estimation of Differential Overqualification." *American Economic Review* 68(3):360–73.

Freeman, Richard B. 1975. "Overinvestment in College Training?" *Journal of Human Resources* 10(3):287–311.

—— 1976. *The Overeducated American.* New York: Academic Press.

Fuchs, Victor R. 1971. "Differences in Hourly Earnings Between Men and Women." *Monthly Labor Review* 94(5):9–15.

—— 1974. "Recent Trends and Long-Run Prospects for Female Earnings." *American Economic Review* 64(2):236–42.

Fullerton, Howard N., Jr. and Paul O. Flaim. 1976. "New Labor Force Projections to 1990." *Monthly Labor Review* 99(12):3–13.

Ghez, Gilbert R. and Gary S. Becker. 1975. *The Allocation of Time and Goods over the Life Cycle.* New York: National Bureau of Economic Research.

Gilman, Harry J. 1965. "Economic Discrimination and Unemployment." *American Economic Review* 55(5/1):1077–96.

Goldfarb, Robert S. 1974. "The Policy Content of Quantitative Minimum Wage Research." *Proceedings of the 27th Annual Meeting of the Industrial Relations Research Association.* pp. 261–68.

Goldstein, Morris and Robert S. Smith. 1976. "The Estimated Impact of the Antidiscrimination Program Aimed at Federal Contractors." *Industrial and Labor Relations Review* 29(4):523–43.

Gordon, David M. 1972. *Theories of Poverty and Underemployment: Orthodox, Radical and Dual Labor Market Perspectives.* Lexington, Mass.: Heath.

Gordon, Nancy M. 1978. "The Treatment of Women in the Public Pension Systems of Five Countries." Working Paper no. 5069-01. Washington, D.C.: The Urban Institute.

Gordon, Nancy M., Thomas E. Morton and Ina C. Braden. 1974. "Faculty Salaries: Is There Discrimination by Sex, Race and Discipline?" *American Economic Review* 64(3):419–27.

Gramm, Wendy L. 1973. "The Labor Force Decision of Married Female Teachers: A Discriminant Analysis Approach." *Review of Economics and Statistics*, 55(3):341–48.

Greenberg, David H. and James R. Hosek. 1976. *Regional Labor Supply Response to Negative Income Tax Programs.* Rand Publication, No. R-1785—EDA.

Greenspan, Alan. 1976. Statement published in the *New York Times*, September 4, 1976.

Griliches, Zvi. 1977. "Estimating the Returns to Schooling: Some Econometric Problems." *Econometrica* 45(1):1–22.

Gronau, Reuben. 1973. "The Intrafamily Allocation of Time: The Value of Housewives' Time." *American Economic Review* 63(4):634–51.

—— 1974. "Wage Comparisons—A Selectivity Bias." *Journal of Political Economy* 82(6):1119–43.

—— 1976. "The Allocation of Time of Israeli Women." *Journal of Political Economy* 84(4):S201–S220.

—— 1977. "Leisure, Home Production, and Work—The Theory of the Allocation of Time Revisited." *Journal of Political Economy* 85(6):1099–123.

Gwartney, James D. and Richard Stroup. 1973. "Measurement of Employment Discrimination According to Sex." *Southern Economic Journal* 39(4):575–87.

Hall, Robert E. 1973. "Wages, Income and Hours of Work in the U.S. Labor Force." In Harold Watts and Glen G. Cain, eds., *Income Maintenance and Labor Supply*, pp. 102–62. Chicago: Markham.

Hallam, Charlotte. 1973. "Legal Tools To Fight Sex Discrimination." *Labor Law Journal* 24(12):803–09.

Hamermesh, Daniel S. 1977a. *Jobless Pay and the Economy.* Baltimore: Johns Hopkins University Press.

—— 1977b. *Unemployment Insurance and Labor Supply.* Michigan State University, Mimeo.

Hanoch, Giora. 1967. "An Economic Analysis of Earnings and Schooling." *Journal of Human Resources* 2(3):310–29.

—— 1976. "Hours and Weeks in the Theory of Labor Supply." RAND Publication, no. R-1787-HEW.

Hansen, W. Lee. 1963. "Total and Private Rates of Return to Investment in Schooling." *Journal of Political Economy* 71(2):128–40.

Hayghe, Howard. 1975a. "Job Tenure of Workers, January 1973." Washington, D.C.: U.S. Department of Labor, Bureau of Labor Statistics, Special Labor Force Report No. 172.

—— 1975b. "Marital and Family Characteristics of the Labor Force, March 1975." *Monthly Labor Review* 98(11):52–56.

—— 1976. "Families and the Rise of Working Wives—An Overview." *Monthly Labor Review* 99(5):12–19.

Hawkins, Beverly J. 1974. "Women, Work and the Law—A Legislative Review." RAND Publication, no. P-5176.

Heckman, James J. 1974. "Shadow Prices, Market Wages and Labor Supply." *Econometrica* 42(4):679–94.

—— 1979. "New Evidence on the Dynamics of Female Labor Supply." In Cynthia B. Lloyd, Emily Andrews, and Curtis L. Gilroy, eds., *Women in the Labor Market*, New York: Columbia University Press.

Heckman, James J. and Robert Willis. 1977. "A Beta-Logistic Model for the Analysis of Sequential Labor Force Participation by Married Women." *Journal of Political Economy* 85(1):27–58.

Heckman, James J. and Kenneth I. Wolpin. 1977. "An Economic Analysis of the Contract Compliance Program." In Orley C. Ashenfelter and Wallace Oates, eds., *Essays in Labor Market Analysis*, pp. 73–103. Jerusalem: Israel Universities Press.

Hedges, Janice N. and Jeanne K. Barnett. 1972. "Working Women and the Division of Household Tasks." *Monthly Labor Review* 95(4):9–14.

Hill, C. Russell. 1973. "The Determinants of Labor Supply for the Working Urban Poor." In Glen G. Cain and Harold W. Watts, eds., *Income Maintenance and Labor Supply*, pp. 182–204. Chicago: Markham.

Hill, C. Russell and Frank P. Stafford. 1974. "Allocation of Time to Pre-School Children and Educational Opportunity" *Journal of Human Resources* 9(3):323–41.

Hill, Martha S. 1978. "Self-Imposed Limitations on Work Schedule and Job Location." In Greg Duncan and James Morgan, eds., *Five Thousand American Families: Patterns of Economic Progress*, 6:151–93. Ann Arbor: University of Michigan, Institute for Social Research.

Hines, Fred, Luther Tweeten and Martin Redfern. 1970. "Social and

Private Rates of Return to Investment in Schooling by Race-Sex Groups and Regions." *Journal of Human Resources* 5(3):318–40.

Hirschleifer, J. 1958. "On the Theory of Optimal Investment Decisions." *Journal of Political Economy* 66(4):329–52.

Hoffer, Stefan N. 1973. "Private Rates of Return to Higher Education for Women." *Review of Economics and Statistics* 56(4): 482–86.

Hoffman, Emily P. 1975. "An Econometric Study of the University of Massachusetts/Amherst Faculty Salary Differentials." Final Report DLMA 91-25-74-27-1, U.S. Department of Labor, Manpower Administration.

Honig, Marjorie. 1974, "AFDC Income, Recipient Rates and Family Dissolution." *Journal of Human Resources* 9(3):303–22.

Hoskins, Dalmer and Lenore E. Bixby. 1973. *Women and Social Security: Law and Policy in Five Countries.* U.S. Department of HEW, Social Security System, Report no. 42. Washington, D.C.

Jencks, Christopher. 1972. *Inequality: A Reassessment of the Effects of Family and Schooling in America.* New York: Basic Books.

Johnson, George E. and Frank P. Stafford. 1974. "The Earnings and Promotion of Women Faculty." *American Economic Review* 64(6):888–903.

Johnston, Denis F. 1973. "Education of Workers: Projections to 1990." *Monthly Labor Review* 96(11):22–31.

Jorgenson, D. W. and Zvi Griliches. 1967. "The Explanation of Productivity Change." *Review of Economic Studies* 34/3(99): 249–283.

Kalachek, Edward D., Wesley Mellow and Fredric Q. Raines. 1978. "The Male Labor Supply Function Reconsidered." *Industrial and Labor Relations Review* 31(3):356–67.

Kalachek, Edward D. and Fredric Q. Raines. 1970. "Labor Supply of Lower Income Workers." *President's Commission on Income Maintenance Programs, Technical Studies.* Washington, D.C.

Kanowitz, Leo. 1969. *Women and the Law: The Unfinished Revolution.* Albuquerque: University of New Mexico Press.

Kanter, Rosabeth Moss. 1977. *Men and Women of the Corporation.* New York: Basic Books.

Kiefer, Nicholas M. 1976. "The Economic Benefits from Manpower Training Programs." Technical Analysis Paper #43, Office of Research and Evaluation, Office of the Assistant Secretary for Policy, Evaluation and Research, U.S. Department of Labor. Washington, D.C.

—— 1979. "Training Programs and the Employment and Earnings of Black Women." In Cynthia B. Lloyd, Emily Andrews, and Curtis L. Gilroy, eds., *Women in the Labor Market.* New York: Columbia University Press.

Killingsworth, Mark R. 1976. "Must a Negative Income Tax Reduce Labor Supply? A Study of the Family's Allocation of Time." *Journal of Human Resources* 11(3):354–65.

—— 1979a. *Neoclassical Labor Supply Models: A Survey.* Princeton: Princeton University Press.

—— 1979b. "Comment." In Cynthia B. Lloyd, Emily Andrews, and Curtis L. Gilroy, eds., *Women in the Labor Market.* New York: Columbia University Press.

King, Allan G. 1977. "Is Occupational Segregation the Cause of the Flatter Experience-Earnings Profiles of Women?" *Journal of Human Resources* 12(4):541–49.

Kniesner, Thomas J. 1976. "The Full-Time Workweek in the United States, 1900–1970." *Industrial and Labor Relations Review* 30(1):3–15.

Kohen, Andrew I., with Susan C. Breinich and Patricia Shields. 1975. "Women and the Economy: A Bibliography and a Review of the Literature on Sex Differentiation in the Labor Market." Center for Human Resource Research, College of Administrative Science, Ohio State University.

Kohen, Andrew I. and Roger D. Roderick. 1975. "The Effects of Race and Sex Discrimination on Early-Career Earnings." Center for Human Resource Research, College of Administrative Science, Ohio State University. Mimeo.

Kosters, Marvin. 1969. "The Effects of an Income Tax on Labor Supply." In Arnold C. Harnberger and M. J. Bailey, eds., *The Taxation of Income from Capital,* pp. 301–24. Washington: Brookings Institution.

Kosters, Marvin and Finis Welch. 1972. "The Effects of Minimum Wages by Race, Age and Sex." In Anthony H. Pascal, ed., *Racial Discrimination in Economic Life,* pp. 103–18. Lexington, Mass.: Heath.

Landes, Elizabeth M. 1977. "Sex Differences in Wages and Employment: A Test of the Specific Capital Hypothesis." *Economic Inquiry* 15(4):523–38.

Lazear, Edward, 1979. "Male-Female Wage Differentials: Has the Government Had Any Effect?" In Cynthia B. Lloyd, Emily

Andrews, and Curtis L. Gilroy, eds., *Women in the Labor Market.* New York: Columbia University Press.

Lecht, Leonard A. 1976. *Changes in Occupational Characteristics: Planning Ahead for the 1980s.* New York: The Conference Board. A Research Report.

Leibowitz, Arleen. 1972. "Woman's Allocation of Time to Market and Non-Market Activities: Differences by Education." Ph.D. dissertation, Columbia University.

—— 1974a. "Education and Home Production." *American Economic Review* 64(2):243–50.

—— 1974b. "Home Investments in Children." *Journal of Political Economy* 82(2/2):S111–S131.

—— 1975. "Women's Work in the Home." In Cynthia B. Lloyd, ed., *Sex, Discrimination, and the Division of Labor*, pp. 223–43. New York: Columbia University Press.

—— 1976. "Years and Intensity of Schooling Investment." *American Economic Review* 66(3):321–34.

—— 1977. "Potential Inputs and Children's Achievement." *Journal of Human Resources* 12(2):242–49.

Leuthold, Jane. 1976. "The Impact of Taxes on the Work Decision of the Two-Earner Family." Paper presented at the American Economic Association Meeting. Atlantic City, N.J.

—— 1978. "The Effect of Taxation on the Hours Worked by Married Women." *Industrial and Labor Relations Review* 31(4):520–26.

Lewis, H. Gregg. 1956. "Hours of Work and Hours of Leisure." *Industrial Relations Research Association, Annual Proceedings*, pp. 196–206.

—— 1974. "Comments on Selectivity Biases in Wage Comparisons." *Journal of Political Economy* 82(6):1145–55.

—— 1975. "Economics of Time and Labor Supply." *American Economic Review* 65(2):29–34.

Lippman, Steven A. and John J. McCall. 1976. "The Economics of Job Search: A Survey," *Economic Inquiry* 14(2):155–87, and 14(3):347–68.

Lloyd, Cynthia B. 1975. "The Division of Labor Between the Sexes: A Review." In Cynthia B. Lloyd, ed., *Sex, Discrimination, and the Division of Labor*, pp. 1–24. New York: Columbia University Press.

Lloyd, Cynthia B. and Beth Niemi, 1976. "Labor Force Participation and Unemployment Revisited: Some New Evidence from the

1970s." Paper presented at the Labor Workshop Columbia University.

——1978. Sex Differences in Labor Supply Elasticity: The Implication of Sectoral Shifts in Demand." *American Economic Review: Papers and Proceedings* 68(2):78–83.

Long, Clarence D. 1958. *The Labor Force under Changing Income and Employment.* Princeton, N. J.: Princeton University Press.

Long, James E. 1976, "Employment Discrimination in the Federal Sector." *Journal of Human Resources* 11(1):86–97.

Lopatka, Kenneth T. 1977. "Developing Concepts in Title VII law." In Leonard J. Hausman, Orley Ashenfelter, Bayard Rustin, Richard F. Schubert, and Donald Slaiman, eds., *Equal Rights and Industrial Relations,* pp. 31–69. Madison, Wisc.: Industrial Relations Research Association.

MacRae, C. Duncan and Elizabeth Chase MacRae. 1976. "Labor Supply and the Payroll Tax." *American Economic Review* 66(3):408–09.

Madden, Janice. 1975. "Discrimination—A Manifestation of Male Market Power?" In Cynthia B. Lloyd, ed., *Sex, Discrimination, and the Division of Labor,* pp. 146–74. New York: Columbia University Press.

—— 1978. "Economic Rationale for Sex Differences in Education." *Southern Economic Journal* 44(4):778–97.

Malkiel, Burton G. and Judith A. Malkiel. 1973. "Male-Female Pay Differentials in Professional Employment." *American Economic Review* 63(4):693–705.

Mallan, Lucy B. 1974. "Changes in Female Labor Force Experience 1961–71 and the Effect on Earnings." Paper presented at the Annual Meeting of the American Economic Association. San Francisco.

Maret-Havens, Elizabeth. 1977. "Developing an Index to Measure Female Labor Force Attachment." *Monthly Labor Review* 100(5):35–38.

Marshall, Alfred. 1938. *Principles of Economics.* London: Macmillan.

Marston, Stephen T. 1975. "The Impact of Unemployment Insurance on Job Search." *Brookings Papers on Economic Activity,* (1):13–60.

Mattila, J. Peter. 1974. "Job Quitting and Frictional Unemployment." *American Economic Review* 64(1):235–39.

Merrett, Stephen. 1966. "The Rate of Return to Education: A Critique." *Oxford Economic Papers* (n.s.) 18(3):289–303.

Michael, Robert T. 1973. "Education in Nonmarket Production."
     Journal of Political Economy 81(2/1):306–27.
Michelotti, Kopp. 1977. "Educational Attainment of Workers, March
     1977." *Monthly Labor Review* 100(12):53–57.
Miller, Herman P. 1965. "Lifetime Income and Economic Growth."
     American Economic Review 55(4):834–44.
Mincer, Jacob. 1962a. "Labor Force Participation of Married
     Women: A Study of Labor Supply." In H. Gregg Lewis, ed.,
     Aspects of Labor Economics, A Report of the NBER, pp.
     63–105. Princeton, N.J.: Princeton University Press.
—— 1962b. "On-the-Job Training: Costs, Returns and Some Implica-
     tions." *Journal of Political Economy* 70(5/2):S50–S79.
—— 1966 "Labor Force Participation and Unemployment: A Review
     of Recent Evidence." In Robert A. Gordon and Margaret S.
     Gordon, eds., *Prosperity and Unemployment*, pp. 73–112. New
     York: Wiley.
—— 1974a. *Schooling, Experience, and Earnings.* New York: NBER.
—— 1974b. "Progress in Human Capital Analyses of the Distribution
     of Earnings." Discussion Paper 74-7504, Columbia University.
—— 1975. "Education, Experience, and the Distribution of Earnings
     and Employment: An Overview." In T. Thomas Juster, ed.,
     Education, Income, and Human Behavior, pp. 71–94. New York:
     McGraw-Hill.
—— 1976. "Unemployment Effects of Minimum Wages." *Journal of
     Political Economy* 84(4/2):S87–S104.
—— 1978. "Family Migration Decisions." *Journal of Political
     Economy* 86(5):749–73.
Mincer, Jacob and Haim Ofek. 1979. "The Distribution of Lifetime
     Labor Force Participation of Married Women." *Journal of
     Political Economy* 87(1):191–202.
Mincer, Jacob and Solomon Polachek. 1974. "Family Investments in
     Human Capital: Earnings of Women." *Journal of Political
     Economy* 82(2/2):S76–S108.
—— 1978. "Women's Earnings Re-Examined." *Journal of Human
     Resources* 13(1):118–34.
Morgenstern, Richard D. and William Hamovitch. 1976. "Labor
     Supply of Married Women in Part-Time and Full-Time Occupa-
     tions." *Industrial and Labor Relations Review* 30(1):59–67.
Munts, Raymond and Irwin Garfinkel. 1974. *The Work Disincentive
     Effects of Unemployment Insurance.* Kalamazoo: Upjohn Insti-
     tute on Employment Research.

Munts, Raymond and David C. Rice. 1970. "Women Workers: Protection or Equality?" *Industrial and Labor Relations Review* 24(1):3–13.

National Center for Education Statistics. 1975. *Earned Degrees Conferred: 1971–1972.* Washington, D.C.

—— 1977a. *Earned Degrees Conferred: Analysis of Trends, 1965–66 through 1974–75.* Washington, D.C.

—— 1977b. *Earned Degrees Conferred, 1974–75.* Washington, D.C.

Niemi, Albert W., Jr. 1975. "Sexist Differences in Returns to Educational Investment." *Quarterly Review of Economics and Business,* 15(1):17–25.

Niemi, Beth. 1970. "Sex Differentials in Unemployment in the U.S. and Canada, 1947–1966." Ph.D. dissertation, Columbia University.

—— 1974. "The Female-Male Differential in Unemployment Rates," *Industrial and Labor Relations Review* 27(3)331–50.

—— 1975. "Geographic Immobility and Labor Force Mobility: A Study of Female Unemployment." In Cynthia B. Lloyd, ed., *Sex, Discrimination, and the Division of Labor,* pp. 61–89. New York: Columbia University Press.

—— 1977. "Recent Changes in Differential Unemployment." *Growth and Change* 8(3):22–30.

Oaxaca Ronald. 1973. "Male-Female Wage Differentials in Urban Labor Markets." *International Economic Review* 14(3):693–709.

Oelsner, Lesley. 1977a. "Supreme Court Backs Seniority Work Rules that May Discriminate." *New York Times,* June 1, 1977, p. 1.

—— 1977b. "Recent Supreme Court Rulings Have Set Back Women's Rights." *New York Times,* July 8, 1977, p. 1.

Office of Management and Budget. 1976. *Special Analyses: Budget of the United States, 1977. Special Analysis M: "Federal Civil Rights Activities,"* Washington, D.C.

O'Neill, June. 1976. "The Equity of Social Security Benefits." Paper presented at Annual Meeting of American Economic Association, Atlantic City, N.J.

Osterman, Paul. 1978. "Sex, Marriage, Children and Statistical Discrimination." Boston University, Mimeo.

Palmer, John and Joseph Minarik. 1976. "Income Security Policy." In Henry Owen and Charles Schultze, eds., *Setting National Priorities: the Next Ten Years,* pp. 505–82. Washington: Brookings Institution.

Pechman, Joseph A. and P. Michael Timpane. 1975. *Work Incentives and Income Guarantees: The New Jersey Negative Income Tax Experiment.* Washington: Brookings Institution.

Perrella, Vera C. 1963. "Marital and Family Characteristics of Workers, March 1963." Washington, D.C.: U.S. Department of Labor, Bureau of Labor Statistics, Special Labor Force Report No. 40.

Perry, Charles R., Bernard E. Anderson, Richard L. Rowan, Herbert R. Northrup, et al. 1975. *The Impact of Government Manpower Programs: In General, and on Minorities and Women.* Manpower and Human Resources Studies, No. 4. Philadelphia: University of Pennsylvania, The Wharton School, Industrial Research Unit.

Phelps, Edmund S. 1972. "The Statistical Theory of Racism and Sexism." *American Economic Review* 62(4):659–61.

Piore, Michael J. 1975. "Notes for a Theory of Labor Market Stratification," In Richard C. Edwards, Michael Reich, and David M. Gordon, eds., *Labor Market Segmentation*, pp. 125–50. Lexington, Mass.: Heath.

Polachek, Solomon W. 1975a. "Potential Biases in Measuring Male-Female Discrimination." *Journal of Human Resources* 10(2): 205–29.

—— 1975b. "Differences in Expected Post-School Investment as a Determinant of Market Wage Differentials." *International Economic Review* 16(2):451–470.

—— 1975c. "Discontinuous Labor Force Participation and Its Effects on Women's Earnings." In Cynthia B. Lloyd, ed., *Sex, Discrimination, and the Division of Labor*, pp. 90–122. New York: Columbia University Press.

—— 1978. "Sex Differences in Education: An Analysis of the Determinants of College Major." *Industrial and Labor Relations Review* 31(4):498–508.

—— 1979. "Occupational Segregation: Theory, Evidence and A Prognosis." In Cynthia B. Lloyd, Emily Andrews, and Curtis L. Gilroy, eds., *Women in the Labor Market.* New York: Columbia University Press.

Polachek, Solomon W. and Francis Horvath. 1977. "A Life Cycle Approach to Migration: Analysis of the Perspicacious Peregrinator." In Ronald G. Ehrenberg, ed., *Research in Labor Economics*, pp. 103–49. Greenwich, Conn.: JAI Press.

"Public Service Jobs—A Way to Put the Untrained to Work." *U.S. News and World Report*, August 5, 1974, p. 62.

Quester, Aline. 1976. "The Effect of the Tax Structure on the Labor Market Behavior of Wives." Paper presented at Eastern Economic Association Meetings, Bloomsburg, Pa.

Renshaw, E. F. 1960. "Estimating the Returns to Education." *Review of Economics and Statistics* 42(3):318–24.

Rivlin, Alice M. 1975. "Income Distribution—Can Economists Help?" *American Economic Review* 65(2):1–15.

Robbins, Lionel. 1930. "On the Elasticity of Demand for Income in Terms of Effort." *Economica* 10(29):123–29.

Rosen, Harvey S. 1976. "Tax Illusion and the Labor Supply of Married Women." *Review of Economics and Statistics* 58(2):167–72.

Rosen, Sherwin. 1969. "On the Interindustry Wage and Hours Structure." *Journal of Political Economy* 77(2):249–73.

Salant, Stephen W. 1977. "Search Theory and Duration Data: A Theory of Sorts." *Quarterly Journal of Economics* 91(1):39–57.

Salop, S. C. 1973. "Wage Differentials in a Dynamic Theory of the Firm." *Journal of Economic Theory* 6(4):321–44.

Sanborn, Henry. 1964. "Pay Differences Between Men and Women." *Industrial and Labor Relations Review* 17(4):534–50.

Sandell, Steven H. 1975. "The Economics of Family Migration." in *Dual Careers: A Longitudinal Analysis of the Labor Market Experience of Women*, vol. 4. Center for Human Resource Research, Ohio State University.

—— 1977. "Attitudes Toward Market Work and the Effect of Wage Rates on the Lifetime Labor Supply of Married Women." *Journal of Human Resources* 12(3):379–86.

Sandell, Steven H. and David Shapiro. 1978. "A Re-Examination of the Evidence." *Journal of Human Resources* 13(1):103–17.

Sawhill, Isabel V. 1973. "The Economics of Discrimination Against Women: Some New Findings." *Journal of Human Resources* 8(3):383–96.

Sawhill, Isabel V., Gerald E. Peabody, Carol A. Jones, and Steven B. Caldwell. 1975. *Income Transfers and Family Structure*. Washington, D.C.: The Urban Institute Paper No. 979-03 (URI 13100).

Schoenberg, Erika H. and Paul H. Douglas, 1937. "Studies in the Supply Curve of Labor." In Earl J. Hamilton, Albert E. Rees, and Harry G. Johnson, eds., *Landmarks in Political Economy*, pp. 229–61. Chicago: University of Chicago Press, 1962.

Schultz, T. Paul. 1975 "Estimating Labor Supply Functions for Married Women." RAND publication, no. R-1265-NIH/EDA.

Schultz, Theodore W. 1961, "Investment in Human Capital." *American Economic Review* 51(1):1–17.

Schweitzer, Stuart O. and Ralph E. Smith. 1974. "The Persistence of the Discouraged Worker Effect." *Industrial and Labor Relations Review* 27(2):249–60.

Shea, John R. 1973. "Welfare Mothers: Barriers to Labor Force Entry." *Journal of Human Resources* 8, Supplement: 90–102.

Simeral, Margaret H. 1978. "The Impact of the Public Employment Program on Sex Related Differentials." *Industrial and Labor Relations Review* 31(4):509–19.

Skolnik, Alfred M. 1975. "Unemployment Insurance Benefits Temporarily Expanded." *Social Security Bulletin* 38(6):42–44.

Smith, Adam. 1776. *The Wealth of Nations* (1937 ed.). New York: Modern Library.

Smith, James P. 1975. "On the Labor-Supply Effects of Age Related Income Maintenance Programs." *Journal of Human Resources* 10(1):25–43.

—— 1977. "Family Labor Supply over the Life Cycle." *Explorations in Economic Research* 4(2):205–76.

—— 1979. "The Convergence to Racial Equality in Women's Wages." In Cynthia B. Lloyd, Emily Andrews, and Curtis L. Gilroy, eds., *Women in the Labor Market*. New York: Columbia University Press.

Smith, Ralph E. 1977. "The Impact of Macroeconomic Conditions on Employment Opportunities for Women." Paper no. 6, prepared for U.S. Congress, Joint Economic Committee, 94th Congress, 2d session.

—— 1979. "Projecting the Size of the Female Labor Force: What Makes a Difference?" In Cynthia B. Lloyd, Emily Andrews, and Curtis L. Gilroy, eds., *Women in the Labor Market*. New York: Columbia University Press.

Smith, Sharon P. 1976. "Government Wage Differentials by Sex." *Journal of Human Resources* 11(2):185–99.

—— 1977. *Equal Pay in the Public Sector: Fact or Fantasy*. Princeton, N.J.: Princeton University Press.

Spence, Michael. 1973. "Job Market Signaling." *Quarterly Journal of Economics* 87(3):355–74.

—— 1974. *Market Signaling: Informational Transfer in Hiring and*

Related Screening Processes. Cambridge: Harvard University Press.

Strand, Kenneth and Thomas Dernberg. 1964. "Cyclical Variation in Civilian Labor Force Participation." *Review of Economics and Statistics* 46(4):378–91.

Strober, Myra H. 1977. "Wives's Labor Force Behavior and Family Consumption Patterns." *American Economic Review* 67(1): 410–17.

Suter, Larry and Herman Miller. 1973. "Income Differences Between Men and Career Women." *American Journal of Sociology* 78(4):962–74.

Task Force on Working Women. 1975. *Exploitation from 9 to 5.* Report of the Twentieth Century Fund Task Force on Women and Employment. Lexington, Mass.: Heath & Co.

Tella, Alfred. 1964. "The Relation of Labor Force to Employment." *Industrial and Labor Relations Review* 17(4):454–69.

—— 1965. "Labor Force Sensitivity to Employment by Age, Sex," *Industrial Relations* 4(2):69–83.

Thurow, Lester C. 1975. *Generating Inequality.* New York: Basic Books.

Tomlinson, Kenneth Y. 1975. "Let's Stop the Unemployment Rip-Off." *Reader's Digest* 107(644):100–4.

Underwood, Lorraine A. 1979. *Women in Federal Employment Programs,* Washington, D.C.: The Urban Institute Paper 5074-1 (URI 24400).

"Unemployment—A Story the Figures Don't Tell." *U.S. News and World Report,* November 18, 1974, pp. 43–45.

U.S. Department of Commerce. Bureau of the Census. 1973. *1970 Census of the Population: Employment Status and Work Experience.* Subject Reports PC (2) 6A. Washington, D.C.

U.S. Department of Health, Education, and Welfare. 1979. *Social Security and Changing Roles of Men and Women.* Washington, D.C.

—— Social Security Administration. 1975. "Reports of the Quadrennial Advisory Council on Social Security." Washington, D.C.

—— 1978. *Report of the HEW Task Force on the Treatment of Women under Social Security.* Washington, D.C.

U.S. Department of Labor. 1969. *Facts About Women's Absenteeism and Labor Turnover.* Washington, D.C.

—— Bureau of Labor Statistics. "Employment in Perspective: Working Women." Report 544, 2, 2d quarter, 1978. Washington, D.C.

—— Employment and Training Administration. 1978. *Employment and Training Report of the President*. Washington, D.C.

—— Manpower Administration. 1974. *Manpower Report of the President*. Washington, D.C.

—— 1975. *Manpower Report of the President*. Washington, D.C.

—— Women's Bureau. 1969. *1969 Handbook on Women Workers*. Bulletin No. 294. Washington, D.C.

—— 1975. *1975 Women's Handbook*. Washington, D.C.

U.S. Equal Opportunity Commission. 1975. *Tenth Annual Report*. Washington, D.C.

U.S. President. 1973. *Economic Report of the President*. Washington, D.C.

Vanek, Joann. 1974. "Time Spent in Housework." *Scientific American* 231(5):116–20.

Wachter, Michael L. 1972. "A Labor Supply Model for Secondary Workers." *Review of Economics and Statistics* 54(2):141–50.

—— 1977. "Intermediate Swings in Labor Force Participation." *Brookings Papers on Economic Activity* (2):545–576.

Waldman, Elizabeth and Beverly J. McEaddy. 1974. "Where Women Work—An Analysis by Industry and Occupation." *Monthly Labor Review* 97(5):3–13.

Wallace, Phyllis. 1976. *Equal Employment and the AT&T Case*. Cambridge: MIT Press.

Weisbrod, Burton A. 1966. "Investing in Human Capital." *Journal of Human Resources* 1(1):5–21.

Welch, Finis. 1975. "Human Capital Theory: Education, Discrimination and Life Cycles." *American Economic Review* 65(2):63–73.

—— 1976a. "Minimum-Wage Legislation in the United States." In Orley Ashenfelter and James Blum, eds., *Evaluating the Labor-Market Effects of Social Programs*, pp. 1–38. Princeton, N.J.: Princeton University, Industrial Relations Section, Department of Economics.

—— 1976b. "Employment Quotas for Minorities." *Journal of Political Economy* 84(4/2):S105–S139.

Welch, Finis and James P. Smith. 1979. "The Overeducated American? A Review Article." *Proceedings of the National Academy of Education* (forthcoming).

Wertheimer, Barbara. 1976. "Search for a Partnership Role: Women in Labor Unions Today." In Jane Chapman, ed., *Economic Independence for Women: The Foundation of Equal Rights*, pp. 183–209. Beverly Hills: Sage.

Wohlstetter, Albert and Sinclair Coleman. 1972. "Race Differences in Income." In Anthony H. Pascal ed., *Racial Discrimination in Economic Life*, pp. 3–81. Lexington, Mass.: Heath.

Woltman, Harry R. and William W. Walton. 1968. "Evaluation of the War on Poverty, the Feasibility of Benefit Cost Analysis for Manpower Programs." Resource Management Report prepared for GAO, 1968.

Zellner, Harriet S. 1974. "The Determinants of the Occupational Distribution of Women." Ph.D. dissertation, Columbia University.

—— 1975. "The Determinants of Occupational Segregation." In Cynthia B. Lloyd, ed., *Sex, Discrimination, and the Division of Labor*, pp. 125–45. New York: Columbia University Press.

—— 1976. "A Report on the Extent and Nature of Employment Discrimination Against Women." Manuscript.

Index